"McHugh, I'm going to beat your ass with this book! It is quite simply *too* good. At once insightful, brilliant, clever, and beautiful, but it is also *deeply* personal and lovely. At the end of the day it is a fierce weapon that should be a staple in every serious chef's kitchen . . . not their cookbook collection."

—John Currence, ex-chef/neo-instigator

"*Cured* doesn't simply serve as a guide to building an enviable and expansive larder, it goes a step further, teaching you how to put it all to use to great effect."

—David Zilber, coauthor of *The Noma Guide to Fermentation*

"Steve McHugh is a philosopher-chef, attuned to the rhythms of the natural world, focused on the transformative possibilities of the kitchen. His courage and keen palate, on display in *Cured*, remind me that recipes are acts of faith and meals are everyday sacraments."

—John T. Edge, author of *The Potlikker Papers*

"This is the book we have all been waiting for. Chef McHugh has long inspired me with his knack for making beautiful, thoughtful, and tasty food. Curing and preserving is an art form that many of the world's cuisines rely on. Steve's deep understanding of these techniques and his willingness to share them are a gift that will keep on giving. From quick-pickled vegetables to smoked nuts, cured fish, and potted meats, this is a cookbook that shows American cooking at its absolute best. This is going to become a book that will be passed down for generations."

—Vishwesh Bhatt, two-time James Beard Award–winning chef and author of *I Am From Here*

CURED

CURED

Cooking with Ferments, Pickles, Preserves & More

Steve McHugh

with Paula Forbes

Photographs by Denny Culbert

TEN SPEED PRESS

California | New York

Introduction

Cure |kyŏŏr|

Verb [with object]

1. To restore, especially restore to health; to remedy.

2. To prepare an ingredient for preservation, such as by salting, drying, smoking, etc.

3. To harden or strengthen a substance, such as cement or rubber; to improve durability.

"Oh, won't you stay . . . just a little bit longer?"
—*Maurice Williams and the Zodiacs, 1960*

Preserved foods are unlike any other ingredient: they're magic dust, special sauce, secret weapons. But you have to know how to use them.

Ingredients that have been preserved through pickling, fermenting, curing, drying, and other methods not only form the backbone of a well-stocked pantry, they're often the crucial element that pushes a dish to the next level. Preservation changes the character of an ingredient, altering textures and concentrating flavors. These processes can also introduce new facets of flavor, adding heat or acid or funk. The essence of the ingredient is intensified, so a small amount goes a long way. A tiny bit of bacon can transform an entire pot of beans; just a drop of fermented hot sauce makes a raw oyster sing.

Have you ever bought a jar of preserved lemons to use in a recipe you found in a magazine and then wondered what to do with the rest of it? Made a big batch of pesto with summer's fresh basil, only to find it unused, frosty, and dull in the back of the freezer months later? Got talked into a jar of beet mustard at the farmers' market that now taunts you from the door of your refrigerator, daring you to use it for . . . what?

This is where I come in. My name is Steve McHugh, and I'm a chef in San Antonio. I love the magic that preserved foods give to dishes, and they've always been at the core of my kitchen, whether it's charcuterie or pickles or jam. When I came up with the idea for this cookbook, I wanted to share with readers not just how to preserve food but *why*: it's such a simple way to improve home cooking. But it was during the pandemic that I realized the potential for a book like this. Curiosity about preserved foods had increased dramatically, and many home cooks were discovering the power of preservation for the first time. It has been generations since people have spent so much time preserving foods at home, and across the country, pantries are lined with jars, bottles, and cans of preserves, whether store-bought or homemade. This is the book that will help you turn those jars into breakfast, lunch, and dinner.

A Note on Shelf Life

Most of the "preserves" in this book are traditional preserves: recipes for pickles and fermentations and jams that are intended to extend the shelf life of whatever fruit or vegetable you are preserving. However, in the interest of education, some recipes—like the quick-cured vegetables on page 187—use a preservation *technique* to change the ingredient's flavor or texture without significantly extending the shelf life of the ingredient. Where applicable, a recipe will note whether it is suitable for freezing and how long it will last in the refrigerator. For information on canning, see page 328.

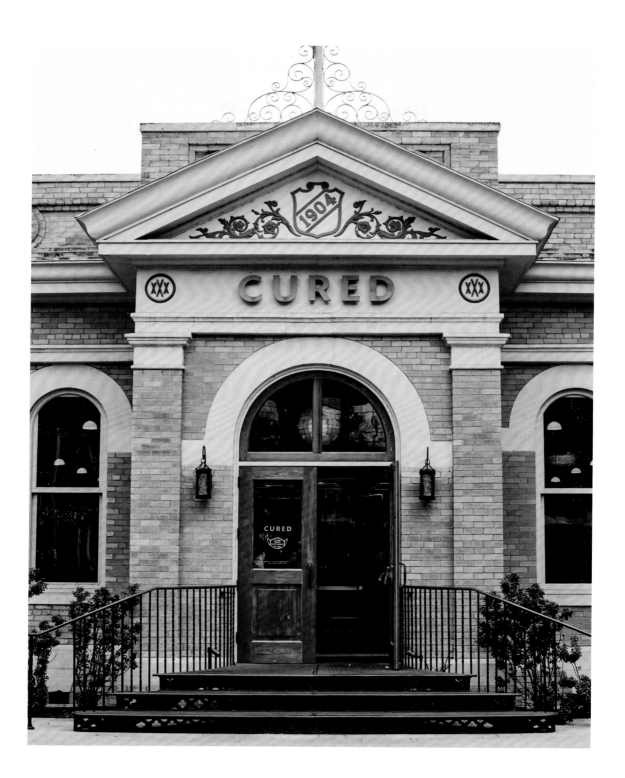

To cure is to strengthen, to bolster reserves. Spending time with loved ones cures our relationship with them, setting bonds like cement as fortification against hard times. To cure is to look toward the future, to anticipate needs, to save a tiny bit of today for tomorrow. That which has been cured has been transformed; paused, changed, and emerged as something new.

I was thirty-three years old when I learned about another type of cure. I had been diagnosed with non-Hodgkin's lymphoma, and the cure I needed was as vicious as it can be beneficial: chemotherapy. Cancer felt like a door slammed in my face, an indication that my time was finite. I had been offered a job opportunity in San Antonio, and I considered turning it down in light of this news. It just made sense to stay in New Orleans, where I had begun my career and established a community around myself over the course of fourteen years. But my oncologist pulled me aside and said, "No one told you to stop living your life." While cancer is a crucible, it might not be a death sentence.

So in 2010 my wife, Sylvia, and I moved to San Antonio after all. The opportunity was too tempting, too good to pass up. Cancer be damned. I had three surgeries and did eight rounds of chemo. Slowly, I got better. And I started thinking about what I wanted my life to look like.

Inside the knowledge that our days are limited, there is a human impulse to prolong the rare and precious moments that bring us joy. An extra glass of wine with friends on a sun-dusted terrace, a few minutes longer in the park with a laughing toddler, walking the long way home on the first warm spring evening: all of these

are attempts to bottle time. We linger—twenty minutes more, ten minutes, five—basking in these moments, staving off the knowledge that they will soon pass.

We do the same with food. Originally, humans preserved food because it was necessary for survival, but in the twenty-first century, we preserve foods for many reasons. For me personally, I just enjoy the process of it. Preservation allows us to carry ingredients with us well past their peak season—strawberry jam on toast is a balm against a cold winter day, and the grilled sausages of summer sparkle with the bright snap of sauerkraut. Chefs love to talk about seasonality, and I'm not going to recommend you buy fresh tomatoes in February or asparagus in November. But you can freeze tomato sauce and pickle asparagus to enjoy these flavors out of season—without stressing the global supply chain or using up enormous resources.

The post-treatment life I envisioned for myself awaited me in an old brick building with high-arching windows in the midst of San Antonio's historic Pearl Brewery property, itself in need of a cure, a return to well-being. I started planning a restaurant that would nod to what cancer gave me and what it cost. The menu would be full of charcuterie, pickles, jams, and mustards alongside peak-season local ingredients: the best of the past and the present combined on a plate. It would reflect my childhood surrounded by brothers on a dairy farm in Wisconsin, my culinary education in New Orleans, and my hard-won future in San Antonio. The space would foster an appreciation for time, providing room for friendships and community to cure, both in the dining room and in the kitchen. It would be the first time I worked for myself, in a restaurant Sylvia and I had dreamed about opening since we first met. A restaurant that captured that precious, fleeting joy of lingering.

We called it Cured.

———

People always ask me what kind of restaurant Cured is, and it doesn't fall neatly into a category. It's a living, breathing thing. Ingredients drive everything we do—we utilize entire animals from our ranchers and try to make the most of peak-season produce. For us, it's smart, sustainable business to preserve, ferment, and can, purchasing produce at the height of its freshness.

Charcuterie is at the center of our menu. It is the vehicle that helps us achieve our goals, which is to buy that 350-pound pig and treat it with the utmost respect. To me, that means using all of the animal. We make hams, we make salami, we make pâtés and sausages. We use every bit.

The same philosophy extends to fruits and vegetables. Cured has a wall of jars in every color imaginable, full of relishes and salsas and pickles and jams and mustards and fermented foods. These make for a killer charcuterie board, sure, but preserved foods inform the entire menu. Our gumbo is made with smoked pork and garnished with pickled okra; the burger is topped with onion jam; fermented hot sauce goes into micheladas and fried chicken.

When the coronavirus pandemic hit in 2020, this type of cooking seemed more vital than ever. We shut down the restaurant for a period, but spring still came, and along with it, the bounty of the farms of South Texas: strawberries, fennel, purple hull peas, beets, cabbage, and more. I got to work, for once alone in the Cured kitchen, and packed away as much of it as possible. Curing then became a promise to my future self, an act of faith that diners would return. And as the world gradually reopened, I was thankful for

Salt

Most cooks these days have a preference between two kinds of kosher salt: Morton or Diamond Crystal. I use Morton at the restaurant, so that's what I used to test these recipes. Recipes where salt content makes a crucial difference—like, say, fermentations—include a weight for the salt. Otherwise, you can salt your dishes to taste. Roughly speaking, if you prefer Diamond Crystal, multiply the volume of salt in any recipe by 1.75. No matter what salt you use, though, I always recommend tasting your dish for seasoning before serving and adjusting as needed.

that ever-evolving wall of jars to welcome guests back into our dining room.

I don't expect you to make your own hams like we do at the restaurant, but I do think home cooks of all skill levels can learn a lot from looking at food through the lens of preservation. What happens when you take the highest quality ingredients you can find, preserve them (or buy them already preserved!), and let that inform how you cook? My guess is you'll start cooking a lot more interesting, flavorful foods—for not a ton more effort.

How to Use This Book

Think of this book as a deck of cards. Its recipes can be shuffled in endless combinations to suit your region, the time of year, and your personal taste. The chapters are organized by technique and, very roughly speaking, are ordered from simplest to most difficult. Likewise, the recipes within each chapter are loosely ordered in terms of difficulty.

Start with the Base Ingredients, which are preserved produce, herbs, flavorings, and even meat and seafood. In your kitchen, you can use store-bought items, or if you're feeling ambitious, you can make these preserves from scratch with the recipe provided. The recipe for each Base Ingredient has several suggested variations that change either what's being preserved or the flavorings you add to it. Once you get more comfortable with preserving food at home, you might even come up with your own variations.

Now that you've got your Base Ingredient—a jar of supermarket mustard, spicy pickles from a local farmers' market, or homemade blackberry jam—it's time to figure out what to do with it. For each Base Ingredient, there are several Application Recipes—my suggestions for ways to showcase these ingredients in dishes you can make for weeknight dinners, Sunday brunch, or, what the heck, Friday happy hour.

And now we shuffle the deck: each of the Application Recipes will work with just about any variation of the Base Ingredient you can get your hands on. The Miso Mushroom Vegetarian Reuben (page 250)? Tastes just as great with spicy fennel kraut or garlicky collards kraut as it does with standard green cabbage sauerkraut. The Simple Frosted Cake (page 164) uses compound butter in both the batter and the frosting, allowing you to add flavor with candied pecans or pumpkin and cinnamon. And the personality of Risotto (page 89) changes dramatically depending on whether you add oven-dried tomatoes, mushrooms, or even citrus.

Starting to see the possibilities? Once you explore the preserved ingredients commercially available, dabble in making your own from scratch, and fine-tune the variations, suddenly the 160-ish recipes in this book become hundreds, thousands. The possibilities are literally endless. And that's what I want you to learn from this book: by incorporating preserved ingredients into your cooking, you unlock limitless possibility in your kitchen.

Adjusting Seasoning to Your Preserves

Now, I know I just said, "Each of the Application Recipes will work with just about any variation of the Base Ingredient." But you've got to be smart about the seasoning. While I've tested these recipes with as many different preserves as possible, there are always going to be outliers. No recipe can account for every possible preserve out there, and you just may be tempted to try these recipes with a hot sauce so spicy it ranks off the Scoville scale or a jar of marmalade you didn't realize was rather bitter when you picked it up at the store. Here's my advice for adjusting the recipes to suit.

First, taste the preserve on its own (assuming it's edible raw). Note whether it's spicier, sweeter, or saltier than you expected. Go into the recipe knowing the preserve's character: If it's terribly salty, use less additional salt than the recipe recommends. If it's very bitter, use a bit more sugar. You may also run into textural differences that can be modified for greater success: a whole-grain mustard may be pureed in a blender or whole-leaf kimchi chopped into smaller pieces.

If you realize something is off after you complete a recipe, you still have options. In my restaurants, I tell my cooks to finish dishes with all kinds of ingredients: salt and pepper, yes, but also sugar, lemon juice, hot sauce, honey, soy sauce, vinegar, butter, Parmesan, and more. The key to balancing flavor is to *literally* balance it: if one side of the flavor spectrum is too heavy, add the opposite flavor to balance the scale. If it's too fatty, add acid. If it's too acidic, add fat. A pinch of salt or a splash of acid can help with too much sweetness. Some sweetness can help with too much salt. The list goes on.

And most of all, trust yourself! You know what tastes good. Believe in that instinct: If something needs more salt, add it. If it's too spicy, maybe water it down a bit. What separates good cooks from great ones is tasting food as you go and learning how to adjust the flavor accordingly. Don't be shy. Grab a spoon and get to work.

Acid

Acid—typically citrus or vinegar—is everywhere in our kitchens. You probably have different vinegars and a bowl of citrus on hand at all times. My refrigerator is full of pickled cucumbers, beets, okra, and green beans. I have jars of mustard and a fruit shrub for throwing together cocktails with ease. And rows of canned tomatoes in my pantry, preserved in their own acid (assisted by lemon).

When we eat fatty, smoky, creamy, or salty foods, our taste buds can get fatigued. That's when I reach for acid, the ultimate balancer. Acid cleanses: it's why we like pickles on sandwiches or tomato sauce with meatballs. Like salt, acid can enhance flavors and make them more pronounced. Okra, eggplant, or green beans might taste boring on their own, but when dressed with a vinaigrette or pickled, the true flavor of the vegetable will emerge. Acid can break down food slightly, introducing tenderness. Mustard is a great example of this: the acid breaks down the hard, dried mustard seeds into a tasty (if pungent!) condiment.

Acid preserves food by helping prevent bacteria growth. But it also has to taste good! The key to a great pickle (or other acidic preserve) is balance. It sounds obvious but you want the pickle to taste like the ingredient being pickled—whether that's cucumbers or okra or green beans—while taking on the textural improvements and bacteria-preventing qualities of the acid.

The acidity of a substance is measured on the pH scale; the lower the pH level, the more acidic the preserve, and the better it prevents spoilage (more on this on page 328). Different acids vary in pH level and also introduce different flavors. A red wine vinegar is going to behave differently in a preserve than rice wine vinegar or apple cider vinegar. Meanwhile, citrus juice introduces fruitiness with higher sugar content and higher pH and is thus better suited to different recipes. After all, you wouldn't dump a bunch of cucumbers into some orange juice and expect to get pickles, right?

So in this section, let's celebrate all things sour.

Base Ingredient: **Vinaigrette**

Vinaigrette as a preserve? It may not last quite as long in the refrigerator as pickles, but vinaigrettes can be a great tool in your arsenal for extending the life of herbs, alliums, fruit, and much more. And they're fabulous additions to any preserves-based kitchen, helping to dress up not just greens but grilled vegetables, pasta salads, marinades, and more. You can even warm up vinaigrettes to serve as a sauce for meats and fish.

In culinary school, I was taught a proper vinaigrette was one part acid to three parts oil. I still use this as a rule of thumb, but there are times when the ratio can be adjusted. When dressing a piece of fish fresh off the grill, I prefer a bit more acid to stand up to the smoke, and when using lime or lemon juice, I will add a touch more oil to counterbalance the flavor of the citrus.

Simple Vinaigrette

We use a fairly neutral olive oil in the restaurants to allow the acid to be the star of our vinaigrettes, but don't be afraid to substitute a nice unfiltered olive oil for a bit more bite, or even a nut oil to change the flavor completely. No matter what you do, though, always use the highest-quality vinegar you can.

MAKES 1 CUP

¼ cup sherry vinegar
2 tablespoons minced shallot
Salt
¾ cup extra-virgin olive oil
Freshly ground black pepper

1 Combine the vinegar and shallot in a small mixing bowl along with a pinch of salt. Let it sit for 1 minute; this allows the shallot to soften slightly.

2 While whisking continuously, slowly drizzle the olive oil into the vinegar-shallot mixture.

3 Season with salt and pepper to taste. Store in an airtight container in the refrigerator for up to 2 weeks.

Vinaigrette Variations

Creamy Dill Vinaigrette: Make the vinaigrette as written, but use only ½ cup olive oil. Add 1 chopped hard-boiled egg (see Note, page 22), 1½ tablespoons Dijon mustard, and 1 cup packed dill fronds to a blender or food processor. With the machine running, slowly drizzle in the vinaigrette, blending until smooth and creamy.

Chipotle Lime Vinaigrette: Make the vinaigrette as written. Add the vinaigrette, 2 chipotle peppers in adobo, 1 tablespoon agave nectar or honey, 1 garlic clove, and the zest and juice of 1 lime to a blender or food processor. Puree until smooth.

Blackberry Vinaigrette: Make the vinaigrette as written using balsamic vinegar in place of sherry vinegar. Add 1 cup blackberries to a mixing bowl and use a big whisk to mash and break up the berries. Add the vinaigrette and whisk together to combine.

Warm Caramelized Onion Vinaigrette: Heat 2 tablespoons olive oil in a large cast-iron pan over medium-high heat. Cook 1 large onion, sliced, stirring, until just golden, about 10 minutes. Reduce the heat to low, add 2 teaspoons honey, and cook, stirring, for an additional 5 minutes. Remove the onions from the heat and let them cool while you make the vinaigrette as written, omitting the shallots. Add the onions to a blender or food processor along with 1 teaspoon mustard powder and the vinaigrette. Blend until smooth.

Easy Ideas for Using Vinaigrette

- Marinate meat or fish
- Dress vegetables before adding to a sandwich
- Dress grain salads
- Drizzle over anything grilled to finish the dish
- Fold into warm rice for a rice bowl
- Drizzle over sautéed vegetables
- Toss with vegetables prior to roasting
- Brush on bread before toasting

Marinated Cheese (or Tofu)

Marinating fresh cheese like mozzarella or feta in a vinaigrette highlights the flavor of both the cheese and the vinaigrette. Cubes of provolone would work well, too, or you can try tofu for a vegan option. This recipe calls for Fresno chiles because of their beautiful red color; fruity, smoky flavor; and heat level that lies somewhere between a jalapeño and a serrano. This is a great snack for serving at a dinner party; pour the marinated cheese into a shallow bowl and serve with toothpicks on the side.

SERVES 6 TO 8 AS AN APPETIZER

1 pound feta, fresh mozzarella cheese, or tofu, cut into ½-inch cubes

1 cup vinaigrette (page 11)

½ Fresno chile, thinly sliced (about ¼ cup sliced)

1 cup loosely packed fresh basil, torn into pieces

¼ teaspoon salt

¼ teaspoon freshly ground black pepper

1 cup pitted Kalamata olives

1   Place the cheese in a bowl and pour the vinaigrette over it. Let sit at room temperature for 20 minutes to help soften the cheese.

2   Fold in the chile, basil, salt, pepper, and olives. Refrigerate for at least 4 hours and no more than 48 hours before serving. The longer the cheese marinates, the softer the cheese will become and the more the flavors will develop.

Grilled Eggplant with Vinaigrette and Fresh Herbs

Eggplant is like a sponge, with the ability to soak up flavors. Here, slices of eggplant are infused with flavor: first, they're brushed with vinaigrette; then, they pick up smoke from the grill. The honey counters the eggplant's bitter tendencies, and a pile of fresh herbs really brightens the whole dish.

SERVES 6

2 medium eggplants (about 2 pounds total), sliced lengthwise into ¾-inch-thick planks

¾ cup vinaigrette (page 11)

Salt and freshly ground black pepper

2 garlic cloves, minced

2 sprigs thyme, stems discarded and leaves chopped

½ cup fresh parsley leaves

¼ cup torn fresh basil leaves

¼ cup fresh cilantro leaves

2 tablespoons fresh dill leaves

2 tablespoons fresh tarragon leaves

1½ tablespoons honey

1 Prepare a hot grill or heat your oven's broiler on high. Brush both sides of the eggplant slices with vinaigrette, reserving what doesn't get used to dress the herbs. Season both sides with a large pinch of salt and plenty of black pepper, and sprinkle with the garlic and thyme.

2 Combine the reserved vinaigrette with the herbs and stir to combine. Set aside.

3 If using a broiler, position the rack 4 to 6 inches below the heat source and place the eggplant slices on a foil-lined sheet pan. (Do not use parchment or a silicone baking mat as these will burn under the heat.)

4 Place the eggplant on the grill or under the broiler until the eggplant is golden brown— even slightly charred in spots. (Keep a close eye on it; it can go from looking uncooked to burned pretty quickly. Start checking around 5 minutes.) Turn the slices over and continue to cook until browned on the other side. The eggplant should take between 10 and 15 minutes to cook, total, depending on exactly how far it is from the broiler or how hot your grill is.

5 Lay the eggplant slices, slightly overlapping, on a serving dish and drizzle with the honey while still warm. Cover the slices with the herb salad and serve.

Pickled Shrimp

Shrimp is a great introduction to pickling proteins. It holds up well in the pickling liquid but still tastes like shrimp when all is said and done. A holiday staple, this is a great make-ahead snack for guests. It would also be lovely topping a summertime salad of Bibb lettuce, finished with fresh herbs, shredded carrots, and sliced radish.

SERVES 6 AS AN APPETIZER
Begin recipe 1 to 3 days before serving.

1 stalk celery, cut into 4 pieces

½ onion, thinly sliced

2 lemons, sliced into thin rounds

3 tablespoons (46g) salt

1 pound medium (21/25) shrimp, peeled and deveined, tails intact

1 teaspoon red pepper flakes

2 garlic cloves

2 teaspoons yellow mustard seeds

1 jalapeño, stemmed and sliced into rounds

2 bay leaves

1 teaspoon freshly ground black pepper

¼ teaspoon fennel seeds

**Vinaigrette (page 11) to cover
(1½ to 2 cups)**

1 Combine the celery, onion, half the lemon slices, salt, and 8 cups of water in a large pot. Bring to a boil.

2 Reduce the heat to a simmer and add the shrimp. Stir the shrimp so that they don't stick together, then cover the pot and remove it from the heat. After 5 minutes, strain the shrimp and discard the water and vegetables. Allow the shrimp to cool slightly.

3 Combine the shrimp, red pepper flakes, garlic cloves, mustard seeds, jalapeño slices, bay leaves, black pepper, and fennel seeds in a large mixing bowl. Stir thoroughly, so the shrimp are coated in the seasonings. Let shrimp cool completely.

4 Put the remaining sliced lemons in a quart jar. Top the lemons with the shrimp mixture and pour in the vinaigrette. Make sure the shrimp are completely submerged in the vinaigrette. Put the lid on the jar and refrigerate for at least 1 day and no more than 3 days.

5 Serve the shrimp in a shallow bowl, doused with the brine, with toothpicks on the side.

Pasta Salad with Tomatillo, Shallots, and Parsley

For years I had never tried a raw tomatillo—typically they're cooked or used in salsas. Then one of our farmers showed up with tons of tomatillos and said, "Try one." I was blown away by the sweet, tangy flavor. Lesson learned: always trust your farmers. The flavor and crunch of the raw tomatillos work well here with the vinaigrette and pasta.

SERVES 6 TO 8 AS A SIDE

3 tablespoons pine nuts

Salt

1 pound fusilli pasta

6 tablespoons vinaigrette (page 11)

3 cups tomatillos (about 1 pound), shucked, cored, and cut into large bite-size pieces

1 cup cherry or grape tomatoes, halved

½ cup sliced shallots

⅓ cup fresh parsley leaves

1½ cups shaved Parmesan

Freshly ground black pepper

1 Bring a large pot of salted water to a boil to cook the pasta.

2 Toast the pine nuts with a pinch of salt in a small sauté pan over medium-low heat until fragrant, about 2 minutes. Be careful not to burn them. Remove from the heat and let cool.

3 Cook the pasta in the boiling water according to the package instructions. Drain and rinse the pasta under cold water, then put it in a large mixing bowl and toss it with the vinaigrette to prevent sticking.

4 Add the tomatillos, tomatoes, shallots, and parsley to the bowl and stir to combine.

5 Fold in the cheese and pine nuts. Season with salt and pepper and serve.

Base Ingredient: **Mustard**

When I was growing up in Wisconsin, mustard was used on everything—didn't matter if it was a hot dog or a casserole. And no wonder, it's a perfect condiment: mustard adds spice and acidity, and it contributes texture to whatever it's paired with. It's endlessly adaptable, too, coming in every flavor you can imagine.

It's also much, much easier to make from scratch than you probably realize. And while there are probably thousands of commercially available mustards out there, it's worth making at home because you can customize the flavor. You can use yellow mustard seeds for a mild mustard and brown or black seeds for a spicier one. You can leave your mustard seeds whole or puree them depending on your preference. And you can add flavors to your mustards, from beer to honey to fruit.

Cured's House Mustard

This recipe calls for you to puree half the mustard seeds in a food processor after soaking, which is how I usually like it. Some of the recipes in this section call for you to puree all the seeds, like the Remoulade (page 21), and some work better if you leave the mustard seeds whole, like the Split Pea Soup (page 25).

MAKES 2½ CUPS
Begin recipe 2 weeks before using.

½ cup yellow mustard seeds

½ cup brown mustard seeds

1 cup plus 6 tablespoons sherry wine vinegar

½ cup honey

¼ cup packed light brown sugar

1 teaspoon (5g) salt

1 Put the mustard seeds and 1 cup of the vinegar in a bowl or jar and cover. Allow the seeds to soak overnight at room temperature. They will absorb nearly all the vinegar.

2 Add half the soaked seeds, the remaining 6 tablespoons vinegar, and the honey to a blender or food processor and puree until smooth.

3 Combine the puree with the remaining soaked seeds, the brown sugar, and the salt in a bowl. Transfer to a jar, cover, and refrigerate for 2 weeks to allow the harshness and heat of the seeds to mellow. After those 2 weeks, the mustard will hold in the refrigerator for up to 4 months.

Mustard Variations

Beer Mustard: Follow the instructions for the mustard, but replace the sherry vinegar with 1 cup beer for soaking and 6 tablespoons malt vinegar for the added vinegar.

Sambal Mustard: Make the mustard recipe using rice wine vinegar instead of sherry. At the blending step, blend all the mustard seeds plus ¼ cup sambal, 1 teaspoon garlic, and 1 teaspoon peeled and chopped fresh ginger.

Sweet Potato Mustard: Replace the mustard seeds with 1 cup mustard powder and skip the soaking stage. Put 1 pound peeled and diced sweet potatoes in a pot of salted water, bring to a boil, and then reduce to a simmer for 10 minutes (or until soft). Drain and cool. Place the cooked sweet potatoes in the blender with the mustard powder, 6 tablespoons vinegar, honey, brown sugar, and salt and blend until smooth.

Cherry Mustard: Heat ½ cup plus 2 tablespoons champagne vinegar and ¾ cup pitted sour cherries in a small saucepan over low heat for 10 minutes. Use this champagne-cherry vinegar mixture for both additions of vinegar in the mustard recipe. When it's time to blend, puree the entire mixture with the honey, brown sugar, and salt. (You can also make this mustard with ¾ cup diced peaches, plums, apples, pears, and more.)

Easy Ideas for Using Mustard

- Combine 2 parts mayonnaise and 1 part mustard for a quick dipping sauce
- Serve alongside hard, flavorful cheeses, like cheddar and aged Gouda
- Fold into macaroni and cheese to amplify the cheese flavor
- Spread on meat before cooking to add flavor and get dried herbs and spices to stick better
- Add toward the end of a braise to perk up the sauce
- Mix with maple syrup for a glaze for roast chicken

Remoulade

I keep remoulade on hand like most folks have ketchup. No seafood boil is complete without this classic French dipping sauce. It's perfect on po'boys, great with boiled meats, and pairs with fish and crab cakes. This is a very versatile recipe: throw in some diced pickles (page 29) and it becomes the tartar sauce of your dreams. Mix in a bit of chopped kimchi (page 253) and you have the missing ingredient for your poke bowl.

MAKES ABOUT 2 CUPS
Begin recipe the day before serving.

1¼ cups mayonnaise

¼ cup finely minced shallots

1 tablespoon prepared horseradish

Juice of ½ lemon

¼ cup mustard (page 19)

1 garlic clove, minced

1 teaspoon white wine vinegar

¼ teaspoon smoked paprika

¼ teaspoon cayenne

½ teaspoon salt

¼ teaspoon celery salt

4 dashes hot sauce (page 262 or store-bought)

Combine all the ingredients in a bowl. Place the remoulade sauce in an airtight container and refrigerate overnight to allow the flavors to develop.

Mustardy Potato Salad with Bacon

What I think sets a great barbecue spot apart from the crowd is when they really nail the sides. I know it sounds simple, but with so much emphasis on producing great meat, sides can be relegated to a back burner. This potato salad is my riff on what you'd find at a Texas barbecue joint. It's smoky, spicy, and acidic—the perfect addition to any plate of barbecue.

SERVES 6 TO 8

3 pounds Yukon gold potatoes, peeled and cut into 1-inch pieces

Salt

8 ounces bacon, diced

⅓ cup mustard (page 19)

1 cup mayonnaise

¼ cup red wine vinegar

Freshly ground black pepper

3 stalks celery, finely chopped

¼ cup finely chopped fresh parsley

¼ cup finely chopped fresh chives

3 large eggs, hard-boiled and roughly chopped (see Note)

1 Put the potatoes in a large pot, salt generously, and cover with water. Bring to a boil and boil until cooked through but not mushy, about 6 minutes. Drain and let cool slightly.

2 While the potatoes are cooling, sauté the bacon in a pan over medium heat and cook until just crisped, about 8 minutes. Use a slotted spoon to transfer the bacon to a paper towel–lined plate. Reserve 2 tablespoons of the bacon fat.

3 Whisk together the reserved bacon fat, the mustard, mayonnaise, and red wine vinegar in a small bowl. Season with salt and pepper to taste.

4 Use a potato masher to halfway mash the potatoes in a large mixing bowl while they're still slightly warm. Make sure you leave plenty of good-size chunks. The goal is to have a potato salad that is half-mashed and half-chunky—this is not a time to use your potato ricer or food mill. Add half the dressing, the bacon, and celery and stir until combined. Refrigerate the salad for at least 1 hour, and up to overnight; refrigerate the remaining dressing as well.

5 Just before serving, fold in the remaining dressing, the chopped herbs, and eggs. Taste and adjust the seasoning as needed. Serve.

Note: I have a surefire method for hard-boiled eggs that I teach all my cooks. Put your eggs in a pot and cover them with water. Add a bit of salt and a drizzle of olive oil; the olive oil permeates the shell while cooking and makes for easier peeling. Bring just to a simmer over medium heat and simmer for 11 minutes. Rinse in cold water until cool enough to handle, then peel.

Split Pea Soup with Whole-Grain Mustard

Split pea soup reminds me of my childhood. There's something soul-satisfying about it, especially during those long Wisconsin winters. This recipe uses whole-grain mustard (page 19) to add a sharpness and acidity not usually found in pea soup.

SERVES 4 TO 6

2 tablespoons extra-virgin olive oil

1 ham hock (1 to 1½ pounds)

1 onion, finely diced

2 stalks celery, finely diced

2 medium carrots, peeled and finely diced

Salt and freshly ground black pepper

1 cup white wine

1 pound dried green split peas, rinsed

1 bay leaf

1 sprig thyme

1 sprig rosemary

¼ to ½ cup whole-grain mustard (page 19; see Note)

Fresh chives, sliced, for garnish

Croutons, for garnish (recipe follows)

1 Heat the olive oil in a large, heavy soup pot or Dutch oven over medium-high heat. Add the ham hock and brown it on all sides, 3 to 4 minutes per side. Remove it from the pot and set aside.

2 Reduce the heat to medium. Sauté the onion, celery, and carrots along with a large pinch of salt and a few cranks of black pepper until softened, about 3 minutes. Add the wine and cook, scraping the bottom of the pot, until reduced significantly, about 6 minutes.

3 Add the split peas to the pot along with 8 cups of water. Stir to combine. Add the browned ham hock, bay leaf, thyme, and rosemary and bring to a boil. Reduce to a simmer and cook, covered, stirring occasionally, until the split peas become tender and begin to fall apart, 1 to 1½ hours. (If the soup gets too thick, add some water to thin it.)

4 Remove the bay leaf and herb sprigs. Remove the ham hock from the soup and let it cool slightly before removing the meat from the bone and chopping it into bite-size pieces. Add the ham meat back to the soup. (Discard the fat and bone or save the bone for stock, page 53.) Add the mustard, stir to combine, and season with salt and pepper to taste. Serve topped with chives and croutons.

Note: Some mustards are spicier than others. I recommend you start with ¼ cup, taste the soup, and add more as needed. You want a prominent but not overwhelming mustard flavor—you'll use more of a sweet mustard.

Croutons

2 tablespoons unsalted butter

2 tablespoons extra-virgin olive oil

2 cups bread, torn into bite-size pieces (sourdough, baguette, or any crusty country loaf)

Salt and freshly ground black pepper

Heat the butter and oil in a large skillet or cast-iron pan over medium heat. Add the bread and toast, turning every minute or so, until golden brown, 4 to 6 minutes total. Season with salt and pepper and serve.

Mustard-Glazed Sheet Pan Chicken with Root Vegetables

People tend to think that chefs eat gourmet meals at home, but the fact is we can be just as exhausted at the thought of getting dinner on the table as everyone else—and at times a bit more so. Thankfully, we have a few tricks up our sleeves. This is a great, easy recipe that's also a good way to clear out random root vegetables you may have hanging around in your refrigerator: fennel, potatoes, sweet potatoes, and winter squash are all at home here. Feel free to mix up the combination; just make sure your sheet pan is full but not crowded.

SERVES 6

2 tablespoons extra-virgin olive oil, plus more for greasing the pan

6 skin-on, bone-in chicken thighs (about 2½ pounds)

Salt and freshly ground black pepper

1 pound fingerling potatoes, halved

1 medium onion, diced

1 medium parsnip, peeled and cut into 1-inch pieces

1 medium carrot, peeled and cut into 1-inch pieces

1 medium rutabaga, peeled and cut into 1-inch pieces

1 to 2 turnips (depending on size), peeled and cut into 1-inch pieces

3 garlic cloves, chopped

1 sprig rosemary, leaves finely chopped

1 teaspoon finely chopped fresh tarragon

½ cup chicken stock (page 51)

¼ cup mustard (page 19)

1   Heat the oven to 425°F. Grease a sheet pan with olive oil.

2   Season the chicken thighs with salt and pepper on all sides and set aside at room temperature for about 20 minutes.

3   Meanwhile, combine the potatoes, onions, parsnips, carrots, rutabaga, turnips, garlic, herbs, and olive oil in a mixing bowl. Season with salt and pepper and toss until well coated. Scatter the vegetables evenly over the prepared sheet pan. Roast the vegetables for 15 minutes.

4   Whisk together the chicken stock and mustard in a small bowl.

5   Place the chicken thighs on top of the vegetables, evenly spaced. Spoon the mustard mixture over each thigh, then drizzle the remaining sauce over the vegetables. Put the pan back in the oven and roast until a thermometer inserted into the chicken reads 165°F, about 45 minutes. Serve the vegetables alongside the chicken.

Base Ingredient: **Pickles**

When it comes to pickles, most people think of cucumbers, but you can pickle just about any fruit or vegetable. At the restaurant, we spend the growing season pickling everything from okra to green beans to watermelon rinds—even butternut squash. And in Texas we have a nearly year-round growing season, so we're pickling pretty much all the time! In this section, you'll find instructions for pickling all of these and more.

If you intend to can your pickles, follow the instructions on page 328 for sanitizing your jars. Otherwise, just make sure you're using a clean, dry vessel made out of nonreactive material—meaning glass, plastic, stainless steel, enamel, or glazed ceramics. You do not want to pickle in containers made from other metals or in porous, unglazed ceramics; the former because acid can react with the metal, impacting the flavor of the pickle, and the latter because the vessel will absorb some of the pickling liquid, potentially allowing bacteria to develop.

Cucumber Pickles

A classic cucumber pickle is a great place to start your pickling adventure. Pickling liquid is basically seasoned vinegar—don't discard it when you're done with the pickles; have fun using it in recipes. It's great when used to make mustards (page 19) and also works nicely in vinaigrette (page 11). Making your own pickling spice also means you can tinker with the flavors—just make sure you don't change the quantity of vinegar or salt in the pickling liquid. Any leftover pickling spice is great used in meat brines (page 197), too.

Always rinse your cucumbers, as this will eliminate any mold spores that could possibly ruin your finished product. Don't use cucumbers that have been coated with wax—it will inhibit the vinegar from creating a proper pickle. Always use cucumbers as close to harvest as possible. Lastly, firmer cucumbers are better—that's why I prefer the small, firm, and nubby pickling varieties of cucumber. Avoid any that have blemishes or have become soft.

MAKES 1 QUART
Begin recipe the day before serving.

3 to 5 pickling cucumbers (1 to 1½ pounds), each cut lengthwise into 4 spears

1 bunch dill

4 teaspoons (21g) salt

2 tablespoons dill seeds

2 cups white wine vinegar

4 teaspoons Pickling Spice (recipe follows, or use store-bought)

1 Put the cucumbers and dill in a quart glass jar or other nonreactive container.

2 To make the brine, combine the salt, dill seeds, vinegar, pickling spice, and 1 cup of water in a small pot and bring to a boil. Boil until the salt dissolves, about 2 minutes. Remove from the heat and carefully pour the hot brine into the jar, making sure the cucumbers are completely covered with brine. (You may have leftover brine, depending on the size of the cucumbers.) Let cool to room temperature.

3 Cover the jar and refrigerate for 24 hours before enjoying. Cucumbers pickled in this manner will last for about 2 months in the refrigerator, but they will lose crunch as time goes on.

Pickling Spice

You can purchase pickling spice at the store, but I prefer the blend below for a nice, round flavor. Some of the spices here are left whole and some are crushed—I use a mortar and pestle to crush spices without powdering them, but you can also pulse them a couple of times in a spice grinder or break them up by hand.

   2 tablespoons black peppercorns

   2 tablespoons yellow mustard seeds

   2 tablespoons coriander seeds

   2 tablespoons allspice berries

   2 tablespoons caraway seeds

   1 (3-inch) cinnamon stick, crushed

   10 whole bay leaves, crushed

   1 tablespoon ground ginger

1 Toast the peppercorns, mustard seeds, coriander, allspice, and caraway in a dry sauté pan over medium-high heat until fragrant, about 3 minutes.

2 Allow the spices to cool before combining with the cinnamon stick, bay leaves, and ground ginger. Store in an airtight container for up to 6 months.

Easy Ideas for Using Pickles

- Slice thinly and add to a sandwich (especially grilled cheese!)
- Wrap in thinly sliced ham and stick through with a toothpick for an easy appetizer
- Mince and combine with mayonnaise for a quick spread or dipping sauce
- Chop and add to egg salad, chicken salad, or pasta salad
- Chop and add to bread dough before baking (sounds weird, but try it!)
- Add as a tangy element in a rice bowl
- Garnish a savory cocktail such as a martini or Bloody Mary
- Serve alongside anything spicy or fatty to provide an acidic counterpoint

Pickle Variations

Vegetable	Preparation	Brine Substitutions/ Additions	Procedure
Okra (12 ounces)	Use whole okra.	Substitute distilled white vinegar for the white wine vinegar. Add a pinch of red pepper flakes.	Proceed with base recipe as written.
Green Beans (12 ounces)	Remove the stems from whole green beans.	Add 1 teaspoon cayenne and 4 whole garlic cloves.	Proceed with base recipe as written.
Cauliflower (12 ounces)	Cut into bite-size florets.	Substitute unpasteurized apple cider vinegar for the white wine vinegar. Add 2 teaspoons ground turmeric and 2 teaspoons mustard powder.	Proceed with base recipe as written.
Green Tomatoes (1½ pounds)	Remove the core from each tomato and cut into ¼-inch-thick slices.	Add ½ teaspoon ground turmeric (which brightens the green color) and 4 garlic cloves.	Proceed with base recipe as written.
Watermelon Rinds (1 pound)	Peel the green, glossy exterior off the rinds and cut into ½-inch dice.	Cut the amount of salt in the base recipe by half. Add 1 star anise pod and 1 tablespoon whole fennel seeds.	Bring the brine to a simmer and add the rinds. Simmer until the rinds turn opaque, about 20 minutes. Proceed with base recipe as written.
Butternut Squash (12 ounces)	Peel, remove and discard seeds, and cut squash into ½-inch dice.	Substitute unpasteurized apple cider vinegar for the white wine vinegar. Add 2 tablespoons light brown sugar, 4 sage leaves, and 2 cardamom pods.	Simmer the brine until the sugar dissolves, add the squash, and simmer until cooked, another 8 minutes. (A toothpick should easily go through the squash, but it shouldn't be soft or mushy.) Proceed with base recipe as written.

Pickle Brine Martini

This cocktail is basically a dirty vodka martini. If you've got pickles in the fridge, though, it's a fun way to start your night—and using your own pickles makes it even more special.

MAKES 1 COCKTAIL

2½ ounces vodka

1 ounce pickle brine (page 30)

½ ounce dry vermouth

Fresh dill, for garnish

1   Chill your martini glass in the freezer for at least 30 minutes.

2   Add the vodka, pickle brine, and dry vermouth to a cocktail shaker filled with ice. Shake the martini for a good 30 seconds, then strain into the chilled glass.

3   Float a small piece of dill on top of the drink.

Romaine and Pickles Salad with Shaved Parmesan

This is a simple salad that shows off the flavor of any pickled vegetable: combine olive oil with pickle brine for a quick dressing, and then chop the pickles and toss them with the greens. The dish changes dramatically depending on what kind of pickle you use.

SERVES 6

½ cup diced pickles (page 29), with 2 tablespoons pickle brine reserved

6 tablespoons extra-virgin olive oil

Salt and freshly ground black pepper

½ cup golden raisins

1 head romaine lettuce, chopped crosswise into 2-inch pieces

4 ounces (about ¾ cup) Parmesan shavings

Croutons (page 25)

1   Whisk together the reserved pickle brine and the olive oil in a small bowl. Season with salt and pepper to taste; keep in mind your pickle brine may be quite salty, so you may not need much additional salt! Stir in the raisins.

2   Put the romaine, pickles, and vinaigrette-raisin mixture in a large mixing bowl. Sprinkle with a pinch of salt and pepper. Toss gently to combine, then add the Parmesan and toss again briefly, trying not to break up the cheese shavings.

3   Transfer to a serving bowl, top with the croutons, and serve.

Cornmeal-Crusted Fried Pickles

The first time I had fried pickles was in New Orleans, when a seafood platter came out of the kitchen covered in them. My mind was blown. At that point I had typically thought of frying as a technique best used for ingredients that need a bit of help on flavor, like catfish or green tomatoes. But here they took something that, in my mind, needed no help and made it texturally better. I could have sat there for hours dunking fried pickles in Remoulade (page 21) and washing them down with cold beer. I suggest you do the same!

SERVES 4 TO 6

1 cup cornmeal

½ cup all-purpose flour

1 teaspoon salt

1 teaspoon freshly ground black pepper

1 teaspoon paprika

½ teaspoon cayenne

12 pickled cucumber spears or other pickled vegetable (page 31)

Vegetable or peanut oil, for frying

Remoulade (page 21) or store-bought ranch dressing, for serving

1 Line a plate with paper towels.

2 Whisk together the cornmeal, flour, salt, pepper, paprika, and cayenne in a shallow bowl or pie dish.

3 Carefully dredge each spear in the cornmeal mixture, pressing it into all sides and making sure each spear is completely covered.

4 Heat 3 inches of oil in a heavy pot or Dutch oven until an instant-read thermometer reads 375°F. (If you don't have an instant-read thermometer, you will know the oil is ready if you drop a couple grains of cornmeal in it and they sizzle dramatically.) Fry the pickles in two batches until golden brown on all sides, about 2 minutes. Use a slotted spoon to remove and set aside on the prepared plate to drain.

5 Serve the fried pickles with a side of remoulade or ranch dressing for dipping.

Pickled "Pimento" Cheese

I didn't try pimento cheese until I was twenty, so perhaps you'll forgive me this slight variation on the classic, which replaces the traditional pimentos with pickles. The acid from the pickles cuts through the creamy cheese spread for an unexpectedly tasty treat.

Do be sure you take the time to grate your own cheddar for this recipe. Lots of preshredded cheeses are coated in cellulose to prevent clumping, and that cellulose will make for a pimento cheese that just doesn't want to come together fully. It's worth a little elbow grease, I promise. (You can also grate cheese in a food processor if you're in a hurry.)

MAKES ABOUT 1 QUART

1 (8-ounce) package cream cheese, softened

½ cup mayonnaise

1 cup finely diced pickles (page 29), with 2 tablespoons pickle brine reserved

1 pound sharp yellow cheddar, grated

1 teaspoon ground white pepper

1 teaspoon hot sauce (page 262 or store-bought)

⅛ teaspoon cayenne

1 teaspoon sugar

1 teaspoon minced garlic

Crackers, for serving (Crackers shown are Twice-Baked Firecracker Saltines, page 264)

1   Using a stand mixer fitted with the paddle attachment, beat the cream cheese on medium speed until smooth. Add the mayonnaise and reserved pickle brine and continue beating until smooth. Reduce the speed to low and add the shredded cheese, mixing until well incorporated.

2   Remove the bowl from the mixer and use a rubber spatula to fold in the pickles, white pepper, hot sauce, cayenne, sugar, and garlic.

3   Refrigerate the pimento cheese for at least 30 minutes before serving. This can be made ahead and refrigerated for up to 4 days.

Pickle Ham Biscuits

Instead of cutting plain biscuits in half and packing them full of ham and pickles, why not incorporate them right into the dough? This recipe makes a great addition to a lunch box or picnic basket because your whole sandwich is baked into the biscuit. Just add mustard (page 19)!

Biscuits can be fickle, though. More often than not, if your biscuits aren't turning out quite right, technique is to blame. First, cold or even frozen butter is much easier to grate, and grated butter makes more tender biscuits. If you're not getting the rise you're looking for, it may be because you twisted the cutter when forming the biscuits, thus sealing up the sides. Dipping the cutter in flour before cutting also helps with this. If you knead the dough for too long, you end up warming up the butter too much, which also impacts the rise. Finally, make sure the biscuits are touching each other and the sides of the pan, if at all possible, so they bake up and not out. With a little practice, soon you'll be making gorgeous, sky-high biscuits.

MAKES 16 BISCUITS

3 cups all-purpose flour, plus more for dusting your work surface

2 teaspoons sugar

1 tablespoon baking powder

1 teaspoon salt

1 teaspoon baking soda

½ cup (1 stick) cold unsalted butter, grated on the large holes of a cheese grater, plus ¼ cup (½ stick), melted

1¼ cups buttermilk

¼ cup shredded cheddar

¼ cup finely diced ham

¼ cup finely diced pickles (page 29)

1   Heat the oven to 425°F. Using a stand mixer fitted with the paddle attachment, combine the flour, sugar, baking powder, salt, and baking soda. Mix on low speed until combined.

2   Add the grated butter and beat on low speed until the mixture resembles cornmeal. It's okay if a few small pieces of butter remain. It's important not to overmix.

3   Add the buttermilk, cheddar, ham, and pickles and mix on low speed until incorporated.

4   Turn the dough out onto a work surface lightly dusted with flour. Dust the top of the dough and your hands with flour. Knead the dough over on itself six or seven times and flatten into a 1-inch-thick round.

5   Use a flour-dusted rolling pin to roll the dough into a ¾-inch-thick round. Dip a 2½-inch round cutter into flour and then use it to cut the biscuits. Reshape the excess dough and continue to cut until all the dough is used up.

6   Put the biscuits in a 12-inch cast-iron pan. Bake for 25 minutes, or until golden brown. Brush with the melted butter and serve.

Base Ingredient: Tomato Sauce

For home cooks and chefs alike, tomato sauce is one of the ultimate foods to put up. Summer in a jar! Homemade tomato sauce has a million culinary applications, and that's before you start adding flavorings to it. Processing tomatoes at their peak is a bit of a pain—especially because it's so hot when they start coming into the restaurant—but come January and February, boy am I glad for all those jars of red sauce.

And if you're not the tomato-processing kind? The grocery store shelf has an almost overwhelming number of options for canned tomatoes, so here's how to find a good one: First, look at the list of ingredients. Is there anything in there other than tomatoes, tomato juice, and *maybe* basil? Avoid! Good old canned tomatoes are great on their own; there's no need for sugars, herbs, or spices. More specifically, avoid anything that lists "calcium chloride" as an ingredient. This is an additive that prevents the tomato from breaking down, giving it a firm texture. But you want tomatoes to break down in tomato sauce!

Basic Tomato Sauce

Tomatoes contain a bit of acid, but not all varieties are acidic enough to can on their own. Typically we use Roma tomatoes for tomato sauce, but any paste variety—or combination of paste varieties—will work. Romas are unfortunately not quite acidic enough to can on their own, though. So I add lemon juice to my tomato sauce, which also serves the purpose of brightening everything up a bit. You can find instructions for canning your tomato sauce on page 328. You can also freeze tomato sauce for up to 6 months.

MAKES 6 CUPS

2 tablespoons extra-virgin olive oil
1 small yellow onion, finely diced
5 garlic cloves, minced

2 (28-ounce) cans whole peeled plum tomatoes or 7 cups diced paste tomatoes (about 4 pounds), peels, cores, and seeds removed
2 tablespoons cold unsalted butter
Juice of ½ lemon
Salt and freshly ground black pepper

1   Heat the olive oil over medium heat in a heavy pot or Dutch oven. Add the onions and cook, stirring occasionally, until soft, about 3 minutes. Add the garlic and sauté for 1 more minute.

2   Add the tomatoes, juice and all, to the pot and increase the heat to medium-high. Swirl about 1 cup of water through the cans to rinse out the last bits of tomato and add that to the pot as well. Bring the sauce to a simmer, reduce the heat to medium-low, and use a wooden

spoon to stir and break up the tomatoes. Cook until thickened, about 30 minutes, stirring occasionally. The tomatoes should be broken up but still slightly chunky.

3 Remove the pot from the heat and add the butter and lemon juice (the cold butter helps the sauce emulsify). Season with salt and pepper.

4 This sauce will keep for 1 week in the refrigerator or up to 6 months in the freezer.

Tomato Sauce Variations

Red Wine Tomato Sauce: Follow the tomato sauce recipe, but use only one (28-ounce) can of tomatoes. At the end of step 1, before adding the tomatoes, add a 750ml bottle of a bold red wine, such as Chianti. Simmer until reduced by one-third, about 15 minutes, scraping the bottom of the pot with a wooden spoon to release any stuck bits. Add the tomatoes and proceed as written.

Creamy Tomato Sauce: Follow the tomato sauce recipe. At the end of step 1, add ¼ cup dry white wine, 1½ cups heavy cream, and ½ cup fresh basil leaves along with the tomatoes. When the sauce is finished, puree in a blender.

Herby Tomato Sauce: Follow the tomato sauce recipe. Use any dried woody herbs, including oregano, rosemary, marjoram, bay leaf, thyme, sage, or savory (see page 97). Add 2 tablespoons total of one to three different herbs when adding the tomatoes.

Garlic Jalapeño Tomato Sauce: Avoid using canned tomatoes with basil to make this variation. Follow the tomato sauce recipe, but double the garlic and add 2 seeded, stemmed, and minced jalapeños. Sauté as written, then at the end of step 1 add ¼ cup all-purpose flour. Sauté briefly, stirring so the flour doesn't burn, then add the tomatoes, 2 tablespoons chili powder, and ½ teaspoon cumin. Omit the butter. This variation will work as an enchilada sauce.

Easy Ideas for Using Tomato Sauce

- Use warm for a dip for grilled cheese sandwiches
- Use as a braising liquid
- Whisk a couple tablespoons into ½ cup vinaigrette (page 11)
- Use as a cooking liquid for shrimp, mussels, or eggs
- Fold into cooked grains like farro or barley along with a handful of chopped fresh herbs
- Thin with stock (page 51) for soup broth
- Use as part of the cooking liquid for risotto (page 89)

Barbecue Sauce

Some Texas barbecue joints eschew sauce, claiming it masks the flavor of the meat, but I think the right sauce accentuates the flavor. Starting with tomato sauce will save you quite a bit of time—you just combine all the ingredients in a pot and watch it come together. The simplest form of cooking! Plus it leaves you more time to have a cold beer and stare at your smoker.

MAKES 1 QUART

2 cups tomato sauce (page 39)

1½ cups packed light brown sugar

½ cup honey

½ cup unpasteurized apple cider vinegar

Juice of 1 lemon

¼ cup Dijon mustard

¼ cup Worcestershire sauce

½ teaspoon cayenne

½ teaspoon chili powder

½ teaspoon smoked paprika

2 teaspoons freshly ground black pepper

Put all the ingredients in a heavy saucepan and simmer, uncovered, over low heat for 30 minutes, making sure to stir every so often to avoid sticking. Serve warm.

Tomato Soup with Greens and Tiny Pasta

This is a hearty vegetarian soup that can be made rather quickly. I like to use fregola, a toasted pasta from the Sardinian region made of semolina, but it can be hard to find; any small pasta will work great. If you don't have an immersion blender, you can always puree your soup in a regular blender and then return it to the pot to finish.

SERVES 6

2 tablespoons unsalted butter

2 garlic cloves, minced

1 tablespoon plus ½ cup thinly sliced (chiffonade) fresh basil

¼ teaspoon red pepper flakes

4 cups tomato sauce (page 39)

4 cups vegetable stock, homemade (page 51) or store-bought

1½ cups fregola pasta (or Israeli couscous, orzo, or other small pasta)

3 cups baby kale

1 tablespoon rice wine vinegar

Salt and freshly ground black pepper

1   Melt the butter in a large pot over medium heat. Add the garlic, the 1 tablespoon sliced basil, and red pepper flakes and cook until fragrant, about 1 minute.

2   Add the tomato sauce and vegetable stock and bring to a simmer. Reduce the heat to medium-low, place a lid on the pot, and simmer for 10 minutes.

3   Turn off the heat and use an immersion blender to puree the soup until smooth. (Note: If you're using a smooth tomato sauce or prefer a chunkier soup, you can skip this step.)

4   Add the fregola and stir to avoid clumping. Bring the soup back to a simmer over medium heat. Place the lid on the pot and cook the pasta in the soup for the amount of time recommended on the package, or until cooked through.

5   Stir in the kale and simmer for an additional 5 minutes. Season with the vinegar and salt and pepper to taste.

6   Remove from the heat and serve in bowls, garnished with the remaining ½ cup basil leaves.

Eggs Baked with Tomato Sauce

This dish calls for a bit of chopped marjoram, an herb that doesn't get used as much as I think it should. It is from the mint family and has a taste and aroma of oregano but is slightly sweeter. Depending on how many people you're feeding, you could add more eggs to this—generally, you want 1 to 2 eggs per person. The bread here is a must because the sauce is great for dipping.

SERVES 3 TO 4

6 large eggs

2 cups tomato sauce (page 39)

½ cup dry white wine

1½ teaspoons chopped fresh marjoram

1 teaspoon chopped fresh thyme

3 cups packed fresh spinach

Salt and freshly ground black pepper

1 cup whole milk ricotta

½ teaspoon red pepper flakes

1 baguette, cut crosswise into thirds, each third sliced lengthwise

3 tablespoons extra-virgin olive oil

10 fresh chives, chopped, for garnish

1   Take the eggs out of the refrigerator and let them sit on the counter while you prepare the rest of the dish—you want them to be room temperature when you put them in the sauce later on.

2   Heat the oven to 400°F.

3   Combine the tomato sauce, wine, marjoram, and thyme in a pot and bring to a simmer over medium heat. Simmer for 8 minutes, stirring occasionally.

4   Add the spinach to the pot and stir until cooked down completely, about 2 minutes. Season to taste with salt and pepper.

5   Spread the ricotta on the bottom of a 12-inch cast-iron pan or a 2-quart casserole. Top the ricotta with the hot tomato sauce.

6   Using a spoon, create six small wells in the top of the tomato sauce and crack an egg into each well. Sprinkle each egg with some of the red pepper flakes and bake until the whites have set but the yolks are still a bit runny, 12 to 15 minutes.

7   While the eggs are baking, place the cut baguettes on a sheet pan and brush with the olive oil, and season with salt and pepper. Bake for 10 minutes, or until nicely toasted.

8   Sprinkle the chives over the eggs and serve with the toasted bread.

Choose Your Own Adventure Meatballs

Along with the tomato sauce variations on page 40, I thought I'd give you a meatball recipe to pair with each. I like to use grass-fed beef, which is lighter in fat but fuller in flavor. The egg, bread crumbs, and cheese help make up for the leaner meat. This recipe goes with the basic tomato sauce; a meatball paired to each sauce variation is below. Try mixing and matching these with store-bought sauces as well!

SERVES 6

1¼ pounds lean ground beef

2 garlic cloves, chopped

2 teaspoons salt

¼ teaspoon freshly ground black pepper

1 large egg, lightly whisked

½ cup whole milk

½ cup unseasoned panko bread crumbs

¼ cup grated Parmesan

2 tablespoons chopped fresh parsley

3 cups tomato sauce (page 39)

1 Heat the oven to 350°F. Lightly grease a sheet pan.

2 Put the beef, garlic, salt, pepper, egg, milk, bread crumbs, cheese, and parsley in a large mixing bowl and use clean hands to mix until just combined. Do not overmix, as this will result in dry meatballs.

3 In a sauté pan over medium-high heat, cook a small tablespoon of the meat mixture and taste. Add salt or pepper to the raw meat mixture as needed.

4 Roll the remaining mixture into 1-inch meatballs. You should have roughly 36 to 40 meatballs.

5 Bake the meatballs on the prepared sheet pan for 15 minutes.

6 While the meatballs are cooking, heat the tomato sauce in a large, deep skillet or shallow Dutch oven.

7 Remove the meatballs from the oven and add them to the sauce along with any fat and juices that have accumulated on the pan. Stir to coat the meatballs with the sauce and cook for an additional 8 minutes.

Meatball Variations
(See tomato sauce variations, page 40)

Red Wine Tomato Sauce Meatballs: Substitute Italian-style bread crumbs for the panko. Serve over cooked pasta and top with dollops of goat cheese.

Creamy Tomato Sauce Meatballs: Replace the ground beef with ground turkey or chicken.

Herby Tomato Sauce Meatball Sandwiches: Substitute 4 ounces of the beef with minced bacon and add 1 teaspoon ground fennel seed. Make open-faced sandwiches by spooning meatballs and sauce over toasted baguettes and top with shredded mozzarella. Place sandwiches under the broiler to melt the cheese. Once melted, finish with red pepper flakes and chopped fresh herbs.

Garlic Jalapeño Tomato Sauce Meatballs: Replace the ground beef with ground pork. Add 2 tablespoons sherry vinegar, 1 teaspoon cayenne, 2 teaspoons smoked paprika, ½ teaspoon ground coriander, a pinch of allspice, and a pinch of dried oregano to the meatball mixture. Serve in the sauce with warm tortillas.

Ice

One of the easiest ways to preserve something is to freeze it. I know, because half the time when my cooks don't know what to do with something, they shove it in the freezer. It's just so much easier than fermenting or curing!

The flip side is that one day you'll find yourself with a freezer full of food you have no plans for. *Why is all this stuff in here?* you'll ponder, pulling out foil-wrapped this and plastic bag–stuffed that. The key is to fill your freezer with purpose: pack it with things you know you'll use.

A freezer can be a second pantry, something I consider vital for simplifying your everyday cooking. With just four frozen ingredients on hand—stock, pesto, yeast dough, and ice cream—you can make lots of different meals, snacks, and treats.

Safe freezing practices come down to temperature, both when the ingredient is frozen and when it thaws. The danger zone is 40° to 140°F, and to freeze (and thaw) food safely, you must get it through this zone quickly. Hot foods, like stock, can be cooled quickly by chilling the cooking vessel in an ice bath before portioning it into containers. Putting a pot of stock straight into the fridge won't cool it down quickly enough—and might warm up your refrigerator and put other foods in danger. When possible, thaw frozen ingredients in the refrigerator.

Wrapping something in plastic or foil is not enough; freeze food in reusable sealable containers or resealable plastic bags. Glass or plastic works nicely; deli containers are cheap, readily available, and come in a variety of sizes. Use the smallest container you can, and squeeze as much air out of it as possible.

Frozen foods don't go bad so much as they go off—if something's been frozen too long, the flavor and texture can get a little weird. The extreme version of this is freezer burn, ice crystals that form on the surface of the food, rendering it discolored with a dried, burned texture. It's best to have a plan for using frozen foods, to label and date your frozen ingredients, and to use the oldest items first.

Base Ingredient: **Stocks**

A good stock can make or break your dish. It's not just about the chicken bones or the ham hocks or the shrimp shells you make them from: stocks get their depth from layers, rounding out meatier flavors with onions and garlic and carrots and a bay leaf or two.

Stocks are the ultimate way to use your freezer as a pantry. Not only should you store ready-to-use stock in the freezer, you can also freeze the ingredients that go into stock until you have enough for a batch. Don't have 2 pounds of chicken bones on hand? No worries: keep a resealable plastic bag in the freezer and add to it when you have leftover chicken bones. When you get to 2 pounds, it's time to make stock. You can do the same when a recipe calls for a half onion or when you're about to leave town and you have herbs that might go bad while you're gone: toss all of it in your freezer stock bag.

Chicken Stock

This liquid gold is the foundation of so many other dishes. If you haven't collected chicken bones in your freezer, you can ask at your butcher counter or see if you can find chicken feet. (Many Asian supermarkets will carry them.) Use cold water for stock, as this lets you bring the temperature up slowly, allowing any impurities in the bones to rise to the surface of the water, where they can be skimmed away. Never let a stock rise above a simmer, as a boil will emulsify any fat attached to your bones, resulting in a fatty stock. It's important not to season stocks, so you can use them in many different recipes. You should also buy low-sodium or sodium-free stocks if using store-bought, so you can control the salt content in your final dish.

MAKES 2 TO 2½ QUARTS OF STOCK

2 pounds chicken bones, feet, necks, and/or gizzards (don't use livers)

1 large onion, peeled and cut in quarters

1 large carrot, peeled and cut into large chunks

2 stalks celery, cut into large chunks

2 bay leaves

1 sprig thyme

1 tablespoon black peppercorns

1   Put the chicken parts, onion, carrot, celery, bay leaves, thyme, peppercorns, and 12 cups of water into a stockpot and bring to a simmer (do not allow to boil). Simmer for 2 hours, skimming off any scum that floats to the surface with a ladle.

2   Set up a colander over a large pot and put a fine-mesh strainer in the colander. Use a ladle to

strain the stock through the mesh strainer into the pot. This is potentially a two-person job: one to hold the pot/strainer setup steady (this person needs to be careful of hot liquid and steam) and the other to ladle the stock.

3 Prepare a large ice bath in the sink that's half ice, half water. (You can use ice packs for this if you like.) Carefully set the pot of hot stock in the ice water and let cool completely. Remove the pot from the ice bath, wipe the outside of the pot dry with a towel, and refrigerate overnight. The following day, remove any fat that has congealed from the surface of the stock.

4 This stock will last, covered, in the refrigerator for 1 week or stored in airtight containers in the freezer for 6 months.

Freeze These to Make Stock Later

Save bones, whole or partial vegetables, herbs that have started to fade (but haven't gone bad yet), and other flavorings to make stock at a later date. Do remember that stocks shouldn't be garbage cans, and be thoughtful about which flavors you add to which stocks. Use the stock chart on the next page for guidance.

· Bones from chickens, pork chops, or steaks
· Shells from shrimp, lobsters, and crabs
· Onions
· Carrots
· Celery
· Garlic
· Green onions
· Leeks
· Savory herbs: thyme, rosemary, parsley, tarragon, cilantro, chives
· Fennel (bulbs, fronds, or stalks)
· Mushrooms

Easy Ideas for Using Stocks

· Use as the broth for soups and stews
· Deglaze a pan after searing meat for a quick sauce
· Cook grains in stock
· Add to leftovers to keep them moist when reheating
· Use as a cooking liquid for savory oatmeal
· Poach vegetables

Easy Ideas for Using Stock Frozen as Ice Cubes

· Finish sautéed vegetables with a splash of stock for a nice glaze
· Treat canine pals on a hot day

Stock Variations

The chicken stock recipe at the beginning of this section is a good starting point for most stocks. To use the chart below, substitute the chicken for other bases like meat, fish, or vegetables; add the same aromatics as listed on page 52 plus any additional aromatics listed below; and adjust the water quantity and simmer time accordingly. These variations yield 2 to 2½ quarts of stock.

Variations	Substitute for the Chicken	Additional Aromatics	Water Volume	Simmer Time
Pork or Beef Stock	Rub 2 pounds pork or beef bones with 2 tablespoons olive oil, then roast for 25 minutes at 350°F. Use tongs to place the bones in the stockpot, then deglaze the roasting pan with 1 cup water, scraping up any browned bits. Add the water to the stockpot. (You can get bones from a butcher or at the farmers' market.)	-	1 gallon	12 hours
Ham Stock	Simmer 2 pounds ham bones, ham hocks, or a combination for 2 hours before adding aromatics, skimming any foam from the surface of the stock. If using ham hocks, pick the meat from the bones and reserve for another use (they'd be great in the Split Pea Soup on page 25 or the Soupe au Pistou on page 65). Return bones to stock.	1 tablespoon coriander seeds, 1 sprig rosemary	1 gallon	2 hours with only ham, add the aromatics and simmer 30 additional minutes
Fish Stock	Rinse 1 pound white fish bones (halibut, grouper, snapper, sea bass, or cod) in a strainer under water for 5 minutes to remove any blood and impurities.	-	12 cups	45 minutes
Vegetable Stock	None. Omit the chicken; include all vegetables listed.	1 sprig parsley	10 cups	1 hour
Mushroom Stock	Roughly chop 1 pound assorted mushroom stems or button mushrooms.	1 sprig parsley	10 cups	1 hour

Bordelaise

Bordelaise is one of those fancy French steak sauces chefs learn in culinary school, but unlike many of those, bordelaise can be made ahead (and even frozen!). I love bordelaise because it's a great supporting player; it's never going to overshadow that amazing steak you've grilled. (Unlike some cloying store-bought steak sauces I could name.) If you swap out the stock on this to match the meat you're serving, you could serve it with something like the Big Holiday Pork Roast (page 203) or alongside your Thanksgiving turkey.

**MAKES 1 CUP, ENOUGH FOR
8 TO 10 SERVINGS OF STEAK**

¼ cup extra-virgin olive oil

1 head garlic, halved horizontally

6 shallots, sliced

1 large carrot, peeled and sliced

3 stalks celery, chopped

¼ cup brandy

2 cups dry red wine

3 cups stock (page 53)

1 bay leaf

2 sprigs thyme

Salt and freshly ground black pepper

1 Heat the olive oil in a large cast-iron pan or heavy pot over medium-high heat.

2 Once hot, place the garlic halves cut-side down in the oil and cook until dark and nearly burned, about 3 minutes. (It's okay if you partially char them.) Remove the garlic from the pan and set aside.

3 Add the sliced shallots and sauté until browned, about 5 minutes. Add the carrots and celery and sauté for an additional 5 minutes.

4 Remove the pan from the heat and add the brandy. Scrape the bottom of the pan with a wooden spoon to release any browned bits while the alcohol burns off, about 2 minutes. Return the pan to the heat. Be prepared: the brandy may catch on fire. If it does, allow the alcohol to burn off before proceeding.

5 Add the wine and bring the sauce to a simmer over medium-high heat. Reduce the heat to medium and cook, continuing to stir and scrape the bottom of the pot, until reduced by half, about 10 minutes.

6 Add the stock, bay leaf, thyme, and reserved garlic halves to the pan and bring it to a simmer. Lower the heat to medium and simmer for 30 minutes.

7 Strain the sauce through a fine-mesh strainer into a pan and reduce the sauce to 1 cup over medium-high heat, about 10 minutes. Season with salt and pepper to taste.

Note: You can make this sauce ahead of time and refrigerate it for up to 5 days or freeze it for up to 1 month.

Hominy Puree with Gravy

Hominy—nixtamalized corn that's been boiled until soft—is one of my favorite ingredients. I first encountered it when I moved to San Antonio. I started goofing around with it and realized that if you cooked it down and pureed it, you'd get a dish with the texture of mashed potatoes but the flavor of corn. Match the stock to whatever you're serving for your main dish (see photo, page 258).

SERVES 6

4 (15.5-ounce) cans white hominy, drained
8 cups stock (page 51)
¼ cup (½ stick) unsalted butter, softened
Salt
Gravy, for serving (recipe follows)

1 Combine the hominy and stock in a pot and bring to a simmer; simmer until the hominy is soft, about 20 minutes.

2 Use a cup measure to remove 4 cups of the cooking liquid, reserving, then drain the hominy in a colander.

3 Put the hominy in a blender and add 1 cup of the reserved cooking liquid and the butter. Blend until smooth, adding more stock if necessary. (Make sure you leave 2 cups of cooking liquid for the gravy.)

4 Season with salt and serve warm with the gravy.

Gravy

½ cup (1 stick) unsalted butter
1 medium onion, diced
1 small jalapeño, stemmed, seeded, and minced
1 garlic clove, minced
¼ cup all-purpose flour
1 teaspoon salt
½ teaspoon freshly ground black pepper
2 cups hominy cooking liquid
1 teaspoon lemon juice
1 tablespoon whole milk

1 Melt the butter in a large sauté pan over medium-low heat. Add the onions and jalapeños and slowly cook until the onions are very soft and golden brown, 20 minutes. Add the garlic and cook for an additional minute.

2 Sprinkle the flour over the onion mixture and stir until combined. Add the salt and pepper and cook for 2 minutes, stirring. Add the cooking liquid and cook until it's thick enough to coat the back of a spoon, about 5 minutes. Add the lemon juice and milk and taste for seasoning.

Note: If you are only making the gravy, you may replace the hominy liquid with 2 cups of stock.

Fennel with Orange and Kalamata Olives

Fennel is one of the most forgiving, versatile vegetables out there: it's amazing raw, cooked, grilled, or braised. It's traditional to pair it with orange to help bring out its delicate anise flavor, which is combined here with the added salty punch of the olives. You can freeze any of the big feathery fronds you don't use for garnish or for stocks.

SERVES 6 AS A SIDE

3 fennel bulbs, about 10 ounces each, trimmed, fronds reserved for garnish, stalks discarded (or saved for stock, page 52)

¼ cup extra-virgin olive oil

1 large sweet onion, thinly sliced

2 garlic cloves, minced

½ teaspoon red pepper flakes

1 teaspoon salt

1 teaspoon freshly ground black pepper

1 cup dry white wine (or ½ cup orange juice and ½ cup water)

1½ cups stock (page 51)

1 orange, unpeeled, cut into wedges

½ cup pitted Kalamata olives

2 tablespoons toasted pine nuts, for garnish

1 Heat the oven to 400°F.

2 Cut the fennel bulbs in half lengthwise, then cut each half into six wedges. Trim most of the core from each fennel wedge, leaving just enough to hold the wedge together.

3 Heat a large sauté pan with straight sides over medium-high heat and add the olive oil. Cook the fennel wedges until browned on both sides, about 5 minutes per side.

4 Reduce the heat to medium and add the onions. Gently use a spatula to move the fennel around the pan, trying not to break the wedges, to allow the onions to fall to the bottom of the pan and cook until just softened, about 5 minutes. Add the garlic, red pepper flakes, salt, and pepper and gently stir to combine.

5 Add the wine and simmer until the wine is almost entirely cooked off, about 10 minutes. Gently stir the mixture with a wooden spoon several times during this process, scraping the bottom to release any flavoring into the wine.

6 Arrange the fennel and onion mixture in a 3-quart baking pan. Add the stock to the pan. Nestle the orange wedges in among the fennel and sprinkle with the olives.

7 Bake until the fennel is tender and the liquid is almost entirely evaporated, about 40 minutes. Remove from the oven and garnish with the pine nuts and reserved fennel fronds. Serve.

Note: This dish can be assembled ahead of time. Complete the recipe through the end of step 6 and refrigerate, covered. The next day bake as written in step 7; it will take 5 to 10 extra minutes coming straight out of the refrigerator.

Baked Rice with Shrimp and Chorizo

A simple paella, this is a dish of layered flavors. The stock is spiked with saffron; the olive oil mingles with the oils from Spanish chorizo; the vegetables are cooked down with tomato paste and smoked paprika. It will look like it's not going to all fit in the pan a couple of times during the cooking process, but I promise if you use a 12-inch cast-iron pan, it will fit.

SERVES 6

3½ cups stock (page 51)

1 teaspoon saffron threads (optional)

½ cup extra-virgin olive oil

12 ounces Spanish chorizo, diced

1½ pounds medium (21/25) shrimp, peeled and deveined, tails intact

1½ teaspoons salt

1½ teaspoons freshly ground black pepper

1 medium onion, diced

4 to 5 garlic cloves, thinly sliced (about 2 tablespoons)

½ cup drained and diced jarred roasted red peppers

1 jalapeño, stemmed and thinly sliced

1 tablespoon tomato paste

2 tablespoons smoked paprika

1 pound Arborio rice

1 cup dry white wine

½ cup frozen peas, thawed

3 tablespoons chopped fresh parsley, for garnish

1 Heat the oven to 450°F.

2 Heat the chicken stock and saffron (if using) in a saucepan and bring to a simmer.

3 Meanwhile, heat a 12-inch cast-iron pan over medium-high heat and add ¼ cup of the olive oil. Sauté the chorizo in the olive oil until the sausage begins to crisp and the oil has taken on a red hue, about 5 minutes. Use a slotted spoon to remove the chorizo and set aside.

4 Season the shrimp with 1 teaspoon of the salt and 1 teaspoon of the black pepper and sauté in the chorizo oil until just opaque, about 3 minutes. Remove the shrimp from the pan and refrigerate until needed.

5 Add the remaining ¼ cup olive oil to the pan along with the onions. Sauté, scraping the bottom of the pan with a wooden spoon to loosen any stuck bits, until the onions are slightly brown, about 5 minutes. Add the garlic and sauté for 1 minute longer. Add the red peppers and jalapeños and sauté for 5 minutes. Finally, add the tomato paste and smoked paprika and continue to stir and cook for 1 minute, or until fragrant.

6 Add the rice, hot stock, wine, reserved chorizo, and the remaining ½ teaspoon each salt and black pepper to the pot and stir to combine.

7 Cover the pan (foil will work if it doesn't have a lid) and bake for 25 minutes.

8 Remove the rice from the oven and top with the shrimp and peas. Bake, uncovered, for an additional 5 minutes.

9 Let the rice rest for 10 minutes, then top with the chopped parsley before serving.

Base Ingredient: **Pesto**

Many cuisines around the world have a chopped herb sauce in their repertoire, but my personal favorite is pesto. It's quick to make and packs a ton of flavor into a tiny amount of space. It's a great way to put up herbs from the garden ahead of a freeze; basil, yes, but any soft herbs (parsley, sorrel, chives) and even some greens (arugula, kale, spinach) make great pestos. Heck, I've been known to turn carrot tops into pesto. A mix of herbs can be nice as well. (Apologies to the Genovese for these detours from tradition.)

Pesto can be stored in deli containers by the cup or pint or, famously, frozen in ice cube trays for individual servings. If you're choosing the latter route, pop them out of the ice cube tray once frozen and store them in a resealable plastic bag with as much air as possible squeezed out of it. This will help prevent freezer burn, allow for easier access, and free up your ice cube tray for other uses.

Basil Pesto

I like a loose pesto, with more olive oil than most. Unfortunately, that means it has too much oil in it to freeze solid! But if you do not intend to use your pesto immediately, you'll need to freeze it, as pesto will brown in the refrigerator. You'll also need to adapt this recipe somewhat: To make freezer pesto, cut the olive oil down to ½ cup and freeze in an airtight container for up to 6 months. To use in the Application Recipes, thaw and whisk in the additional ½ cup olive oil prior to using.

MAKES 1 PINT

2 cups packed fresh basil leaves, or 8 to 10 sprigs, or 2 ounces leaves

⅓ cup pine nuts

1 garlic clove

⅔ cup shredded Parmesan

1 cup extra-virgin olive oil

Salt and freshly ground black pepper

Juice of ½ lemon

1 Pulse the basil, pine nuts, garlic, and cheese in a food processor until combined and crumbly looking, about 10 pulses.

2 Drizzle the olive oil into the mixture while continuing to pulse. You should end up with a loose puree. Season with salt, pepper, and lemon juice.

Easy Ideas for Using Pesto

- Add a pesto ice cube to vinaigrette
- Whisk into a soft cheese for a dip
- Top a pizza
- Fold into mashed potatoes
- Add to sautéed vegetables
- Fold into mayonnaise for a sandwich spread
- Spread on crostini
- Use as the dressing for pasta salad
- Add to chicken salad

Pesto Variations

Instead of . . .	Use . . .
Basil	Chives, cilantro, parsley, arugula, dill, sorrel, watercress, carrot tops, spinach, kale
Pine Nuts	Peanuts, walnuts, hazelnuts, macadamia nuts, almonds, pecans (or do as the French do and leave out the nuts and cheese!)
Parmesan	Feta, Pecorino, Asiago, aged Gouda, queso fresco, cotija, or Manchego

Shaved Summer Squash Salad with Pesto and Pepitas

This salad just screams summer, with its bright colors and many textures. We always have some version of a squash salad at Cured during the summer, because at a certain point we inevitably have more squash than we know what to do with. And I don't think people know how good raw summer squash can taste!

SERVES 4

2 pounds zucchini and yellow squash, ends trimmed

Salt

¾ cup goat cheese, softened

¼ cup roasted salted pepitas

⅓ cup pesto (page 60)

Freshly ground black pepper

1 Use a peeler to cut the squash into paper-thin ribbons, making sure each strip includes a little bit of the colorful peel. Stop when you reach the seeds and discard the seedy center.

2 Toss the ribbons gently in a colander with a big pinch of salt. Allow to drain in the sink for 10 minutes.

3 Either distribute the squash among individual plates or pile onto a serving dish. Dot the salad with small dollops of goat cheese and sprinkle with pepitas.

4 Drizzle the pesto over the salad and grind some pepper over the top. Serve.

Pesto-Topped Grilled Oysters

The quantity of pesto and cheese you need will vary slightly based on the size of the oysters you're using. Our larger Gulf oysters will require more, while East and West Coast oysters are typically smaller and will require less. Cooking times will vary slightly as well.

SERVES 4 TO 6

Rock salt (optional)

1 cup pesto (page 60)

2 dozen freshly shucked oysters, detached and replaced on the half shell for easier eating

½ cup grated Parmesan

1   Prepare a charcoal or gas grill to high heat. Place the rock salt (if using) on a serving dish large enough to hold 2 dozen oysters.

2   Spoon roughly 1½ to 2 teaspoons pesto on top of each oyster, depending on the size, and place them directly above the hottest part of the grill, taking care not to spill the pesto. Grill the oysters until the pesto is beginning to bubble and the oysters are starting to curl around the edges.

3   Top each oyster with a large pinch of the grated Parmesan and grill for 1 minute longer.

4   Place the grilled oysters on top of the rock salt and serve hot.

Soupe au Pistou

This is a summertime soup you can make in the winter, thanks to your store of frozen pesto—or the French pistou, sans pine nuts and cheese. The smoky ham, the medley of vegetables, and the bright flavor of basil make this a hearty bowl of sunshine on a cold day.

SERVES 4 TO 6

1 smoked ham hock (about 1 pound)

2 quarts chicken stock or ham stock (page 51)

2 tablespoons extra-virgin olive oil

1 large onion, diced

1 garlic clove, minced

1 medium tomato, diced

1 small zucchini, diced

1 small yellow squash, diced

8 ounces green beans, tips removed and cut into ½-inch pieces (yellow wax or any other similar bean will also work)

1 cup orzo or macaroni (or similar small pasta)

1 (15.5-ounce) can white beans, drained

1 teaspoon chopped fresh thyme

Pinch of red pepper flakes

Salt to taste

1½ cups pesto (page 60)

1 Bring the ham hock and chicken stock to a simmer in a large pot. Simmer, covered, for 45 minutes. Remove from heat. Use tongs to remove the ham hock and set aside.

2 Let the ham hock cool slightly and then separate the meat from the bone and discard the skin and any cartilage. Roughly chop the meat and set aside. (You may save the bone for stock, page 53, or discard.)

3 Heat the olive oil in a large soup pot over medium heat. Add the onions and sauté for 10 minutes, until golden. Add the garlic and sauté for 1 additional minute.

4 Add the tomato to the pot and sauté for 10 minutes, smashing it with the back of a wooden spoon to break up the pieces.

5 Add the zucchini and yellow squash to the pot and cook, stirring periodically, until soft but not mushy, 20 minutes.

6 Pour the stock into the pot and add the reserved ham hock meat along with the green beans, orzo, white beans, thyme, and red pepper flakes. Bring to a simmer and cook until the pasta is cooked through, 10 minutes.

7 Taste the soup and season with salt as needed. (You may not need much if the ham hock is very salty.)

8 Spoon large ladles of soup into serving bowls and top each with a nice healthy dollop of pesto.

Pesto and Ricotta Stuffed Shells with Tomato Sauce

This dish looks like a lot of work, but it comes together pretty easily. It's a fantastic pantry meal (assuming you've got pesto in your freezer!). You can make it ahead and freeze the whole thing in the pan, too. Just thaw it before baking; once thawed, it will take 15 to 20 minutes longer to bake than called for here.

SERVES 6 TO 8

1 (12-ounce) box jumbo pasta shells (you will use about 24 shells for the recipe, but some will split while boiling, so boil more than you need)

1 large egg

1½ cups ricotta

1½ cups pesto (page 60)

¾ cup grated Parmesan

1 teaspoon salt

½ teaspoon freshly ground black pepper

1 tablespoon extra-virgin olive oil

Bolognese (recipe follows), Red Wine Tomato Sauce (page 40), Herby Tomato Sauce (page 40), or 4 cups store-bought pasta sauce

½ cup torn fresh basil leaves

1 Heat the oven to 375°F.

2 Bring a large pot of heavily salted water to a boil. Cook the pasta shells in the boiling water for 2 minutes less than the package instructions, as they will continue cooking in the oven.

3 Lightly whisk the egg in a medium mixing bowl. Then add the ricotta, pesto, Parmesan, salt, and pepper and whisk until fully incorporated.

4 When the pasta has finished cooking, drain and rinse it under cold water, until cool enough to handle. Toss the shells gently in a mixing bowl with the olive oil to prevent them from sticking to each other.

5 Cover the bottom of a 9 by 13-inch lasagna pan (or other 3-quart casserole) with the Bolognese.

6 A piping bag works well for filling the shells but is not strictly necessary. You can also use a resealable plastic bag with the corner cut off or a spoon. Fill each of your cooked shells with about 3 tablespoons of the cheese mixture. You should get about 24 filled shells. Nestle the stuffed shells into the sauce, seam-side up.

7 Bake until the sauce is bubbling and the cheese filling has browned in places, 30 minutes. You can brown the shells a bit more under the broiler if you like.

8 Remove from the oven and let sit for 10 minutes. Sprinkle the basil leaves over the top and serve.

Bolognese

¼ cup extra-virgin olive oil

1 pound lean ground beef

1 teaspoon salt

1 teaspoon freshly ground black pepper

1 small onion, diced

2 carrots, peeled and diced

2 stalks celery, diced

2 garlic cloves, minced

¾ cup whole milk

1 (28-ounce) can whole peeled tomatoes in puree or ½ recipe tomato sauce (page 39)

½ cup dry white wine

2 cups chicken stock (page 51)

1   Add 2 tablespoons of the olive oil to a large pot over medium-high heat. Add the ground beef and sear, without stirring, until browned, about 6 minutes. Season with the salt and pepper. Cook, stirring frequently, until the meat is cooked through, 8 more minutes.

2   Add the remaining 2 tablespoons olive oil to the pot along with the onions, carrots, and celery and sauté for 5 minutes. Add the garlic and sauté for 1 additional minute.

3   Add the milk to the pot, stir to combine, and bring to a simmer. Reduce the heat to low and simmer until the liquid has almost entirely evaporated, about 10 minutes.

4   Add the tomatoes, wine, and chicken stock and bring the mixture back to a simmer.

5   Reduce the heat to low and cook, uncovered, for 2 hours, stirring occasionally, until still moist but not soupy.

6   Taste and adjust the seasoning.

Base Ingredient: Yeast Dough

A simple rich yeast dough is an invaluable addition to your freezer pantry. Its uses are nearly infinite, making it a valuable ingredient to have on hand for any meal (including dessert!).

A few notes for yeast dough success: You can take this Base Recipe straight into any of the Application Recipes that follow or freeze it until ready to use. If frozen, thaw overnight in the refrigerator and then proceed with the Application Recipe. And finally, know that yeast doughs vary greatly depending on the weather, temperature, and particularly humidity. Don't be surprised if your results vary slightly each time you make this base dough, or if you need to use a little more flour or knead a little longer to get similar results from time to time.

Freezer Yeast Dough

This dough is enriched with butter and egg yolk to help increase its fat content, thus helping it stand up to the drying effects of freezing and thawing. The richness also makes this dough an excellent candidate for both savory and sweet applications.

MAKES 1½ POUNDS DOUGH

1 packet (¼ ounce/2¼ teaspoons) active dry yeast

¼ cup warm but not hot water, about 110°F

½ cup whole milk

¼ cup (½ stick) unsalted butter

¼ cup sugar

½ teaspoon salt

2½ cups all-purpose flour

2 egg yolks

1 large egg

1 Dissolve the yeast in the warm water in a small bowl. Let sit until small bubbles form on the surface, 10 to 15 minutes.

2 Heat the milk in a small saucepan until steaming (do not allow to boil). Remove from the heat and add the butter, sugar, and salt. Stir until the butter has melted.

3 Add the milk mixture, the yeast mixture, and 1 cup of the flour to the bowl of a stand mixer fitted with paddle attachment. Mix on low speed until incorporated. Stop the mixer and use a rubber spatula to scrape down the sides of the bowl. Turn the mixer speed up to medium and mix for 5 additional minutes. Remove the bowl from the mixer, place it in a warm part of the kitchen, and cover with a towel or plastic wrap. Let rise until the dough doubles in size, about 1 hour.

4 Once the dough has doubled in size, reattach the bowl to the stand mixer, this time with the dough hook attached. Add the egg yolks and whole egg. Turn the mixer on low speed and

slowly add the remaining 1½ cups flour, a few tablespoons at a time, until a dough forms and it is light and soft (you may have to scrape the sides down with a rubber spatula a couple of times to achieve this). If the dough has not come together yet, add a few more tablespoons of flour, one at a time, until it comes together on the hook and looks less soupy.

5 Knead the dough on medium-low speed until it is smooth and compact, 6 to 8 minutes. Knead briefly by hand in the bowl to form the dough into a ball. If you plan on using the dough now, continue on to the Application Recipes on the following pages.

6 If you're planning on freezing the dough, form it into a 1-inch-thick disk and wrap it in plastic wrap. Place this in a resealable plastic bag and freeze until needed. To thaw, refrigerate overnight and proceed with the Application Recipe. The dough will last 1 month in the freezer.

Easy Ideas for Using Yeast Dough

Thaw the dough overnight in the refrigerator. Let double in size at room temperature, and then:

- **Pizza:** Heat your oven as high as it can go. Roll the dough into three or four rounds, top with pizza toppings, and bake on a sheet pan. Pizzas are done when the dough is puffed and brown in spots and the cheese has melted, 4 to 8 minutes, depending on size.

- **Dinner Rolls:** Partition the dough into 1½-inch balls and place on a greased sheet pan. Brush with melted butter, let rise once again until doubled, about 1 hour, then bake in a 375°F oven until golden, about 15 minutes.

- Mezcal Lime Pecan Sticky Buns, page 155

- Mini Kolaches, page 136

Grissini

Grissini are like dressed-up breadsticks. I've made some suggestions below, but you can really go nuts with the toppings. You could even go sweet with these, using some of the infused sugars on page 122. This recipe is fun to make (and eat!) with kids.

MAKES ABOUT 3 DOZEN BREADSTICKS
If using frozen dough, begin recipe 1 day before serving.

1 recipe yeast dough (page 68)

1 egg white

1 tablespoon cold water

½ cup toppings of your choosing: sesame seeds, poppy seeds, sea salt, dried minced garlic, red pepper flakes, fresh cut herbs, chopped olives, or a combination

1 If you are working with frozen dough, thaw the dough overnight in the refrigerator. If you're starting with fresh dough, begin with step 2.

2 Roll the dough into a ball and place in a greased bowl. Cover it with a towel and place it in the warmest part of the kitchen until doubled in size, 1 to 2 hours, depending on the temperature of your kitchen.

3 Heat the oven to 425°F. Line two sheet pans with parchment paper and spray them lightly with cooking spray.

4 Punch down the dough and place it on a floured work surface. Let it rest for 10 minutes.

5 Divide the dough in half. Roll half the dough into a ½-inch-thick rectangle about 8 inches by 12 inches.

6 Beat the egg white with the cold water and brush this mixture on top of the dough.

7 Sprinkle the dough with half the desired toppings and use a rolling pin to gently press them into the surface of the dough.

8 Using a pizza wheel or a sharp knife, cut the dough into 8-inch-long strips roughly ½ inch wide. Lay the strips on a prepared sheet pan about ½ inch apart. Pick up one end of the grissini and twist it four or five times as shown in the photo.

9 Repeat steps 4 to 8 with the remaining dough. Let the grissini rest for 20 minutes at room temperature before baking.

10 Bake until golden brown, about 12 minutes. Remove from the oven and let cool before eating.

The Big Club Sandwich

A gigantic sandwich can be a fun cocktail party snack when cut into many small portions, or a nice lunch to bring to a picnic when cut into bigger servings. You can of course vary the fillings to your taste—swap the Swiss for cheddar, or go vegetarian with a variety of roasted vegetables in place of the meat. The only thing that matters with the big sandwich is that you go BIG.

SERVES 8 TO 12 AS A PARTY SNACK
If using frozen dough, begin recipe 1 day before serving.

1 recipe yeast dough (page 68)

¼ cup extra-virgin olive oil

1 sprig rosemary, leaves roughly chopped

1 teaspoon flaky sea salt

½ cup mayonnaise

½ cup stone-ground mustard (page 19 or store-bought)

2 large tomatoes, thinly sliced

8 ounces thinly sliced smoked ham or coppa

8 ounces thinly sliced Swiss cheese

8 ounces thinly sliced Genoa salami

2 avocados, halved and cut into ¼-inch-thick slices

12 ounces sliced bacon, cooked and cooled

4 ounces sprouts (I prefer onion sprouts)

Toothpicks, for serving (optional)

1 If you are working with frozen dough, thaw the dough overnight in the refrigerator. If you're starting with fresh dough, begin with step 2.

2 Roll the dough into a ball and place it in a greased bowl. Cover it with a towel and place it in the warmest part of the kitchen until doubled in size, 1 to 2 hours, depending on the temperature of your kitchen.

3 Grease a 9 by 13-inch pan with 2 tablespoons of the olive oil and gently transfer the dough to the pan. Use your fingers to punch down the dough, continuing to poke at it and spread it until you have a rectangle that is nearly the size of the pan. (Do not let your fingers go all the way through the dough.) Let the dough rise until it fills the pan and has puffed up slightly, about 2 hours.

4 Heat the oven to 425°F.

5 Dimple the top of the dough with your fingers. Drizzle the dough with the remaining 2 tablespoons olive oil and sprinkle it with the rosemary and salt.

6 Bake until golden brown, 25 minutes. Cool for 5 minutes in the pan, and then use a spatula to remove the bread and transfer it to a rack to cool completely.

7 Use a long serrated knife to carefully cut the bread in half horizontally.

8 Spread the mayonnaise on the top half and the mustard on the bottom. Layer the tomatoes over the mustard, followed by the ham, cheese, salami, avocado slices, bacon, and sprouts, in that order. Place the mayonnaise half of the bread over the toppings and cut the sandwich into individual square sandwiches. (It may help to put a toothpick in each serving before cutting, both to serve as guidelines and to keep the sandwich together as you cut.)

Cinnamon Sugar Fritters

With the dough in the freezer ahead of time, this is one of those recipes that comes together so easily yet results in flavor one hundred times more than the effort you put into it. Try these fritters with one of the infused sugars on page 122, or for a New Orleans twist, cover them in a mountain of powdered sugar.

MAKES 12 FRITTERS
If using frozen dough, begin recipe 1 day before serving.

1 recipe yeast dough (page 68)

2 tablespoons cinnamon

½ cup sugar

Vegetable or peanut oil, for frying

1 If you are working with frozen dough, thaw the dough overnight in the refrigerator. If you're starting with fresh dough, begin with step 2.

2 Roll the dough into a ball and place in a greased bowl. Cover it with a towel and place it in the warmest part of the kitchen until doubled in size, 1 to 2 hours, depending on the temperature of your kitchen.

3 Whisk the cinnamon and sugar together in a medium bowl. Set aside.

4 Line a plate with paper towels. Heat 1½ inches of oil in a large, heavy pot until an instant-read thermometer reads 350°F. (If you don't have an instant-read thermometer, you can check the temperature by sticking a wooden spoon or skewer into the oil; if bubbles form on the surface, it's ready.)

5 While the oil is heating, lightly flour a work surface. Roll the dough into a ½-inch-thick rectangle about 16 inches by 12 inches. Cut the dough in half lengthwise and cut each half into six equal-size strips. You'll end up with twelve dough rectangles.

6 Flour your hands and pick up one of the pieces. Slightly stretch the dough into a square with your fingers and slip it into the oil. Use a slotted spoon to move it around, turning it after 1 minute. Fry on the other side for 1 additional minute. Both sides should be golden brown.

7 Use a wire spider or tongs to remove the fritter from the hot oil and place it into the bowl with the cinnamon sugar. Toss to coat. Transfer the fritter to the paper towel–lined plate to cool slightly. Repeat with the remaining dough.

8 Serve with Cajeta (page 148) or Peach Jam (page 131), for dipping.

Base Ingredient: **Ice Cream**

When I first learned how to make ice cream, I was blown away by how easy it was. You do need some kind of ice cream maker, but once you've got that, there's really not much to it. And the ability to customize your own flavors is well worth the trouble of acquiring special equipment! This vanilla recipe, for example, would be a great base for chopped-up leftover holiday candy, or a swirl of jam (page 131) or caramel (page 147) toward the end of the churning. Plus, with no stabilizers or preservatives, homemade ice cream has better texture and flavor.

Vanilla Ice Cream

MAKES 1 QUART
Begin this recipe 1 day before serving.

2½ cups heavy cream

1 cup whole milk

1 vanilla bean, split lengthwise

8 egg yolks

¾ cup sugar

Pinch of salt

1   Bring the cream, milk, and vanilla to a simmer in a medium saucepan over medium heat, stirring occasionally. Do not let boil. Remove from the heat and let steep for 30 minutes.

2   Whisk together the egg yolks, sugar, and salt in a medium mixing bowl.

3   Remove the vanilla bean from the cream mixture and bring it back to a simmer. Use a paring knife to scrape the vanilla seeds from the bean into the cream.

4   Whisking constantly, slowly add half the cream mixture into the egg yolks. Pour the contents of the egg bowl into the remaining cream mixture in the saucepan and return to the stove. (This process brings the temperature of the egg yolks up gradually and keeps cooked egg bits out of your ice cream.)

5   Continuing to whisk, heat the ice cream base over medium-low heat until it steams (or until the temperature reaches 180°F on an instant-read thermometer). Pour it into a bowl and let cool to room temperature. Refrigerate, covered, for 4 hours.

6   Churn the ice cream in an ice cream maker according to the manufacturer's instructions, until velvety and soft.

7   Enjoy at this "soft serve" stage or scrape the ice cream into a sealable container and freeze for 6 hours or until firm. This will keep in the freezer in a sealable container for 3 to 4 weeks.

Ice Cream Variations

Peach Ice Cream: Dice 2 ripe peaches and put them in a small bowl with 1½ tablespoons sugar. Stir to coat and let sit 10 minutes. Mash the peaches slightly with the back of a fork. After the vanilla ice cream has been made but before the final freeze, fold the peaches and their juices into the ice cream. Freeze in a sealable container for 6 hours or until firm.

Horchata Ice Cream: Prior to making the vanilla ice cream recipe, toast ½ cup uncooked long-grain white rice and 2 cinnamon sticks that have been broken in half in a saucepan over medium-low heat, stirring constantly until fragrant, about 3 minutes. Remove from the heat and add 2½ cups heavy cream and 1 cup whole milk. Steep for 30 minutes, strain through a fine-mesh strainer, and proceed with the vanilla ice cream recipe as written from step 4.

Dulce de Leche Ice Cream: Skip step 1 of the vanilla ice cream recipe, omitting vanilla. Substitute ¾ cup Dulce de Leche (page 147 or store-bought) for the sugar.

Warm Summer Fruit Sauce

I love a warm fruit sauce with ice cream; like a fruit pie à la mode without all the trouble of making a crust. And the contrasting temperatures really bring out the flavors of both the fruit and the ice cream.

MAKES 2 CUPS

1 pound fruit (berries and stone fruit work great), fresh or frozen and thawed, pitted and cut into bite-size pieces as needed

½ cup sugar

Zest and juice of 1 lemon

Pinch of salt

Ice cream (page 76)

Combine the fruit, sugar, lemon zest and juice, and salt in a medium saucepan and bring to a simmer over medium heat. Simmer, stirring occasionally, until the fruit begins to fall apart (it should not fall apart completely), about 8 minutes. Let cool slightly before serving warm over ice cream.

Boozy Milkshakes

My wife, Sylvia—who dreams up a lot of the cocktails we serve at the restaurant—has created some truly inventive pairings for the ice creams in this chapter. Peach amaro milkshakes? Dulce de leche and Scotch? Not your everyday boozy milkshakes, for sure.

MAKES 4 MILKSHAKES

1 quart ice cream (page 76)

½ cup whole milk

6 ounces liquor (options for pairing follow)

1 cup whipped cream

1 Place four parfait or soda glasses in the freezer.

2 Refrigerate the ice cream for 30 minutes to soften slightly.

3 Add the milk and liquor to a blender, and then scoop the ice cream on top. Mix on a low speed until smooth.

4 Divide the milkshakes among the chilled glasses and top with a dollop of whipped cream.

Ice Cream Flavor	Liquor Pairings (choose one)			
Vanilla	Rye whiskey	Coffee liqueur	3 ounces vodka, 3 ounces Kahlúa	
Peach	Southern Comfort	Bourbon	Amaro, such as Nonino or Montenegro	3 ounces vodka, 3 ounces Grand Marnier
Horchata	Tequila	Mezcal	Dark rum	RumChata
Dulce de Leche	Scotch	Tequila	3 ounces vodka, 3 ounces Irish cream	

Ice Cream Terrine

An ice cream terrine is a showstopper of a dessert, but it couldn't be easier to throw together, or more infinitely customizable. Three different but complementary ice cream flavors come together with nuts, cookies, candies, and fruit into something akin to a make-ahead sundae. You could incorporate all kinds of recipes from this book here: the Ice Cream Cake-wiches (page 83) in place of the ladyfingers, for example, or smoked nuts (page 288), marmalades (page 138), granola (page 111), you name it. And, of course, you can substitute your favorite store-bought ice cream flavors here as well.

SERVES 10

1½ cups peach ice cream (page 77)

⅓ cup whole almonds or other nuts

1 (7-ounce) package ladyfingers or ½ recipe Ice Cream Cake-wiches (page 83)

1½ cups vanilla ice cream (page 76)

⅓ cup malt balls or other bite-size candies

1½ cups horchata ice cream (page 77)

⅓ cup pitted and halved cherries (fresh, if possible)

1 Refrigerate the peach ice cream for 30 minutes.

2 Spray a 9 by 5-inch loaf pan with cooking spray and line it with plastic wrap. Leave long ends of plastic extended over the sides of the pan; it will make wrapping the terrine and lifting it out later easier.

3 Mash the peach ice cream in a mixing bowl with a fork until soft and workable. Fold in the almonds. Spoon the ice cream into the prepared loaf pan and use a small offset spatula to smooth the surface. Top the ice cream with a layer of ladyfingers or cake. Freeze the terrine and refrigerate the vanilla ice cream for 30 minutes.

4 Mash the vanilla ice cream in a mixing bowl with a fork until soft and workable. Fold in the malt balls. Spoon the ice cream into the loaf pan and use a small offset spatula to smooth the surface. Top the ice cream with a layer of ladyfingers or cake. Freeze the terrine and refrigerate the horchata ice cream for 30 minutes.

5 Repeat the mashing process with the horchata ice cream and fold in the halved cherries. Spoon the ice cream into the loaf pan and use a small offset spatula to smooth the surface. Top the ice cream with a layer of ladyfingers or cake.

6 Fold the plastic over the terrine and place into the freezer for at least 4 hours.

7 Remove the terrine from the freezer 20 minutes before serving. Carefully lift it out of the loaf pan using the plastic wrap and cut into thick slices to serve.

Ice Cream Cake-wiches

Cured's pastry chef, Latoya Boisley, helped with these cakey cookies that are perfect for ice cream sandwiches. Dense and rich, you can mix and match these flavors with your favorite ice creams for unlimited combinations. Try the peanut butter cake variation with butter pecan ice cream in the fall, chocolate ice cream for the holidays, or strawberry ice cream in the summer, for example. An offset spatula is key to spreading the batter all the way to the edge of the pan, ensuring a thin, even cake.

EACH CAKE PLUS 1 QUART ICE CREAM MAKES 12 ICE CREAM SANDWICHES

2 cups all-purpose flour

½ teaspoon salt

1 cup (2 sticks) unsalted butter, softened

1 cup granulated sugar

1½ cups packed light brown sugar

4 large eggs

1 teaspoon vanilla

¼ cup rainbow sprinkles

1 quart ice cream (page 76)

1   Heat the oven to 350°F, with a baking rack positioned in the center of the oven. Grease a 13 by 18-inch sheet pan (jelly roll pan) and line it with parchment paper.

2   Sift together the flour and salt in a small mixing bowl.

3   Using a stand mixer fitted with the paddle attachment, beat the butter, granulated sugar, and brown sugar on medium speed until pale and creamy, about 3 minutes. With the mixer running, add the eggs, one at a time, until combined, then add the vanilla.

4   Add the flour mixture to the butter mixture in three stages. Beat on medium speed until combined after each addition, scraping down the sides of the bowl in between. Fold in the rainbow sprinkles with a rubber spatula until just barely combined.

5   Scrape the batter into the prepared sheet pan and smooth the top with an offset spatula. Dip the spatula periodically in a container of warm water to help spread it as smoothly and evenly as possible. Bake until the cake is set and a toothpick inserted in the middle comes out clean, about 35 minutes. Let cool completely.

6   Remove the ice cream from the freezer 5 minutes before assembling the sandwiches.

7   Use the parchment to move the cake to a cutting board and cut in half horizontally.

8   Scoop dollops of the ice cream evenly over one-half of the cake. Use a clean offset spatula to spread the ice cream into an even layer. Place the other half of the cake on top of the ice cream, with the top facing down. Wrap the cake and the cutting board together in plastic wrap (this will help you move it) and freeze for 6 hours.

9   Remove the cake from the freezer and remove the plastic. Trim the edges so everything is nice and squared, and then cut into twelve small sandwiches. Wrap the individual sandwiches with plastic wrap and freeze until ready to serve.

Cake Variations

Peanut Butter Cake: Omit the sprinkles and vanilla. In place of 1 cup butter, use ½ cup (1 stick) butter and 1 cup creamy peanut butter.

Chocolate Cake: Omit the sprinkles and vanilla. In place of 2 cups flour, use 1¼ cups flour and 1 cup cocoa powder.

Dry

Dehydration has to be one of the oldest ways to preserve food. Drying food in the sun or by a fire is a very simple and fairly foolproof process, and one early humans had easy access to. Of course, these days we use a dehydrator or an oven to dry ingredients, but the science behind this preservation technique remains the same.

The key to a lot of preservation methods is managing moisture. Where there is moisture, there is opportunity for harmful bacteria, mold, and other spoilage to occur. By removing the moisture, you remove that opportunity.

There are other benefits to dehydrating foods as a method of preservation. Dehydrated ingredients are lighter and smaller than their fresh counterparts, making them easier to transport (and taking up less room in your pantry!). The texture also changes, even when reconstituted; a reconstituted dried mushroom is meatier than it was fresh, and dried slices of citrus turn crisp and jewel-like, almost like little rounds of stained glass.

But the main reason I like to work with dried ingredients is flavor. Dehydrating an ingredient compounds its flavor in often surprising ways. Take trout: Fresh trout is very delicate and you don't taste its oils prominently. Dry (or smoke, a related technique) that same fish and you get something else entirely: whoa, man, *that* is a fish. Dehydration can bring out flavors you didn't even know were present. And it can turn something kind of mediocre, like slightly out-of-season tomatoes, into something spectacular.

The key to dehydration is timing: you want the ingredient to dry quickly so as not to spoil, but you also can't dry it too quickly or the heat will cook it. Food dehydrators are pretty affordable (although some of them do take up quite a bit of room) and work by heating ingredients slightly while blowing a fan over them. The recipes in this chapter are either dehydrated in your home oven, in the case of the dried tomatoes, mushrooms, and citrus, or the ingredients are purchased dried, including dried herbs and spices.

Base Ingredient: Oven-Dried Produce

I love to make these low-and-slow dried tomatoes in the oven when tomatoes are not quite at their peak season. Plus, you don't have to buy a food dehydrator to do it! The oven-dried tomatoes and all variations will keep for 1 week at room temperature, 1 month refrigerated, and 6 months in the freezer.

Reconstituting Store-Bought Dried Produce

If you are working with store-bought dried tomatoes or mushrooms, follow the instructions on the packaging to reconstitute them prior to using in the Application Recipes. If you are using store-bought sundried tomatoes that have been packed in oil and other seasonings, I recommend you rinse them off prior to using. Also be aware they are higher in sodium, so you'll need less salt in your dish.

Oven-Dried Tomatoes

This method allows you to introduce flavor while concentrating what's naturally in the tomatoes. If your oven has a dehydrator mode, you can use it for this recipe, whereas a convection oven will speed up the process. Just be sure to keep an eye on things and remove the tomatoes from the oven before the sugar burns.

MAKES ABOUT 2 CUPS

2 pounds Roma tomatoes (6 to 8 tomatoes)

1 tablespoon light brown sugar

2 teaspoons salt

1 teaspoon freshly ground black pepper

Leaves from 5 sprigs thyme

2 tablespoons extra-virgin olive oil

1 Heat the oven to 300°F. Line a sheet pan with parchment paper or foil.

2 Cut the tomatoes in half. (Quarter them if exceptionally large.) Arrange them cut-side up on the prepared sheet pan.

3 Combine the sugar, salt, pepper, and thyme leaves in a small bowl. Sprinkle the mixture evenly over the tomatoes. Drizzle the olive oil over the tomatoes.

4 Dry the tomatoes for 4 to 5 hours in the oven, removing them when they are dried but still pliable. The timing will vary depending on the size of the tomatoes.

5 Let cool and store in an airtight container in the refrigerator.

Oven-Dried Produce Variations

Oven-Dried Figs: Stem and halve 2 pounds fresh figs. Place them on a rack and brush them with a small amount of balsamic vinegar and dust them lightly with powdered sugar. Put the rack on a sheet pan and dry in a 200°F oven until dried but still pliable, about 4 hours.

Oven-Dried Mushrooms: Clean any dirt off 2 pounds fresh mushrooms using a small brush or towel. You can dry whole mushrooms, but I prefer to slice them to ensure even drying. Use mushrooms that are fresh, as the older a mushroom becomes, the more liquid it holds, and you run the risk of steaming them instead of drying them. Heat the oven to 200°F and dry the mushrooms on a rack placed over a sheet pan until completely dried, 1 to 2 hours.

Oven-Dried Shallots: Slice 2 pounds shallots into ¼-inch-thick rings. Combine them in a bowl with 2 teaspoons salt and 2 teaspoons vegetable oil. Stir to combine. Spread the shallots out on a parchment paper– or foil-lined sheet pan and dry in a 325°F oven, stirring two or three times, until dry and crisp, about 3 hours.

Oven-Dried Citrus: Slice 2 pounds citrus into ⅛-inch-thick slices. Put the slices on a rack placed over a sheet pan and bake in a 200°F oven until thoroughly dried, flipping the slices over halfway through drying. Lemons and limes will take about 4 hours, oranges 5 hours, and grapefruit 6 hours or longer, depending on their size. Citrus will be dried but still pliable and will crisp as it cools.

Easy Ideas for Using Oven-Dried Produce

Savory (Tomato, Mushroom)

• Add to soups, stews, and braises

• Reconstitute and add to scrambled eggs

• Make into an easy pasta sauce: soak the dried ingredient in hot water for 20 minutes; then chop, sauté in butter, and add a splash of wine and some chopped herbs

• Add to stuffings and bread puddings

• Add to pasta salad

Alliums (Shallots, Onions)

• Chop and fold into a combination of equal parts mayonnaise and sour cream, adding any fresh, chopped herbs you might have on hand; let sit in the refrigerator overnight for an easy dip

• Add to marinades

• Add to soups

• Add to rice and other grains while cooking

Fruit (Citrus, Figs)

• Steep in hot water for a quick infused beverage

• Dice and add to pancake batter

• Reconstitute in wine for a sauce for cakes or ice cream

• Dice and add to pound cakes

• Reconstitute with equal parts dried and fresh fruit for a fruit filling for cakes

• Dice and add to granola

• Dice and add to muffin recipes

• Garnish cocktails

Risotto

I think of risotto as a technique, and one that lends itself to many applications. Because of the slow addition of liquid, it's a perfect base to highlight oven-dried produce. Tomatoes and mushrooms will work best here, but you might try alliums as well. In Italy, you'll sometimes even see citrus risotto as a side for seafood—cut the quantity back to 1 cup dried citrus for that, though, or else your risotto might get pretty intense.

SERVES 4

6 cups stock (page 51 or store-bought)

3 tablespoons extra-virgin olive oil

6 tablespoons (¾ stick) unsalted butter

1 small onion, minced

3 garlic cloves, minced

2¼ cups Arborio rice

3 sprigs thyme

1½ cups diced oven-dried produce (page 87)

2 cups dry white wine

Salt and freshly ground black pepper

1 cup grated Parmesan

1   Bring the stock to a simmer in a large saucepan over medium-high heat. Keep warm.

2   In a separate pot, heat the olive oil and 3 tablespoons of the butter over medium heat. When the butter begins to foam, add the onion and sauté until golden, 6 to 8 minutes.

3   Reduce the heat to low. Add the garlic, rice, and thyme sprigs and sauté for an additional 5 minutes, until it is fragrant but has not taken on any color. Next, stir in the oven-dried produce, then the wine. Cook, stirring, until the wine has almost entirely evaporated, 5 minutes.

4   Add 2 cups of the hot stock to the pot; you want the rice to be just covered. Cook the rice, stirring frequently, adding more stock as needed to cover. Repeat until all the stock has been used up, about 20 minutes total. The rice should be cooked through (but not mushy) and coated in a creamy sauce. If the rice is still crunchy, add a bit of hot water and continue cooking. When the rice is done, remove and discard the thyme sprigs.

5   Remove the rice from the heat, season with salt and pepper to taste, and fold in the Parmesan and remaining 3 tablespoons butter. Serve immediately.

Spoon Bread

Spoon breads are great: super versatile, very forgiving, easy to make, and quick to knock out in a pinch. Somewhere between a custard and a cornbread, spoon breads are a great vehicle for all kinds of savory flavorings. You can serve this as a side to just about anything or as the main course along with a salad. This will work best with oven-dried tomatoes, mushrooms, or alliums.

SERVES 6

¼ cup (½ stick) cold unsalted butter, diced, plus more for the baking dish

2½ cups whole milk

1 cup cornmeal

1 cup diced oven-dried produce (page 87)

3 large eggs

2 teaspoons chopped fresh parsley

1 teaspoon salt

½ teaspoon freshly ground black pepper

1½ teaspoons baking powder

1 Heat the oven to 375°F. Butter an 8-inch square baking dish.

2 Bring the milk to a simmer in a medium saucepan over medium heat (do not allow it to boil). Whisk in the cornmeal and cook for 3 minutes, stirring constantly. Remove from heat and stir in the oven-dried produce.

3 Let the mixture cool for 10 minutes, then add the diced butter, eggs, parsley, salt, pepper, and baking powder. Stir for 1 full minute to help thicken the batter.

4 Pour the mixture into the prepared baking dish and bake until golden brown, 25 to 40 minutes. (The bake time will depend on the moisture content of the dried produce you choose to incorporate.) Serve immediately.

Saucy Poached Halibut

The oven-dried produce is used both to infuse the fish with flavor *and* to make a simple, quick sauce to go on top of it. This dish punches way above its weight—easy enough for a weeknight but tastes like a fancy restaurant dish thanks to the concentrated flavors in the dried produce. And if you *really* want to emphasize the dried produce flavor, serve this on top of a matching Risotto (page 89).

SERVES 6

3 skinless halibut fillets (about 8 ounces each), halved lengthwise

1 teaspoon salt

½ teaspoon freshly ground black pepper

3 tablespoons extra-virgin olive oil

¼ cup diced onion

6 garlic cloves, sliced

2½ cups savory oven-dried produce, such as tomato or mushroom (pages 87 or 88), cut into ½-inch pieces

¼ cup chopped fresh parsley, stems reserved

3 tablespoons unsalted butter

3 tablespoons drained capers

1 Season the fillets with the salt and pepper on both sides and let sit at room temperature for 10 minutes.

2 Heat the olive oil in a wide pot over medium heat. Add the onions and sauté until translucent, about 3 minutes. Add 4 cups water, the garlic, oven-dried produce, and reserved parsley stems and bring to a simmer. Simmer for 6 minutes.

3 Add the fish to the pot, submerging the fillets in the broth (add more water if necessary). Simmer the fish, covered, until it flakes when pierced with a fork, 8 minutes. Remove the fish from the pot with a slotted spoon and set aside, covered, while you finish the sauce.

4 Strain the poaching liquid and reserve the vegetables. Discard the parsley stems and place the rest of the vegetables in a medium bowl. Add the butter and stir until melted. Taste and adjust seasoning if necessary.

5 Serve the fish topped with a spoonful of the vegetable mixture and sprinkle with the chopped parsley and capers.

Upside-Down Cake with Dried Fruit

Here, dried citrus, figs, or other fruit is caramelized underneath a rich cake that, when flipped over, is covered in a decadent sauce. This cake is best right out of the oven but can be made up to 4 days in advance; just leave it in the pan until ready to serve and reheat for 10 to 15 minutes in a 250°F oven before inverting and slicing.

MAKES ONE 9-INCH CAKE

½ cup (1 stick) unsalted butter, softened

¾ cup packed light brown sugar

1 teaspoon vanilla extract

2 cups loosely packed oven-dried fruit (page 88)

2 tablespoons dark rum, bourbon, or orange juice

1½ cups all-purpose flour

½ teaspoon baking powder

¼ teaspoon salt

1 cup granulated sugar

3 large eggs

1 Heat the oven to 350°F. Use 1 tablespoon of the butter to grease a 9-inch cake pan.

2 Combine the brown sugar, vanilla, and 1 cup water in a small saucepan and bring to a simmer over medium heat. Add the dried fruit and simmer for 2 minutes. Use a slotted spoon to remove the fruit from the syrup and set aside in a bowl. Continue cooking the syrup for 1 more minute to reduce it, then remove it from the heat. Carefully add the rum (it may sizzle a bit) and set aside to cool.

3 Sift together the flour and baking powder in a medium bowl. Add the salt and whisk briefly to combine. Set aside.

4 Using a stand mixer fitted with the paddle attachment, beat the remaining 7 tablespoons butter and the sugar together on medium-low speed for about 2 minutes. Add the eggs, one at a time, mixing until fully incorporated and scraping the sides of the bowl with a rubber spatula after each addition.

5 With the mixer on low speed, add the dry ingredients to the butter and egg mixture one large spoonful at a time. Halfway through, stop the mixer and use a spatula to scrape down the sides. Mix until just combined.

6 Arrange the fruit on the bottom of the prepared pan and drizzle with ½ cup of the reduced syrup (save the rest of the syrup for serving).

7 Spoon the batter on top of the fruit and smooth the surface with an offset spatula.

8 Bake the cake until a toothpick inserted in the middle comes out clean, 35 minutes. Let it cool for 10 minutes before inverting onto a large plate. (It may help to run a knife around the edge of the cake first.) Drizzle the remaining syrup over the cake and serve warm in large wedges. (Don't let it cool completely in the pan or else the syrup will harden and it will be hard to get out.)

Base Ingredient: Dried Herbs

In recent years, cooking with dried herbs has become a little passé. But when I was growing up, everyone cooked with dried herbs. I don't think I saw fresh basil until I went to culinary school. And while I love fresh herbs—as you've probably guessed from the dozens of recipes in this book that call for them—there are a lot of instances when dried herbs are actually preferable. In New Orleans, for example, there's a lot of what we call "pot cooking," long-simmered dishes like beans, gumbos, or jambalayas that really benefit from the presence of dried herbs. So my chef brain goes to dried herbs when I'm cooking things low and slow.

Herbs are easy to dry at home, as they dry out pretty quickly. So while you could dry herbs in a dehydrator, I often just tie up a bunch and hang it in a sunny window. If you have an oven with a pilot light, you can also spread out herbs on a sheet pan and leave them there overnight. (In the restaurant, we tie a kitchen towel to the oven door handle to remind everyone that something's in the oven, so they don't accidentally turn it on and scorch the herbs!)

How to Substitute Dried Herbs for Fresh: ¼ teaspoon dried herbs for every tablespoon fresh. (See how concentrated that flavor gets during the drying process?!)

Some Herb and Spice Blends I Use Frequently

Mix small amounts of the following together; let your nose be your guide on the proportions!

- For fish, pork, chicken, or vegetables: basil, fennel seeds, and lavender

- For lamb or dishes with goat cheese: basil, oregano, tarragon, and anise seeds

- For southern US flavors: oregano, crushed bay leaves, paprika, sassafras, and cayenne

- For grilling: rosemary, cracked black pepper, onion powder, and sea salt

Easy Ideas for Using Dried Herbs

- Use in marinades
- Add to vinaigrettes (page 11); soak woody herbs in the vinegar along with the shallots
- Add to tomato sauce while cooking (page 39)
- Add to soups and stews
- Fold into compound butters (page 158)
- Add to bread dough or sprinkle over the top after the loaf is formed
- Combine with salt, pepper, and olive oil for a dip for bread
- Season vegetables before roasting or grilling

Polenta with Herbed Oil

This polenta takes its inspiration from spaghetti night, specifically everyone's favorite accompaniment: good old-fashioned garlic bread. Herbs are steeped in a combination of butter and olive oil, along with garlic and red pepper flakes, to infuse the polenta with tons of flavor.

SERVES 6

2 teaspoons salt

1½ cups yellow polenta
(or coarse-ground cornmeal)

¼ cup extra-virgin olive oil

¼ cup (½ stick) unsalted butter

6 garlic cloves, roughly chopped

**2 tablespoons dried herbs, such as
oregano, basil, thyme, marjoram,
rosemary, or a combination (page 97)**

1 teaspoon red pepper flakes

1 Combine 6 cups water and 1 teaspoon of the salt in a heavy-bottomed pot and bring to a boil. Slowly whisk in the polenta. Cook, stirring, until slightly thickened, 1 to 2 minutes, then reduce the heat to low. Cover and cook, stirring periodically to prevent from sticking to the bottom of the pan, until the polenta is tender and thoroughly cooked, 45 minutes to 1 hour. (If the mixture becomes too thick during cooking, add ½ cup water or so to thin it.)

2 Meanwhile, heat the oil and butter in a small saucepan over medium-low heat until the butter is melted. Add the garlic and cook, stirring, until fragrant but not browned, about 5 minutes. Add the herbs and cook, stirring, for 2 minutes more. Add the red pepper flakes and remaining 1 teaspoon salt, stir for about 15 more seconds, then remove from the heat.

3 Add half the oil mixture to the polenta and stir to combine. Transfer to a serving bowl and use the back of a spoon to create a swirl-shaped indentation on top of the polenta. Carefully spoon the rest of the herbed oil over the top of the polenta, allowing it to settle into the swirl pattern. Serve.

Homemade Breakfast Sausage

People think making sausage is complicated, but homemade breakfast sausage is as easy as making burgers. You can customize the flavors and veer sweeter or spicier as you please. I do very much recommend using white pepper in your breakfast sausage—there's something about it that just gives it that perfect breakfast-y flavor. You can substitute black pepper, though, if you must.

MAKES ABOUT 2 POUNDS

1½ pounds ground pork

½ cup unseasoned panko bread crumbs

1 large egg

2 teaspoons salt

3 tablespoons dried herbs, such as sage, basil, rosemary, marjoram, or a combination (page 97)

1 garlic clove, minced

½ teaspoon ground white pepper (black can be substituted if necessary)

¼ teaspoon ground ginger

3 tablespoons maple syrup

1 tablespoon extra-virgin olive oil

1   Using a stand mixer fitted with the paddle attachment, beat the ground pork, bread crumbs, and egg on low speed until thoroughly combined.

2   Add the salt, herbs, garlic, white pepper, and ground ginger and continue mixing on low for 1 minute.

3   Add the maple syrup and mix for 3 minutes on low speed, and then turn the speed up to high for 1 minute, or until the mixture becomes nice and sticky.

4   Form the sausage into 2-inch balls—you should have 16 to 18 balls. Flatten these into patties about ½ inch thick. Refrigerate the patties for at least 20 minutes and up to 24 hours to allow the flavors to develop. At this point you could freeze the sausage patties, wrapped tightly in plastic and stored in an airtight container, for up to 2 months. Thaw the patties completely before cooking.

5   To cook the patties, heat the olive oil in a cast-iron pan over medium heat. Depending on the size of your pan, you may have to work in batches. You want to leave enough space in between each patty to make flipping easier. Cook until browned on one side, about 3 minutes. Flip and cook for another 2 minutes, until completely browned. Serve warm.

Crispy, Herby Smashed Potatoes

In this dish, dried herbs add flavor and amplify the crispy, crunchy texture of the potatoes. This is one of my favorite ways to eat potatoes—I've served these in all my restaurants, alongside beef, pork, chicken, you name it. Great for breakfast, too, in lieu of hash browns.

SERVES 4 TO 6

2 pounds small potatoes (about 30 potatoes, 1 to 2 inches in diameter)

1 tablespoon plus 1 teaspoon salt

¼ cup extra-virgin olive oil, plus more for brushing the pan

2 tablespoons dried herbs, such as ground bay leaf, rosemary, thyme, sage, parsley, or a combination (page 97)

¼ teaspoon freshly ground black pepper

1   Combine the potatoes and 1 tablespoon of the salt in a large pot with water to cover and bring to a boil over high heat. Reduce to a simmer and cook until the potatoes are tender and easily pierced with a small knife or skewer, about 25 minutes.

2   While the potatoes are cooking, line a sheet pan with aluminum foil and lightly brush it with olive oil.

3   Once the potatoes are fully cooked, drain them in a colander. Let cool completely.

4   Heat the oven to 450°F. Put the cooled potatoes on the prepared pan and use the bottom of a glass or a clean dish towel to flatten them to a thickness of about ½ inch.

5   Spoon the remaining ¼ cup olive oil over the potatoes and season with the remaining 1 teaspoon salt, the dried herbs, and pepper. Roast the potatoes for 15 minutes, then turn them and roast 15 minutes more. The potatoes should be deep brown and crispy. Serve immediately.

Braised Short Ribs with Oranges and Dried Herbs

Braises are really where dried herbs shine; they hold up during the long, low, and slow cooking process. I also like to add a fishy element to braises—not so much you can tell it's there, but just enough to add a shadow of flavor and a big hit of umami. Often I do this with anchovies (and you might try it with smoked seafood, page 307), but I also really love to use fish sauce, as I do here.

SERVES 6

¼ cup extra-virgin olive oil

12 English-style bone-in short ribs, cut about 3 inches in length (about 6 pounds total)

2 teaspoons salt

1 teaspoon freshly ground black pepper

1 large onion, sliced

2 carrots, peeled and diced

6 garlic cloves

1 dried ancho chile

1 (28-ounce) can whole peeled tomatoes

1 orange, cut crosswise into slices, or 8 dried orange slices (page 88)

3 tablespoons dried herbs, such as Mexican oregano, rosemary, bay leaves, thyme, or a combination (page 97)

2 cups dry red wine

6 cups beef stock (page 53, chicken or vegetable will do in a pinch)

2 tablespoons fish sauce (optional)

1 Heat the oven to 350°F.

2 Heat the olive oil in a large Dutch oven over medium-high heat. Season the beef on all sides with the salt and pepper. Sear the short ribs until completely browned and caramelized, about 4 minutes per side. (Depending on the size of your Dutch oven, you may have to work in batches.) Remove the short ribs from the oil and set aside.

3 Add the onions and carrots to the pot and cook until the onions soften, 4 minutes. Add the garlic and sauté for 1 additional minute.

4 Add the ancho chile, tomatoes, orange slices, dried herbs, and red wine. Bring the mixture to a simmer and cook for 3 minutes. Add the beef stock, fish sauce (if using), and browned short ribs to the pot. Bring everything to a simmer.

5 Cover the Dutch oven and cook in the oven for 3 hours.

6 Let the braise rest, still covered, for 20 minutes. This allows the juices to make their way back to the center of the short ribs.

7 Use a slotted spoon to carefully remove the ribs from the broth and set aside. Strain the cooking liquid through a fine-mesh strainer into a bowl and use the back of a spoon to press the solids so you get all the liquids. Skim any fat from the top of the liquid.

8 Serve the short ribs with mashed potatoes or the Polenta with Herbed Oil (page 98). Top with the reserved cooking liquid.

Dried Spices

This section is about mixing and matching spices, how they play off one another, and how they interact with ingredients. My goal is to help you think about using spices in your cooking, and to get you to discover your own favorite spice blend.

When it comes to dried spices, freshness is key. While spices are shelf stable and won't go bad, necessarily, the flavor dissipates the longer they sit on the shelf. I recommend buying only what you need, or the smallest amount you can, so you always cook with the freshest possible spices. In recent years, more and more grocery stores have installed bulk spice sections, which helps in buying small amounts. (Most grocery stores go through their bulk spices fairly regularly, or at least more quickly than you will at home.)

Toasting whole spices also helps boost their fragrance and flavor. Use a dry sauté pan or cast-iron pan over medium heat, and shimmy the pan over the burner so that the spices are constantly moving. After a minute or two, the spices will become very fragrant. They can burn quickly, so keep an eye on them and let cool before using.

When it comes to blending spices, I like to start with a foundation spice and build from there. For example, the Creole seasoning I have been making for years is heavy on paprika, a relatively mild spice that adds flavor but also acts as a medium to disperse stronger flavors like celery salt, cayenne, allspice, garlic powder, and onion powder. In other blends, you might see turmeric, annatto, ancho and other mild chile powders, ground tea leaves, sesame seeds, smoked paprika, poppy seeds, and cocoa performing the same function. Sugar and salt can also form the base of a spice blend, but you'll need to keep your eye on the quantities so as not to overwhelm your dish.

Base Ingredient: **Dried Spice Blends**

To formulate your own spice blends, start with ¼ cup foundation spice or a ¼-cup combination of foundation spice and salt and/or sugar. Start building your spice blend knowing which spices are more potent and also which ones you really want to shine in the finished dish. The suggested quantities in the chart below make a small amount, so you won't be stuck with a spice blend that doesn't quite come out the way you want it. When you do land on a blend that you love, though, you can increase the volume based on your usage.

My basic spice blend formula is ¼ cup foundation spice, 2 tablespoons medium-potency spice, 1 tablespoon high-potency spice, and 1 teaspoon super-high-potency spice. Below, I've recommended some spice combinations for paprika-, turmeric-, chile powder–, and annatto-based spice mixes. Mix and match four to five of the following for about ½ cup spice mix:

Foundation Spices (¼ cup)	Paprika	Turmeric	Chile Powder	Annatto
Medium-Potency Spices (2 tablespoons)	Light brown sugar, cumin, dried oregano	Dried parsley flakes, ground fenugreek, cinnamon	Sugar, cumin, dried basil, dried thyme, dried oregano, cinnamon	Dried cilantro, cumin, dried orange peel, dried Mexican oregano
High-Potency Spices (1 tablespoon)	Black pepper, garlic powder, ground celery seed	Black pepper, onion powder, curry powder, ground cardamom	Onion powder, lime powder (see Note), garlic powder, black pepper	Ancho powder, garlic powder, onion powder, black pepper
Super-High-Potency Spices (1 teaspoon)	Ground fennel seed, ground cloves, cayenne, saffron	Ground fennel seed, nutmeg, ground cloves, ground star anise, ground ginger	Ground coriander, red pepper flakes	Ground mace, ground ginger, ground coriander, ground allspice
Uses	Beef, lamb, pork	Chicken, fish, vegetables	Beef, shrimp	Poultry, pork

Note: You can make homemade lime powder by running dried lime wheels (page 88) through a spice grinder, if you like, or order online.

Cured's Pumpkin Chili

If you know anything about Texas chili, you know one thing: no beans. But no one ever said anything about pumpkin! Cured started serving this chili after one of our farmers showed up with a ton of pumpkins, which hold up beautifully next to the spicy beef and add lovely texture.

SERVES 6

2 tablespoons vegetable oil

1 medium onion, diced

3 garlic cloves, minced

2 pounds lean ground beef

1 teaspoon salt

1 teaspoon freshly ground black pepper

1 (12-ounce) bottle of your favorite pumpkin beer

2 cups chicken stock (page 51)

2 chipotle peppers in adobo, roughly chopped

1 poblano pepper, stemmed and seeded, diced

1½ teaspoons dried oregano

3 cups peeled and diced pumpkin (about ¾ pound)

1 large tomato, diced

2½ tablespoons unsalted dried spice blend (page 105) or a variety of chile-based store-bought spice blends will work well

1½ cups sour cream, for serving

1 cup chopped fresh cilantro (optional), for serving

1 Heat the vegetable oil in a large pot over medium-high heat. Add the onions and sauté until translucent, about 3 minutes. Add the garlic and sauté for 1 additional minute.

2 Add the ground beef to the pot along with the salt and pepper and cook the beef until browned through, stirring to break up the meat, about 8 minutes.

3 Add the beer, chicken stock, chipotle and poblano peppers, oregano, pumpkin, tomato, and spice blend and bring to a boil. Reduce the heat to low and simmer, stirring periodically, for 30 minutes, until stew-like but looser than a typical Texas chili.

4 Remove from the heat and taste, adding salt and pepper if needed. Serve in bowls topped with sour cream and cilantro (if using).

Spiced Rice with Zucchini, Carrots, and Cilantro

Aromatic basmati rice, vegetables that lend sweetness, and bright cilantro are supporting players to almost any spice blend you come up with. Curry blends, Middle Eastern spices, Cajun seasoning, and chile rubs: anything you have on hand will work, so long as it's unsalted.

SERVES 6

2 cups basmati rice

3 tablespoons unsalted butter

1 small onion, finely diced

3 garlic cloves, minced

1 cup peeled and finely diced carrot (about 2 carrots, depending on size)

2 tablespoons unsalted dried spice blend (page 105)

4½ cups stock (page 51)

2 cups diced zucchini (about 2 small or 1 medium zucchini)

1¼ teaspoons salt

½ bunch cilantro, leaves roughly chopped

1 Rinse the rice under cold water until the water runs clear. Drain well.

2 Melt the butter in a large pot over medium heat. Add the onion and sauté until soft, 2 minutes. Add the garlic and sauté for 1 minute more.

3 Add the carrot and sauté for 2 minutes more. Next, add the rice and sauté in the butter until all the grains are coated.

4 Add the spice blend and stir to coat the rice. Next, add the stock, zucchini, and salt. Stir to combine. Bring the liquid to a boil, reduce the heat to low, stir one more time, and then cover with a lid and cook for 15 minutes. Remove the pot from the heat and let sit, covered, for 8 minutes.

5 Remove the lid, fold in the cilantro, and serve.

Grilled Pineapple Skewers with Spiced Honey

Spicing fruit is a tradition I didn't encounter until I moved to San Antonio, but boy am I glad this city introduced me to the concept. These grilled pineapple skewers are great as an appetizer, but they would also make an excellent accompaniment to roasted pork (page 203) or brighten up a taco. If you're using wooden skewers, soak them in water for about half an hour before grilling, which will prevent them from catching on fire. Rosemary sprigs also work well as skewers here. Finally, don't be afraid of getting some color on these! The charred bits taste great.

SERVES 8 AS AN APPETIZER, MORE AS A CONDIMENT

1 pineapple (about 3½ pounds)

½ cup honey

Zest and juice of 1 lime

1 tablespoon dried spice blend (page 105)

½ teaspoon salt (omit if using a salted spice blend)

8 skewers, either metal, wooden, or rosemary sprigs

1   Slice off the top and bottom of the pineapple. Use a serrated knife to remove the peel, starting at the top and working your way down in a spiral. Remove any remaining "eyes" using a small knife or tomato corer. Cut the pineapple in half from top to bottom, then cut each half into 4 spears. Cut out the cores.

2   Whisk together the honey, lime juice, spice blend, and salt (if using) in a small bowl.

3   Skewer the pineapple wedges, stopping about 1 inch from the end to prevent the wooden skewers from catching on fire. This also makes them easier to handle. Lay the skewers on a sheet pan and brush with the glaze on all sides.

4   Prepare a grill for medium-high heat.

5   Place the skewers directly over the flames, at an angle to the grill grates. Grill for 3 minutes, and then turn, brush with more glaze, and grill for an additional 3 minutes. Turn the skewers over and grill for 1 minute longer.

6   Remove the skewers from the grill and place on a platter. Drizzle with any remaining glaze and sprinkle with lime zest.

Base Ingredient: Granola

Granola is one of those things where most store-bought versions pale in comparison to homemade. There are some good granolas available for purchase out there, but they can be quite pricey. If you're used to the store-bought stuff, you might be surprised at how tasty homemade can be. Plus, when you make your own granola, you can customize it, adding any nuts, fruit, or other additions you like. Chocolate chips, anyone?

Cured's Almond Granola

This is the almond granola we serve at the restaurant, and it forms a great base for improvisation. The key to a good granola is to not let it go stale, so keep this in an airtight container and eat it quick!

MAKES 4 CUPS

2½ cups old-fashioned rolled oats

¾ cup sliced almonds

½ cup all-purpose flour

1 teaspoon salt

½ cup (1 stick) unsalted butter, melted

1 cup packed light brown sugar

2 tablespoons molasses

½ teaspoon vanilla extract

1 Heat the oven to 300°F. Line a sheet pan with parchment paper or aluminum foil.

2 Combine the oats, almonds, flour, and salt in a large mixing bowl.

3 In a separate mixing bowl, whisk together the butter, brown sugar, molasses, and vanilla. Pour this over the dry ingredients and use a rubber spatula to combine until the oats are well coated.

4 Spread the mixture evenly on the prepared pan and bake for 40 minutes until toasted and golden, stirring and turning the oats halfway through.

5 Remove the pan from the oven and let the granola cool completely before breaking it into bite-size crumbles. Store in an airtight container for up to 2 weeks.

Granola Variations

Instead of . . .	Use one of . . .					
Oats (Only replace half of the oats)	Wheat flakes	Rye flakes	Buckwheat groats (soaked overnight)	Quinoa		
Almonds	Coconut flakes	Sunflower seeds	Pumpkin seeds	Pecans	Walnuts	
Flour	Just about any flour will work here, including gluten-free flours.					
Butter	Olive oil	Coconut oil	Half oil/half nut butter			
Brown sugar	Granulated sugar	Sugar in the raw	Cane sugar	Date sugar	Coconut Sugar	
Molasses	Maple syrup	Honey	Barley malt syrup	Sorghum	Agave nectar	

Or add in . . .	Such as . . .				
Dried fruit Add ½ cup to the wet ingredients, then proceed.	Raisins	Cherries	Chopped apricots	Cranberries	Chopped dried figs

Easy Ideas for Using Granola

- Make a layered yogurt and fruit parfait
- Sprinkle over ice cream
- Add to salads
- Sprinkle over French toast or pancakes, or fold into batter before cooking
- Sprinkle over oatmeal
- Use as a garnish for some soups—try any squash soup, pureed vegetable soups, or even chili (page 106)

	Sesame seeds	Cocoa nibs	Flaxseeds
rown rice syrup	Jam, thinned with water to the consistency of molasses		
	Goji berries	Chopped dates	Chopped dried apples

Roasted Squash with Granola

I love roasted squash; my mom used to make it a lot when I was a kid. The texture is so much better than boiled or sautéed squash. You can swap the butternut for any winter squash, and while it's amazing right out of the oven, it would also be nice cooled and tossed with arugula for a fall salad.

SERVES 4

2 pounds butternut squash, peeled, seeded, and cut into 1-inch pieces

¼ cup extra-virgin olive oil

2 tablespoons light brown sugar

½ teaspoon ground coriander

¼ teaspoon cayenne

Salt and freshly ground black pepper

3 sprigs rosemary

½ cup granola (page 111)

1 orange, cut into 6 wedges

1   Heat the oven to 400°F. Line a sheet pan with parchment paper or aluminum foil.

2   Place the squash, olive oil, brown sugar, coriander, cayenne, and a large pinch of salt and pepper in a large mixing bowl and stir to combine until the squash is evenly coated.

3   Place the squash in the prepared pan and add the rosemary sprigs. Roast for 40 to 50 minutes, turning the pieces of squash with a spatula halfway through. You want the squash quite dark but not burned; look for caramelized, crispy edges.

4   To serve, place the squash in a serving dish and sprinkle with the granola. Serve with orange wedges for squeezing over the top.

Rainbow Slaw with Granola

I love winter greens, but so many recipes require you to cook them forever! Not this one. Massaging the dressing into the greens helps break them down. Plus, with all the different colors, it really stands out at the dinner table.

SERVES 6 TO 8

1 bunch dinosaur kale (also known as lacinato or Tuscan kale)

1 bunch Swiss chard

3 carrots, peeled and grated (about 1 cup)

1 small yellow beet, peeled and grated (about 1 cup)

1 bulb fennel, trimmed and grated (about 1 cup)

6 tablespoons mayonnaise

6 tablespoons Greek yogurt

½ cup pickle brine or lemon juice

2 teaspoons prepared horseradish

1 tablespoon salt

1 teaspoon freshly ground black pepper

1 cup granola (page 111)

1   Cut off and discard the woody stems from the kale and Swiss chard. Roll the leaves up and thinly shred the greens with a knife—the thinner, the better. Rinse the shredded greens in cold water and dry using a salad spinner. The greens need to be thoroughly dry; wrap and gently press them in a clean kitchen towel if you need to. Combine the greens in a large bowl with the shredded carrots, beets, and fennel.

2   Whisk together the mayonnaise, yogurt, pickle brine, horseradish, salt, and pepper in a small bowl.

3   Pour the dressing over the salad, and using clean hands, massage the greens with the dressing for a couple of minutes. Refrigerate the salad for at least 2 hours and up to 8 hours.

4   Top with the granola and serve.

Granola Dutch Baby

Dutch babies are like a magic trick: super-simple ingredients go into a hot oven and emerge transformed as the pillowy pancake of your dreams. Your Dutch baby will fall after you pull it from the oven, and that is okay, but boy are they spectacular before that happens. These eggy breakfast treats can be dressed with sweet or savory toppings, but I love to use granola, which sets into the batter and forms a streusel-y topping for the pancake. And it's excellent, like most granola dishes, topped with a scoop of yogurt and some fresh berries.

MAKES ONE 12-INCH PANCAKE, SERVING ABOUT 2

4 large eggs

½ cup all-purpose flour

1 tablespoon sugar

Pinch of salt

½ cup whole milk

2 tablespoons unsalted butter

1 cup granola (page 111)

Yogurt and fresh berries, for serving

1 Place a 12-inch cast-iron pan on the center rack of a cold oven and heat to 425°F.

2 Whisk the eggs in a medium mixing bowl. Add the flour, sugar, and salt and whisk until any lumps have disappeared. Add the milk and whisk to combine.

3 Remove the pan from the oven and add the butter. Roll it around so that the sides and bottom of the pan are coated. Use a rubber spatula to scrape the batter into the pan, and then sprinkle the batter with the granola. Bake for 10 minutes. The Dutch baby will rise dramatically.

4 Remove the pan from the oven and let it sit for 2 minutes. The pancake will fall a bit; this is to be expected. Cut it into wedges and serve with yogurt and berries.

Granola Pie

This pie takes its inspiration from pecan pie but, texturally, blows it out of the water. It's the combination of ingredients that does it: you've got the nuts but also the oats and other ingredients in your granola that team up to make something truly spectacular. It's decadent, but it's also very easy to make. Bring this to Thanksgiving, and you'll definitely secure a return invite next year.

MAKES ONE 9-INCH PIE

½ cup sugar

1 tablespoon cornstarch

½ cup light corn syrup

¼ cup molasses

1 tablespoon vanilla extract

3 large eggs, beaten

½ cup chocolate chips of your choice (optional; see Note)

1 cup granola (page 111)

1 (9-inch) Pie Crust (recipe follows)

½ teaspoon coarse sea salt, for finishing (optional)

1 Heat the oven to 325°F.

2 Whisk together the sugar and cornstarch in a medium mixing bowl. Then add the corn syrup, molasses, vanilla, and eggs and whisk to combine.

3 Fold the chocolate chips (if using) and granola into the filling. Pour this mixture into the prepared pie crust.

4 Bake on the center rack for 1 hour, until just barely set.

5 Allow to cool for at least 1 hour to set and sprinkle with the sea salt (if using).

Note: Dark chocolate balances the sweetness of the pie but does make it a bit more intense than milk chocolate.

Pie Crust

2 cups all-purpose flour

5 teaspoons sugar

Pinch of salt

6 tablespoons (¾ stick) cold unsalted butter, finely diced

3 tablespoons cold water

1 Heat the oven to 325°F.

2 Using a stand mixer fitted with the paddle attachment, beat the flour, sugar, salt, and butter on low speed until you have a gritty consistency like cornmeal.

3 With the mixer still running, slowly add the cold water until a dough forms. Use your hands to form the dough into a flat disk about 1 inch thick and wrap in plastic wrap. Place the dough in the refrigerator for at least 1 hour.

4 On a floured work surface, use a rolling pin to roll the dough into an 11-inch circle. Carefully place the dough in a standard 9-inch pie plate. Stop here for the granola pie; for all other pie crusts in this book, continue to the next step.

5 Line the dough with parchment paper, add pie weights (or dried beans), and bake for 10 minutes.

6 Allow to cool completely before adding pie filling.

Sugar

I have the world's worst sweet tooth. Seriously, anything with sugar is A-plus in my book. The fact that it's also a top-tier preservation medium doesn't hurt, either. Sugar preserves foods in much the same way salt does: it draws water out. And water, as you learned in the last chapter, is the enemy when it comes to preservation. Sugar also inhibits microbial activity, so once you've preserved something in sugar, bad bacteria are going to have a heck of a time getting to it. This is why at Cured we often top individual jars of chicken liver mousse with a thin layer of jelly—not only does it taste good, it gives it an extra layer of protection from spoilage.

The simplest version of this type of preserve is infused sugar: you take an ingredient that goes well with sweets, like mint, and pack it in sugar. This process, called sugaring, brings a lot of flavor, and it's a preservation method that's been around for centuries.

Sugar is especially effective at preserving fruits, of course, and the bulk of this chapter looks at jams and marmalades. Sugar pulls moisture out of the fruit and then dissolves in it, creating a liquid that is saturated with sugar. This supersweet syrup helps delay spoilage as well. Canning jams and marmalades prevents spoilage even further (see page 328). And finally in this chapter, we'll look at caramels, which occur when sugar is cooked down and caramelized, and then dairy is added; or, sometimes, when dairy is cooked down until its own natural sugars caramelize. This section will explore both types.

In addition to its preservation qualities, sugar is nearly as effective at improving flavor as salt can be. If you take a bowl of cut strawberries, for example, and sprinkle them with a little bit of sugar, they will not taste significantly sweeter. But they *will* taste significantly more like strawberries! They'll also get a bit of textural improvement and color enhancement out of it, too. This same trick works on all kinds of fruit, even tomatoes.

Base Ingredient: **Infused Sugars**

Infused sugars are super-versatile and handy ingredients to have on hand. They make a great addition to coffee or tea in the morning, you can sprinkle them over a half grapefruit for breakfast, or you can use them in place of regular sugar in a baking recipe. The Application Recipes in this section highlight the flavors infused into the sugar, but there's no reason you couldn't use a vanilla sugar in blondies (page 216), for example, or a warm spice-infused sugar in the Granola Pie (page 118). As ever, experiment with infused sugars and you'll be richly rewarded.

Vanilla-Infused Sugar

Vanilla beans are pricey, and I don't like to let anything go to waste. Whenever a recipe calls for the seeds of a vanilla bean, this is how I repurpose the emptied pod. It won't be quite as flavorful without the seeds, but it will still taste really good.

MAKES 3 CUPS
Begin this recipe 1 week before using.

1 vanilla bean, with or without the seeds, halved lengthwise and widthwise

3 cups sugar

Put the vanilla bean halves in a quart jar and cover with sugar. Shake well and let sit at room temperature for 1 week before using, shaking the jar each day. Store at room temperature.

Infused Sugar Variations

Citrus-Infused Sugar: Using a peeler, remove the zest of 1 orange, 1 lemon, and 3 limes in strips. Spread the zest strips evenly over a parchment paper–lined sheet pan and bake at 175°F for 30 minutes. Let cool for 2 minutes, then combine with 3 cups sugar.

Mint-Infused Sugar: Tie 4 sprigs of fresh mint together with a piece of twine and hang upside down at room temperature until the leaves are dry, about 3 days. Remove the leaves from the sprigs and either finely chop them or grind them in a mortar with a pestle with 1 tablespoon of sugar. Combine the mint leaves with 3 cups sugar.

Warm Spice–Infused Sugar: Combine 3 star anise pods, 3 cinnamon sticks that have been broken in half, ¾ teaspoon ground cardamom, 1 teaspoon ground nutmeg, and 3 cups sugar.

Easy Ideas for Using Infused Sugar

• Add to coffee or tea

• Rim cocktails

• Sprinkle on toast

• Use in baking recipes

• Sprinkle over oatmeal

• Use to decorate cakes and cookies

• Heat equal parts infused sugar and water together until the sugar dissolves for a simple syrup to flavor cocktails or lemonade

Pomegranate Molasses Sidecar

The sugar here cuts any bitterness from the cognac while bringing out the citrus flavors of the cocktail. A riff on a classic, this sidecar replaces the traditional orange liqueur with pomegranate molasses. It's a sweet-tart syrup you can get at Middle Eastern grocery stores.

MAKES 1 COCKTAIL

1 lemon wedge

½ cup infused sugar (page 122)

2 ounces cognac

¾ ounce lemon juice

½ ounce pomegranate molasses

1   Rub the lemon wedge around the rim of a coupe glass and discard.

2   Fill a small plate with the infused sugar. Dip the rim of the coupe glass into the sugar to coat the entire rim.

3   Fill a cocktail shaker halfway with ice and add the cognac, lemon juice, and pomegranate molasses. Shake vigorously for 20 seconds. Strain into the coupe glass through a cocktail strainer and enjoy.

Sugar-Crusted Orange Cranberry Muffins

Everyone knows the top of the muffin is the best part! So make them even better with a crunchy-sweet infused sugar top. You can let these cool before eating, but why wait? A warm muffin is an amazing thing.

MAKES 12 MUFFINS

⅔ cup dried cranberries

½ cup orange juice

1⅓ cups all-purpose flour

2 teaspoons cornstarch

½ cup sugar

½ teaspoon baking powder

½ teaspoon baking soda

¼ teaspoon salt

2 large eggs

⅓ cup vegetable oil

2 tablespoons whole milk

Zest of ½ orange (about 1 teaspoon)

3 tablespoons infused sugar (page 122)

1   Heat the oven to 375°F. Line a 12-count muffin tin with baking cups.

2   Place the dried cranberries in a small bowl and pour the orange juice over them. Let soak for 10 minutes.

3   Meanwhile, using a stand mixer fitted with the whisk attachment, combine the flour, cornstarch, sugar, baking powder, baking soda, and salt on low speed.

4   Add the eggs one at a time, whisking between each addition. Scrape down the sides of the bowl with a rubber spatula, and then add the oil, milk, orange zest, and cranberry–orange juice mixture. Whisk until smooth.

5   Divide the batter among the baking cups, filling each three-quarters of the way.

6   Sprinkle the tops of the muffins with the infused sugar and bake until a nice sugar crust has formed and a toothpick inserted into the center of a muffin comes out with wet crumbs attached, 20 minutes.

Sugar-Rolled Tahini Cookies

These great big, soft, chewy cookies are a sort of cross between peanut butter cookies and snickerdoodles. The tahini gives them a subtle nuttiness without overwhelming the infused sugar.

MAKES 16 COOKIES

2¾ cups all-purpose flour

1 teaspoon baking soda

2 teaspoons cream of tartar

½ teaspoon salt

1 cup granulated sugar

½ cup packed light brown sugar

½ cup (1 stick) unsalted butter, softened

½ cup well-stirred tahini

2 large eggs

⅓ cup infused sugar (page 122)

1 Heat the oven to 400°F. Line two sheet pans with parchment paper.

2 Whisk together the flour, baking soda, cream of tartar, and salt in a medium mixing bowl. Set aside.

3 Using a stand mixer fitted with the paddle attachment, beat the sugars, butter, and tahini on medium speed until the mixture is several shades lighter, about 5 minutes.

4 Alternate between adding one-third of the dry ingredients and adding an egg, one at a time, mixing until incorporated and scraping down the sides of the bowl with a rubber spatula between each addition. After the last flour addition, mix until combined.

5 Put the infused sugar in a small bowl. Form cookies by rolling about 3 tablespoons of dough into a ball, and then roll the ball in the infused sugar. Evenly space 8 dough balls on each of the prepared sheet pans.

6 Bake until puffed and set, 10 to 12 minutes. The cookies will look slightly underbaked when ready. Let cool completely on the sheet pan.

Earl Grey Tea Crème Brûlée

Tea time meets dessert in this unexpected (but not too crazy) riff on a classic crème brûlée. This should work with all of the infused sugar variations—you could also use English breakfast tea or green tea for this, if you like.

MAKES FOUR 6-OUNCE CRÈMES BRÛLÉE

2½ cups heavy cream
½ cup plus 4 teaspoons infused sugar (page 122)
2 Earl Grey tea bags
6 large egg yolks

1   Combine the cream and ½ cup of the sugar in a medium saucepan over medium-high heat. Stir until the sugar dissolves (do not allow the mixture to boil), then remove from the heat. Transfer the cream mixture to a liquid measuring cup. Add the tea bags and steep for 10 minutes. Press the tea bags against the side of the cup with the back of a spoon prior to removing, and discard.

2   Prepare an ice bath in a large mixing bowl. In a separate smaller bowl, whisk the egg yolks. Slowly pour the warm cream mixture into the eggs while continuing to whisk. When all the cream has been incorporated, place the small bowl into the ice bath to cool. It should take about 25 minutes to reach room temperature.

3   Heat the oven to 325°F.

4   Divide the mixture equally among four 6-ounce ramekins and place them in a large roasting pan. Pour water into the roasting pan until it comes halfway up the sides of the ramekins. Tightly cover the roasting pan with foil and bake until the custards are set when jiggled, 45 minutes. Remove the ramekins from the roasting pan and let them cool in the refrigerator for at least 2 hours or overnight.

5   Sprinkle 1 teaspoon of the remaining sugar on top of each custard, shaking it so it reaches to the sides. Brown the tops of the ramekins with a kitchen torch, keeping the flame about 2 inches from the custard so that it doesn't burn. You want a nice mahogany color. If you don't have a torch, heat the broiler on your oven to high and position the rack so that the ramekin tops are 2 inches away from the heat. Keep a close eye on the custards and remove when the tops are caramelized and mahogany colored.

Base Ingredient: Jam

I have so many memories of my mom making jam when I was a kid. We grew strawberries on our farm, and it was my responsibility to weed the strawberry patch. For me, jam is the absolute best way to eat strawberries. But peaches are more common here in Texas, so we make a lot more peach jam at the restaurant. We also make a lot of prickly pear jam, apple jalapeño butter, and Pearl Jam (we're located in the old Pearl Brewery, after all!) as nods to our surroundings. We even make an onion jam to serve on charcuterie boards, burgers, grilled meats, and more.

Peach Jam

Jam is not a time to use photo-ready fruit; on the contrary, I find that almost overripe fruit that is just starting to bruise makes the sweetest, most flavorful jam. All jams can be strained through a fine-mesh strainer if you prefer your jams without pulp. And finally, if you'd like to can your jams, see page 328 for instructions. Otherwise, this jam will keep in the refrigerator for a month or longer.

MAKES ABOUT 1 QUART

2½ pounds very ripe peaches
(6 to 7 peaches)
1½ cups sugar
3 tablespoons lemon juice

1 Halve the peaches and cut the halves into four wedges.

2 Combine the peaches and sugar in a large mixing bowl and let sit at room temperature for 4 hours. Stir every hour or so.

3 At this point, you can either mash the jam with a potato masher for a chunkier jam or process the jam in a blender or food processor for a smoother jam. Some recipes, like the Jam and Sambal–Glazed Spiral Ham (page 135) or the Mix-and-Match Jam Cocktail (page 133), work better with a smoother jam.

4 Bring the peaches, any juices that have collected, and the lemon juice to a simmer in a heavy pot and cook on medium-low heat, stirring frequently, until the jam is thick and most of the liquid has evaporated, about 25 minutes. You'll know your jam is done when you drag a wooden spoon across the bottom of the pot and the trail remains clear for several seconds. Let cool completely.

Jam Variations

Strawberry Jam: Combine 2½ pounds strawberries that have been hulled and halved with 1¼ cups sugar. Let sit at room temperature for 1 hour, stirring once halfway through. Substitute 2 tablespoons lime juice for the lemon juice. Cook on medium-low heat, stirring frequently, until the jam is thick and most of the liquid has evaporated, about 15 minutes. Let cool completely.

Prickly Pear Jelly: Wearing gloves, peel 2 pounds prickly pears (7 to 10) and cut them into quarters. Combine the pear quarters with 1½ cups sugar and let sit at room temperature for 1 hour, stirring once halfway through. Put the pears and any liquid that has collected into a pot along with the juice of 1 lime and bring to a simmer. (Do not boil or it may turn brown.) Simmer and reduce for 45 minutes for a syrup or a full hour for jelly. Strain hot through a fine-mesh strainer to remove the seeds and let cool completely.

Apple Jalapeño Butter: Combine 1 cup water and 2 cups sugar in a heavy pot. Bring to a simmer over medium heat and simmer until the sugar dissolves. Add 3 unpeeled apples that have been cored and cut into quarters, and 1 small jalapeño that has been halved lengthwise, stems and seeds removed. Simmer until the apples are tender, about 20 minutes. Run the apple mixture through a food mill and return the milled mixture to the pot. (Discard the peels.) Simmer until thickened, 2 to 3 minutes. Let cool completely.

Pearl Jam: Combine three 12-ounce bottles of Pearl (or equivalent light-bodied lager), 2 tablespoons rice wine vinegar, 1 star anise pod, and the zested strips from 1 orange in a large pot over high heat. Bring to a boil. In a small bowl, whisk together ½ cup sugar with a 1¾-ounce packet of low-sugar pectin. Whisk this into the boiling beer mixture. Add an additional 2 cups sugar to the pot and boil for 1 minute. Reduce the heat to medium-low and simmer for 5 minutes.

Use a slotted spoon to remove the star anise and orange zest. Let cool completely, skimming any scum that forms on the surface of the jam.

Onion Jam: Heat 2 tablespoons olive oil in a large, heavy pot over medium-low heat and add 1½ pounds sliced red onions (3 to 4 onions). Sauté the onions, stirring constantly with a wooden spoon, until golden brown and caramelized, about 25 minutes. Add ¼ cup packed light brown sugar and stir to combine. Cook for an additional 5 minutes, until mahogany in color. Add another ½ cup light brown sugar, ½ cup balsamic vinegar, and 1 sprig of thyme. Cook the jam, stirring periodically, until the liquid has reduced to a sticky syrup, about 45 minutes. Remove from the heat, discard the thyme, and allow to cool completely.

Easy Ideas for Using Jams

- Make a simple jam sauce by simmering equal parts wine or water with jam until syrupy; good with roasts, pancakes, cakes, and more
- Top ice cream
- Serve with meats and cheeses
- Use as a layer between cakes and in jelly rolls
- Top baked brie
- Serve with yogurt
- Add to grilled cheese
- Fill donuts or sandwich cookies
- Whisk into a vinaigrette

Mix-and-Match Jam Cocktail

I love a cocktail that uses ingredients you probably have lying around the house. This may seem like just a three-ingredient cocktail, but its personality changes depending on what jam you have and what type of liquor you pair with it. The jam adds sweetness but also fruity flavor and body, while the club soda lightens everything up.

MAKES 1 COCKTAIL

2 ounces liquor (see pairings below)
1½ tablespoons jam (page 131)
¼ cup club soda

1   Add the spirit and jam to a cocktail shaker with ice.

2   Shake well to allow the ice to melt and the jam to break up, at least 20 seconds. Strain the cocktail into a collins glass filled with ice.

3   Top with the club soda.

Jam	Spirit
Peach	Bourbon
Blueberry	Gin
Blackberry	Mezcal
Strawberry	Vodka
Prickly Pear	Tequila
Apricot	Rum

Jam and Sambal–Glazed Spiral Ham

Some spiral hams can be on the saltier side, so a nice sweet-spicy glaze counterbalances that. The glaze is the simplest version of a pepper jelly, and using the jam and sambal means you don't have to go through the trouble of cooking a separate sauce. This is a real showstopper for a holiday gathering.

SERVES 15 TO 20 GUESTS
(LEFTOVERS FREEZE NICELY)

1 (7- to 10-pound) spiral ham
2¾ cups fruit jam (page 131)
¼ cup sambal
1 teaspoon ground ginger

1 Take the ham out of the refrigerator 1 hour before cooking so it can come up to room temperature.

2 Heat the oven to 350°F.

3 Bring the jam, sambal, ginger, and 1 cup water to a simmer in a saucepan. Simmer until thickened, stirring occasionally, about 10 minutes.

4 While the glaze is cooking, put the ham in a racked roasting pan. Pour 2 cups water in the bottom of the pan.

5 Spoon the glaze over the top of the ham, between 1 and 1½ cups, and use a brush to coat all of its sides. It's okay if some slides off, but get as much on the ham as you can. Reserve the rest of the glaze for later.

6 Use aluminum foil to make a tent over the ham. You want the foil to lock in the steam from the bottom of the pan but not touch the ham itself.

7 Bake until a thermometer inserted into the thickest part of the ham reads 140°F, about 1½ hours.

8 Remove the ham from the oven and remove the foil. Turn the oven temperature up to 450°F.

9 Coat the ham with an additional layer of glaze and return it to the oven for 8 to 10 minutes. When the glaze on the ham is starting to caramelize, remove it from the oven. Let it rest for 15 minutes and serve with any leftover glaze on the side.

Mini Kolaches

Kolaches, small fruit-filled pastries, are a Texas breakfast tradition, thanks to Czech immigrants who popularized them across the state. These come together quickly because of the freezer dough (page 68). You can thaw them overnight and shape them in the morning for an impressive breakfast treat that looks like way more work than it is. I like to use an assortment of jams in one batch to get a nice mix of colors and flavors. I also like to cook them until they're slightly darker than truck-stop-bakery kolaches, but you can pull yours from the oven a few minutes early if you prefer.

MAKES 16 KOLACHES

Yeast dough (page 68), thawed
1 cup jam (page 131)
1 egg white, lightly whisked

1   Roll the dough into a ball and place it in a greased mixing bowl. Cover it with a towel or plastic wrap, and place it in the warmest part of the kitchen until the dough doubles in size, 1 to 2 hours, depending on the temperature of your kitchen.

2   Heat the oven to 350°F and grease a sheet pan.

3   Lightly flour a work surface and scrape the dough onto it. Sprinkle a bit more flour over the dough, and then roll it into a 6 by 16-inch rectangle. Cut the dough in half lengthwise, then cut each half into eight 3 by 2-inch rectangles.

4   Place these on the prepared pan, evenly spaced, and let rise until doubled in size, about 45 minutes.

5   Use your thumb or a small spoon to press an indentation large enough to hold a tablespoon of jam into the center of each kolache. Fill the indentations with jam. Brush the edges of the dough with the egg white and bake until golden brown, about 15 minutes.

Base Ingredient: **Marmalade**

The difference between a jam and a marmalade is you leave the fruit's rind in the mix—this adds amazing texture and flavor, with a hint of bitterness. We make a lot of marmalades at the restaurant around the holidays, when grapefruit and other citrus start heading our way from the Rio Grande Valley.

After you've made a few marmalades, you'll start to recognize the proper texture on sight. But until then, here's a trick for making absolutely sure your marmalade is ready: put three small ceramic plates in the freezer for an hour. When you think the marmalade is done, remove one of the plates and put a teaspoon of the hot marmalade on the plate. If it wrinkles slightly when you touch it with your finger, it's ready. If not, cook the marmalade 2 minutes longer and test again. Repeat until the thickness is correct. (This is why you start with three plates.)

Grapefruit Marmalade

I fell in love with grapefruit when I moved to Texas. Grown in the Rio Grande Valley, our famous red grapefruit thrives because of fertile soil, a subtropical climate, and tons of sun. You want to choose grapefruit that look a tiny bit beat up—these "beauty marks," caused by the leaves of the tree bumping the fruit repeatedly in the South Texas breeze, are said to indicate sweeter fruit.

MAKES 2 QUARTS

2½ pounds grapefruits (4 to 5 total)
Pinch of salt
3½ cups sugar
Juice of 1 lemon

1 Separate the grapefruit into two groups. Cut one group in half across the meridian and slice them into half moons as thinly as possible, removing any seeds as you go. Cut the slices again crosswise, twice—you will end up with thin wedges.

2 Place the wedges in a heavy pot with water to cover and add a pinch of salt. Bring to a boil over high heat. Reduce the heat to medium-low and simmer for 5 minutes.

3 Remove the pot from the heat and let sit for 10 minutes. Drain the wedges in a strainer. (You do not need the liquid.)

4 Peel the other half of the grapefruits and discard the peels. Coarsely chop the pulp, removing the seeds as you go.

5 Cook the pulp, any accumulated juices, the cooked grapefruit slices, sugar, lemon juice, and 5 cups water in a large, heavy pot over medium heat, stirring periodically, until thickened and syrupy, 40 minutes. Cool completely before eating.

Marmalade Variations

Orange Marmalade: Remove the ends from 1½ pounds oranges (3 to 4 large oranges, more if smaller) and slice thinly. Follow the marmalade recipe through step 3. When you get to step 4, put the orange slices, 3½ cups sugar, 2 cups orange juice, ¼ cup lemon juice, and 5 cups water into a large pot. Simmer until thick and syrupy, 1½ hours. (This takes longer to cook down than the grapefruit marmalade because of the liquid added by the orange juice.) Optional: Add ¼ cup orange liqueur to the finished marmalade.

Cherry Orange Marmalade: Follow the Orange Marmalade variation. Use 12 ounces oranges (2 to 3 oranges) in the beginning of the recipe, and add 12 ounces pitted cherries when you add the orange juice in step 4.

Tomato Marmalade: Peel, seed, and dice 12 ripe Roma tomatoes. Tie 10 peppercorns, 1 bay leaf, and the zest strips from 1 orange in a cheesecloth and set aside. Heat 2 tablespoons extra-virgin olive oil in a large, heavy pot over medium heat. Add ¼ cup tomato paste and sauté for 1 minute. Add 5 tablespoons red wine vinegar and ⅓ cup sugar and cook until syrupy, about 2 minutes. Add the cheesecloth bundle, tomatoes, 1 minced jalapeño (stemmed and seeded), and juice of the zested orange. Bring to a simmer and cook until thick and syrupy, about 45 minutes. Remove the cheesecloth bundle and discard. Let cool completely.

Easy Ideas for Using Marmalade

- Spread on toast, scones, or biscuits
- Whisk into marinades and vinaigrettes
- Serve on a cheese plate
- Thin with water or liquor to make an easy glaze for a cake
- Use as a filling between two layers of cake
- Add a spoonful to glaze sautéed shrimp (along with a spoonful of chili sauce, if you like!)

Marmalade Goat Cheese Semifreddo

I love semifreddoes. They're like ice cream, with an airy texture, but you don't need an ice cream maker! This recipe does dirty a lot of dishes, but the end result is spectacular and well worth the effort. I like to serve semifreddoes with garnishes like crumbled cookies, whipped cream, additional marmalade as a sauce, or some fresh fruit.

SERVES 10

1½ cups heavy cream

3 large eggs, separated

2 tablespoons sugar

8 ounces goat cheese, softened

½ cup marmalade (page 138)

1 Line a 9 by 5-inch loaf pan with plastic wrap.

2 Using a stand mixer fitted with the whisk attachment, beat the cream on medium-high speed until you get soft peaks, about 2 minutes. Scoop the whipped cream into a separate container and refrigerate while you prepare the other ingredients. Clean the stand mixer bowl.

3 In a separate large mixing bowl, whisk the egg yolks with the sugar until pale and fluffy.

4 Back in the stand mixer, whisk the egg whites on medium speed until medium peaks are achieved, about 4 minutes. (When the whisk is lifted out, the peaks should curl over slightly.)

5 In a small mixing bowl, whisk together the goat cheese and marmalade. Gently fold this into the egg yolk mixture. Next fold in the whipped cream, followed by the egg whites. Use a rubber spatula to scrape the mixture into the prepared loaf pan and smooth the top. Freeze for at least 4 hours to set, and up to 48 hours before serving.

6 Remove the semifreddo from the freezer 20 minutes prior to serving. Invert onto a cutting board, remove the plastic wrap, cut into thick slices, and serve.

Chipotle Marmalade Chicken Wings

Everyone needs a go-to sports-watching recipe, and this is mine. The chipotle gives these wings a hit of smoke, so they feel a little grilled without you having to actually go outside and grill, a nice trick in bad weather.

SERVES 6

5 pounds chicken wings

2 tablespoons salt (31g), or 2 quarts Basic Meat Brine (page 197)

¾ cup chipotle peppers in adobo, chiles roughly chopped

4 teaspoons lime juice

½ cup marmalade (page 138)

Chopped cilantro and lime wedges, for garnish

1 Salt the chicken wings all over (or submerge under the brine) and refrigerate for 4 hours.

2 Whisk together the chipotle, lime juice, marmalade, and ¼ cup water in a large mixing bowl. Transfer half the glaze to another large bowl.

3 Heat the oven to 400°F. Line two sheet pans with parchment paper or aluminum foil.

4 Add the raw chicken wings to one of the bowls and stir in the sauce until coated. Place the wings on the prepared sheet pans. Discard this bowl of glaze. Bake the wings until cooked through and the skin is golden brown, about 40 minutes. Put the cooked wings in the other bowl of glaze and stir the wings again to coat. Transfer to a serving bowl, scatter the cilantro leaves and lime wedges over and around the wings, and serve with any remaining glaze on the side.

Marmalade Rosemary Thumbprint Cookies

It's hard to improve on a classic, but the rosemary in this dough means these cookies are about more than just a sweet filling. Between the pineyness of the herb and the slightly bitter marmalade, these are more of a sophisticated teatime cookie than an after-school snack.

MAKES ABOUT 2 DOZEN COOKIES

1¾ cups all-purpose flour

¼ teaspoon salt

½ teaspoon finely chopped fresh rosemary

¾ cup (1½ sticks) unsalted butter, softened

½ cup powdered sugar

¼ cup marmalade (page 138)

1   Heat the oven to 375°F. Line a sheet pan with parchment paper.

2   Sift the flour and salt into a medium mixing bowl. Stir in the chopped rosemary.

3   Using a stand mixer fitted with the paddle attachment, beat the butter and powdered sugar on medium speed until pale and fluffy, about 3 minutes.

4   Turn the mixer speed to low and slowly spoon in the flour mixture. Scrape down the sides of the mixer periodically with a rubber spatula.

5   Remove the mixing bowl from the mixer and cover with a towel. Let sit at room temperature for 10 minutes. This will let the dough relax and help prevent the cookies from cracking during baking.

6   Roll approximately 1 tablespoon of dough into a 1-inch ball and place it on the prepared sheet pan. (Space the cookies about 1 inch apart.) Make a well in the cookie with the end of a wooden spoon or your thumb. (The smoother your dough ball is, the less likely it will crack when you make your indentation.) Repeat until all the dough has been used. Fill each divot with about ½ teaspoon marmalade.

7   Bake the cookies until the edges are golden brown, 12 to 13 minutes. Let cool completely on a rack before serving.

Base Ingredient: **Caramel**

Some recipes are just magic. As a young chef, I was always so amazed by pastry chefs turning seemingly basic ingredients into pure dessert gold. There are lots of different methods for making a caramel sauce; the variations in this section cover several. Most caramels have a step in which they sputter or grow rapidly in volume; these have been noted in the recipe and variations below, so do take care with these steps. Finally, as tempting as it is, do not touch or taste caramel until it has cooled. It's much, much hotter than you think.

Caramel Sauce

MAKES 2½ CUPS

1½ cups sugar
1 tablespoon light corn syrup
1 cup heavy cream
¼ cup (½ stick) cold unsalted butter, diced

1 Combine the sugar, corn syrup, and ¼ cup water in a medium saucepan over medium heat. Bring the mixture to a simmer, stirring until the sugar has dissolved.

2 Bring the sugar to a boil without stirring again, just swirling the pan periodically, until a dark amber color is achieved, 7 to 10 minutes. (If you have a candy thermometer, you want it to measure 340°F.) Remove from the heat.

3 Use caution in this next step as the liquid will bubble: Pour the cream into the sugar slowly while whisking continuously. When all the cream has been added, whisk in the butter. If the cream seizes during this process, put the pan back on a low burner and stir until the lumps dissolve.

4 Allow the caramel to cool for 15 minutes in the pot before serving or refrigerating. It will keep in a sealed container in the refrigerator for 2 weeks.

Caramel Variations

Butterscotch: Combine 1½ cups sugar, ⅓ cup light corn syrup, 3 tablespoons unsalted butter, 1 teaspoon salt, and ¼ cup water in a medium saucepan over medium heat. Bring to a simmer, stirring until the sugar dissolves. Bring to a boil again, without stirring, just swirling the pan periodically, until it's a deep amber color (7 to 10 minutes, or when you hit 340°F on a candy thermometer). **Use caution in this next step as the liquid will bubble:** Pour ¾ cup heavy cream into the sugar slowly while whisking continuously. Stir in ½ teaspoon vanilla extract and 1½ tablespoons Scotch (optional). Let cool completely.

Dulce de Leche: Make a double boiler by filling a pot three-quarters full of water and placing a metal bowl that fits snugly in the pot on top. The water should touch the bowl but not overflow the pot. Bring the water to a simmer. Pour two

14-ounce cans of sweetened condensed milk into the bowl. Cook for 3 hours, stirring periodically with a rubber spatula. The dulce de leche should be a dark amber and very thick. Remove from the heat and let cool completely.

Cajeta: Combine 4 cups goat milk, 1 cup packed dark brown sugar, and ¼ teaspoon salt in a saucepan. Bring to a simmer and stir until the sugar dissolves. Combine 2 tablespoons goat milk, ½ teaspoon baking soda, and 2 teaspoons vanilla extract in a small bowl. **Use caution in this next step as the liquid will double in volume:** Carefully pour the baking soda mixture into the pot and stir. Cook the cajeta until it has thickened and turned a dark caramel color, 30 to 45 minutes. Let cool completely.

Easy Ideas for Using Caramel

- Drizzle on ice cream
- Serve with pretzels or fresh fruit
- Stir into coffee
- Swirl into brownie batter before baking
- Add to s'mores
- Use as a filling for sandwich cookies

Caramel-Glazed Carrots

Way better than your average glazed carrots, this recipe also works well with parsnips. Don't skip the almonds; they add great texture and help cut the sweetness.

SERVES 6 AS A SIDE

2 tablespoons unsalted butter

3 pounds carrots, peeled and cut on a diagonal into ¼-inch-thick slices

¼ cup caramel (page 147)

½ teaspoon salt

Juice of 1 orange (about ¼ cup)

4 tablespoons chopped fresh parsley

5 tablespoons toasted almond slivers

1   Melt the butter in a large sauté pan over medium-high heat. Add the carrots, caramel, salt, and orange juice. Bring to a simmer and cook, uncovered, shaking the pan occasionally, for about 12 minutes. At this point the carrots should be cooked through. Remove the pan from the heat and allow to cool slightly before serving.

2   Carefully pour the carrots into a serving dish and garnish with the parsley and slivered almonds.

Cured's Famous Cajeta Eggnog

Cured opened two days before Christmas in 2013, and this eggnog was on the menu from the very beginning. We make it with cajeta (page 148), but this recipe works beautifully with any of the caramels in this section. Make sure you start it around Halloween so it's ready for the Christmas season.

MAKES 4 QUARTS
Begin recipe at least 4 weeks before serving.

12 large eggs

1 cup caramel (page 147)

1 teaspoon ground allspice

¼ teaspoon ground cloves

¼ teaspoon ground ginger

1 teaspoon ground nutmeg

2 tablespoons vanilla extract

2 dashes Angostura bitters

1 cup dark rum

1 cup brandy

½ cup almond liqueur

½ cup walnut liqueur

2 quarts heavy cream

1   Whisk the eggs and caramel together in a medium mixing bowl. Pass the mixture through a fine-mesh strainer into a large mixing bowl. Whisk in the allspice, cloves, ginger, nutmeg, vanilla, and bitters.

2   While continuing to whisk, pour in the rum, brandy, almond liqueur, and walnut liqueur.

3   Whisk in the cream and divide the mixture among four 1-quart jars and refrigerate.

4   Shake the jars occasionally for 30 days for flavors to develop.

Caramel-Drizzled Bundt Cake

This deceptively simple cake may seem like your typical Bundt cake, but it's actually a showstopper that smells intoxicating while baking and develops a lovely sugary, buttery outer crust. The almond extract makes it; the caramel is a supporting player.

MAKES ONE 10-INCH BUNDT CAKE

2½ cups all-purpose flour

2 teaspoons baking powder

1 teaspoon salt

1 tablespoon vanilla extract

½ teaspoon almond extract

¾ cup packed dark brown sugar

¾ cup granulated sugar

1½ cups (3 sticks) unsalted butter, softened

4 large eggs, at room temperature

¾ cup sour cream

1¾ cups caramel (page 147)

1 Heat the oven to 350°F. Grease a 10-inch (12-cup) Bundt cake pan.

2 Combine the flour, baking powder, and salt in a medium mixing bowl.

3 Using a stand mixer fitted with the paddle attachment, beat the vanilla, almond extract, brown sugar, granulated sugar, and butter on medium speed until fluffy, about 4 minutes. Add the eggs one at a time, beating between each addition until incorporated, and then scraping down the sides of the bowl with a rubber spatula.

4 Reduce the mixer speed to low. Add one-third of the flour mixture and beat until just combined. Add one-third of the sour cream and beat until just combined. Repeat two more times with the remaining flour and sour cream. You may need to scrape the sides of the bowl with a spatula once or twice.

5 Transfer the batter to the prepared pan and smooth the top with a spatula.

6 Bake for 1 hour. Check doneness by inserting a wooden skewer; if it comes out with moist crumbs, the cake is done. Transfer to a rack to cool for 15 minutes and then flip onto the rack to cool completely.

7 Heat the caramel sauce in a small pot until warm. Drizzle 1 cup of the warm glaze over the cake and serve with additional sauce on the side.

Mezcal Lime Pecan Sticky Buns

Cinnamon rolls are great and all, but these buns combine three things I love about Texas: pecans, citrus, and mezcal. You could leave out the mezcal if you want, but it really gives the caramel a lovely smoky, floral note.

MAKES 16 MORNING BUNS

Yeast dough (page 68), thawed

3 tablespoons mezcal (optional)

1 cup caramel (page 147)

1 cup sugar

Zest of 2 limes

1 cup chopped pecans

1 Roll the dough into a ball and place it in a greased bowl. Cover the bowl with a towel and place it in the warmest part of the kitchen to rise until the dough doubles in size, 1 to 2 hours, depending on the temperature of your kitchen.

2 Meanwhile, whisk the mezcal (if using) and the caramel together in a small bowl and set aside.

3 Likewise, whisk the sugar, lime zest, and ¼ cup water together in a small bowl and set aside.

4 Spray a 9 by 13-inch pan with cooking spray. Spoon the mezcal-caramel mixture (or just the caramel, if not using the mezcal) into the pan and tilt it back and forth until the bottom is evenly coated with caramel.

5 Once it has doubled, punch down the dough on a lightly floured work surface. Roll it into a ½-inch-thick rectangle, about 8 by 18 inches.

6 Evenly spread the sugar and lime zest mixture over the surface of the dough, leaving about ½ inch bare around the border. Sprinkle with the pecans. Carefully roll the dough from the longer end; you will end up with an 18-inch-long log. Use a very sharp knife to cut the log into 16 rounds. Place the rounds on top of the caramel, evenly spacing them. They will look like they are absolutely swimming in caramel; don't worry about that. Let the dough rise again, covered, until the rounds are slightly puffed and touching each other, 1 to 2 hours.

7 Heat the oven to 350°F. Bake until the tops of the buns are golden brown, about 30 minutes. Let cool 10 minutes in the pan, then use a knife to loosen the sides. Place a rectangular serving tray over the top of the pan and invert the buns onto it. Serve warm.

Fat

Fat is a two-for-the-price-of-one preservation technique. You get both the ingredient being preserved *and* the fat it's preserved in. Fat can preserve an ingredient in a few different ways, but all of them function the same way: the fat creates a seal around the ingredient, preventing harmful molds and bacteria from entering. Throughout this book, we've discussed moisture as the enemy, but air can also bring potential spoilage. Thankfully, fat seals out both.

In some cases, this process is relatively simple. Compound butter (page 158) is an easy way to preserve everything from basil to cherry tomatoes to citrus zest to shallots and other alliums. It doesn't form an airtight seal, as confits do (more on these in a second), so you need to freeze compound butters. But the fat both keeps incorporated ingredients tasting fresh and allows their flavor to carry to anything the butter touches.

Confits are more complex, but they're also more effective. Whether it's something as simple as garlic confit, or a more complicated duck confit, the process is about the same. Ingredients are submerged in fat or oil (and in the case of that duck, submerged in its own rendered fat) and then cooked at a low temperature for a long time. The fat functions like the airlocks discussed on page 239 in the fermentation chapter: it's a one-way street for the moisture that slowly dissipates from the ingredient, bubbling up through the fat.

As far as bacteria are concerned, fat is a nearly impenetrable layer. But you need to make sure you use a clean utensil *every single time* you fish an ingredient out of confit. Every. Single. Time. Otherwise, you risk introducing the very contaminants you worked so hard to keep out!

Confits also just taste great. They're salty, they're fatty, and you can introduce other flavors—garlic, whole spices, herbs—while accentuating the flavor of the main ingredient. Like all good preservation techniques, fat-preserved ingredients have improved texture and flavor, and their flavors go far when incorporated into a dish. And when you pair that with using the confit fat as your cooking oil, well. Sky's the limit!

Base Ingredient: Compound Butter

People think of compound butters as a very cheffy ingredient, but they honestly couldn't be easier to make. It's just butter with flavorings in it: that's it. And since the uses for compound butters are nearly limitless, it's definitely worth having a few different kinds in your freezer! And do store them in the freezer, tightly wrapped in plastic: unlike the other preservation methods in this chapter, the fat in compound butter does not completely seal the flavorings from the environment, leaving some of them exposed. A frozen assist is in order. Most compound butters will last 3 months when stored this way.

When it's time to cook, think of compound butter as a shortcut. Say you're grilling some pork chops and you don't want to make a sauce, or you're knocking out some French toast on a Sunday morning and you've got some sweet compound butter in the freezer. In either case, chop a knob off your compound butter and you're good to go.

Cured's House Compound Butter

This all-purpose savory compound butter is what we use at the restaurant. After the recipe, you'll find two sweet and two savory variations. Always, always, always use unsalted butter for compound butters, and season to taste.

MAKES SLIGHTLY MORE THAN 1 POUND, OR ABOUT 2¼ CUPS

2 teaspoons extra-virgin olive oil

4 garlic cloves, minced

2 tablespoons minced shallot

2 teaspoons red pepper flakes

2 teaspoons chopped fresh thyme leaves

1 teaspoon chopped fresh tarragon leaves

1 teaspoon orange zest

2 teaspoons unpasteurized apple cider vinegar

1 teaspoon salt

½ teaspoon sugar

1 pound (4 sticks) unsalted butter, softened

1 Heat the olive oil in a sauté pan over medium heat. Add the garlic and shallots and sauté for 1 minute, stirring. Remove the pan from the heat and let cool completely.

2 Use a rubber spatula to scrape the shallot mixture into the bowl of a stand mixer fitted with the paddle attachment, along with the red pepper flakes, thyme, tarragon, orange zest, vinegar, salt, sugar, and butter. Mix on low speed until thoroughly combined.

3 Place two 1-foot-long pieces of plastic wrap on a clean cutting board or countertop, and use

a spoon to create a 2-inch-wide line of the butter down the center of each piece of plastic. Roll the plastic around each line, creating cylinders roughly 2 inches in diameter. Twist up the ends, label, and freeze.

4 When ready to use, peel back the plastic, cut off the desired portion size, and rewrap. Use to top freshly cooked pork, chicken, fish, or vegetables. The butter will melt down and baste the dish, forming an instant sauce.

Compound Butter Variations

Roasted Tomato Compound Butter: Before making the compound butter, toss 4 pints cherry tomatoes with 2 teaspoons extra-virgin olive oil, 2 minced garlic cloves, 1 teaspoon sugar, 1 teaspoon freshly ground black pepper, and 2 teaspoons salt on a sheet pan lined with parchment paper or aluminum foil. Bake at 400°F for 40 minutes, until the tomatoes burst and are caramelized, then let cool completely. Puree the tomato mixture in a food processor. Add this puree to 1 pound butter, along with ¼ cup chopped fresh basil leaves, and proceed with the recipe from step 3.

Jalapeño Avocado Butter: Before making the compound butter, sauté ¼ cup olive oil and 2 minced jalapeños (stemmed and seeded) over medium heat until soft. Add 2 minced garlic cloves and sauté 30 seconds more. Let cool completely. Combine 1 pound butter with the cooked jalapeño mixture, 2 ripe avocados, and the zest of 2 limes, and proceed with the recipe from step 3.

Pumpkin Compound Butter: Combine 1 pound butter with 1 cup pumpkin puree (canned is fine), ¼ cup honey, 1 tablespoon cinnamon, 1½ teaspoons ground ginger, 1 teaspoon ground cloves, 1 teaspoon ground nutmeg, and 1½ teaspoons salt. Proceed with the recipe as written from step 3.

Candied Pecan Compound Butter: Before making the compound butter, stir together 3 tablespoons light brown sugar, ½ teaspoon cinnamon, a big pinch of salt, a splash of vanilla extract, and 1 teaspoon water in a sauté pan and heat until it begins to bubble slightly. Add 1 cup pecan pieces to the syrup and cook until the pecans are coated and sticky and no syrup pools in the bottom of the pan, 4 to 5 minutes. Transfer the candied pecans to a sheet pan lined with parchment paper and use a spatula to spread them out. Let cool completely. Combine 1 pound butter with the candied pecans and ½ cup maple syrup, and proceed with the recipe from step 3.

Easy Ideas for Using Compound Butters

- Use (almost) anywhere you would use regular butter
- Make a butter board by spreading the compound butter on a nice cutting board and decorating with complementary chopped herbs, nuts, spices, and other seasonings; serve with bread
- Top pancakes or French toast
- Use as an easy cheater sauce for meat or fish
- Fold into rice or mashed potatoes
- Use to finish steamed, sautéed, or roasted vegetables

Flavor-Packed Cornbread

This recipe is great because it works with both sweet and savory compound butters. If you're partial to sweet cornbreads, use the Pumpkin Compound Butter. Savory? That Jalapeño Avocado Compound Butter makes a cornbread that's begging to be served alongside Pumpkin Chili (page 106).

MAKES ONE 10-INCH ROUND CORNBREAD

1 cup all-purpose flour

2 cups yellow cornmeal, preferably stone-ground

2 tablespoons light brown sugar

1 tablespoon baking powder

1 teaspoon baking soda

1 teaspoon salt

2½ cups buttermilk

2 large eggs

½ cup compound butter (page 158), melted

1 tablespoon vegetable oil

1 Put a 10-inch cast-iron pan in the center rack of the oven and heat to 400°F.

2 Sift the flour, cornmeal, brown sugar, baking powder, baking soda, and salt into a medium mixing bowl.

3 Whisk together the buttermilk, eggs, and butter in a large mixing bowl.

4 Add the dry ingredients to the wet and stir until combined. Let the batter sit for 10 minutes before baking.

5 Remove the cast-iron pan from the oven and add the vegetable oil, swirling to coat the bottom and sides. Scrape the batter into the pan, spreading it all the way to the sides with a spoon or spatula. Place the pan back in the oven and bake until a toothpick inserted into the center comes out clean, about 30 minutes. Remove from the oven and let cool for 15 minutes in the pan before serving.

Cavatelli with Vegetables and Herbs

One of my best arguments for keeping compound butter in your freezer is that you can combine a little flavored butter and hot pasta water to make the world's simplest pasta sauce. It's a trick we use all the time in the restaurants. Add some vegetables, cheese, and herbs and you've got dinner.

SERVES 6

1 pound cavatelli pasta

1 pound fresh asparagus

1 large zucchini, ends trimmed

1 cup savory compound butter (page 158), softened to room temperature

1½ cups halved cherry tomatoes

2 tablespoons extra-virgin olive oil

Salt and freshly ground black pepper

2½ teaspoons chopped fresh tarragon

2½ tablespoons chopped fresh basil

Zest of 1 lemon

⅓ cup grated Parmesan (optional)

1 Bring a large pot of salted water to a boil. Cook the pasta according to the package instructions.

2 While the pasta water comes to a boil, trim the tough bottom 2 inches of the asparagus. Cut the asparagus at a sharp diagonal from the bottom up into ¼-inch-thick pieces. Place in a large serving bowl. Cut the zucchini in half crosswise and use a peeler to create ½-inch-wide strips by peeling down the sides of the zucchini, making sure to include a bit of the green peel in each strip. When you get to the seeds, switch to the other side of the zucchini and repeat. Discard the seedy center and put the strips into the mixing bowl as well.

3 Add the compound butter, tomatoes, and olive oil to the bowl.

4 When the pasta is cooked, spoon out 3 tablespoons of pasta water and add it to the bowl. Drain the pasta and add it to the bowl and stir until the butter melts and everything is combined. Season with salt and pepper, and add the tarragon, basil, and lemon zest. Stir thoroughly.

5 Sprinkle the Parmesan over the top (if using) and serve.

Simple Frosted Cake

Sometimes all you need is a nice, simple frosted cake. This cake gets richness and flavor from the pecan or pumpkin compound butters, although you could certainly use plain butter if you prefer. You need to let the cake cool completely before frosting, but you can make the cake a day or two before serving. Just refrigerate it in the pan you baked it in, wrapped tightly so it doesn't go stale.

**MAKES ONE 9-INCH ROUND CAKE
OR AN 8-INCH SQUARE CAKE (SEE NOTE)**

**½ cup sweet compound butter
(page 159), softened**

¾ cup sugar

1 teaspoon lemon zest

¼ teaspoon salt

1¼ cups cake flour

¼ teaspoon baking soda

½ teaspoon baking powder

3 large eggs

1½ teaspoons vanilla extract

⅔ cup heavy cream

Frosting (recipe follows; see Note)

1 Heat the oven to 350°F. Grease a 9-inch cake pan or 8-inch square baking pan.

2 Using a stand mixer fitted with the paddle attachment, beat the butter, sugar, lemon zest, and salt on medium speed until light and fluffy, 5 minutes.

3 Meanwhile, sift the flour, baking soda, and baking powder into a small mixing bowl.

4 With the mixer on low, alternate adding one egg and the flour mixture in three parts, mixing until smooth and scraping down the sides of the bowl with a rubber spatula between each addition.

5 Add the vanilla and half of the cream. When the cream has been fully incorporated, add the other half and mix until just combined.

6 Scrape the batter into the prepared pan. Jiggle the pan slightly to get the batter to even out. Bake until a toothpick inserted in the center comes out clean, about 35 minutes.

7 Let cool completely on a rack. If you are making a round cake, slide a knife around the edge and invert onto a flat surface to frost. (If the surface of the cake domed significantly while baking, you may need to use a long, serrated knife to cut off the dome and flatten the surface.) The 8-inch square cake may be frosted in the pan, for more of a snacking cake.

8 Using a palette knife or offset spatula, dollop a quarter of the frosting on top of the cake, then spread it evenly from side to side. Add another quarter and continue until the top is covered and frosting is spread all the way to the sides.

9 Take another swipe of the frosting and slowly begin to spread it around the outside of the cake, working from the bottom edge up. Continue to add frosting as you work your way around the cake until it's completely covered. Use all the frosting.

10 Smooth out any rough edges, as well as where the top and sides of the cake meet. Use a spatula to carefully move the frosted cake to a cake stand or serving plate.

Frosting

**2 cups sweet compound butter
(page 159), softened**
4 cups powdered sugar, sifted
Pinch of salt

1   Using a stand mixer fitted with the paddle attachment, beat the butter on medium speed for 2 minutes.

2   Add 2 cups of the powdered sugar and beat on low speed until incorporated. Scrape the sides of the bowl with a rubber spatula, and then turn the mixer up to medium and continue beating for 2 minutes.

3   Scrape the sides down again and add the remaining 2 cups sugar and the salt. Mix on low speed until incorporated, then turn the mixer up to medium speed and mix for 2 minutes.

Note: If you're using an 8-inch square pan for this and intend to frost it in the dish, you only need a half recipe of frosting.

Chicken Liver Mousse

Chicken liver mousse is a staple of the charcuterie boards at Cured, and it couldn't be easier to make at home. You can make this with Cured's House Compound Butter (page 158) for a classic mousse, but it works equally well with the Roasted Tomato Butter and, surprisingly, the Avocado Jalapeño Butter. You might even try it with the sweeter variations for a holiday cocktail party. Chicken liver mousse is surprisingly versatile!

SERVES 6 TO 8
Begin recipe the day before serving.

1 pound chicken livers, drained and rinsed under cold water

2 large eggs

1 teaspoon salt

½ teaspoon freshly ground black pepper

1 cup compound butter (page 158), softened

Bread or crackers, for serving

1 Heat the oven to 300°F. Bring several cups of water to a simmer in a small saucepan and keep hot.

2 Grease a 1-quart casserole or gratin dish with butter and place in the refrigerator. Puree the chicken livers, eggs, salt, and pepper in a blender or large food processor until smooth, about 20 seconds.

3 Add the softened butter and puree for another 20 seconds.

4 Pour the mixture into the chilled dish and cover with foil. Put a roasting pan in the oven and put the dish in the pan. Pour the hot water in the roasting pan until it comes halfway up the sides of the dish.

5 Bake until the mousse is just barely set. It should be mostly firm yet still slightly jiggly in the center when you wiggle the pan. The exact bake time will vary depending on the size and depth of your dish, but start checking at 40 minutes.

6 Allow the mousse to cool for 30 minutes at room temperature.

7 Refrigerate the mousse, covered, for 12 hours to set.

8 Remove the mousse from the refrigerator 1 hour before serving. Serve with bread or crackers.

Note: You may also serve the mousse in individual ramekins; bake these for 25 minutes.

Base Ingredient: Vegetables Confit

Many kinds of ingredients can be used in a confit, but in this section I'm focusing on those that pack a lot of flavor: garlic, tomatoes, fennel, chiles, and carrots. Both the oil and the vegetable can be used in dishes, and the recipes here make spectacular use of both. Just make sure you store these preserves in the refrigerator, and use a clean utensil anytime you dig into them.

Garlic Confit

A tip for this and all confits: use the smallest vessel you can to save how much oil is necessary to cover your ingredients.

MAKES ABOUT 1 CUP FINISHED CONFIT, PLUS THE OIL

3 heads garlic, cloves peeled and ends trimmed (about 30 cloves)

3 sprigs thyme

¾ cup extra-virgin olive oil (or enough to cover the ingredients)

1   Heat the oven to 250°F.

2   Combine the garlic, thyme, and olive oil in a small ovenproof cooking vessel with a lid, like a Dutch oven. You can also cover the dish with foil.

3   Cook, covered, until soft and golden, about 1½ hours. Let the garlic cool to room temperature in the oil.

4   Spoon the garlic along with the oil into an airtight, covered glass jar. This will keep in the refrigerator for up to 2 weeks.

Easy Ideas for Using Vegetables Confits

• Add to mashed potatoes

• Top baked potatoes

• Top pizzas

• Fill omelets

• Add to pasta

• Fold into rice

• Dice and add to meatloaf or meatballs

Vegetables Confit Variations

	Vegetable Prep	Seasoning	Bake Time
Fennel	Trim fronds from 3 heads and cut heads in half lengthwise	6 sprigs thyme, 3 sprigs tarragon, 1 teaspoon red pepper flakes, 1 teaspoon salt, 1 teaspoon freshly ground black pepper, zest of 1 orange	275°F for 2 hours
Cherry tomato	2 pints whole cherry tomatoes	5 fresh basil leaves, 1 sprig rosemary, 3 garlic cloves, ½ teaspoon salt, ½ teaspoon freshly ground black pepper	250°F for 1 hour
Chile	4 cups whole chiles, such as jalapeños or serranos	6 garlic cloves, ½ teaspoon salt	250°F for 2 hours
Carrot, parsnip, or turnip	1½ pounds peeled carrots, parsnips, or turnips	2 halved serranos, zest of 1 orange, 1 tablespoon coriander seeds, 1 teaspoon salt	275°F for 3 hours

Savory Bread Pudding with Mushrooms

The key to a good bread pudding is making sure the ratio of bread to nonbread ingredients is just right. So many become boring bricks because there's just too much bread! This savory bread pudding is packed with flavorful ingredients, including sausage, onions, mushrooms, herbs, and your choice of vegetables confit. Bonus? It can be served for breakfast or dinner, depending on whether you use breakfast or Italian sausage—perfect for Christmas morning or a Sunday supper.

**MAKES ONE 9 BY 13-INCH PAN OF
BREAD PUDDING**

2 tablespoons confit oil

1 pound bulk breakfast or Italian sausage (page 100 or store-bought; optional)

1 medium onion, diced (about 1 cup)

2 cups thinly sliced assorted mushrooms (button, portobello, and shiitake)

6 cups ½-inch cubes day-old crusty white bread

1 teaspoon chopped fresh thyme

6 large eggs

3 cups heavy cream

1 teaspoon salt

¼ teaspoon freshly ground black pepper

2 tablespoons unsalted butter

¾ cup vegetables confit (page 169), cut into ½-inch pieces as needed

1 Heat 1 tablespoon of the confit oil in a sauté pan over medium-high heat. Add the sausage (if using). Use a spatula to break the sausage into bite-size pieces and brown until cooked thoroughly, about 10 minutes. Put the sausage in a mixing bowl. Drain all the oil from the pan except for 1 tablespoon.

2 If not using the sausage, add the 1 tablespoon confit oil to the pan now. Heat the pan over medium heat. Add the onions and cook until softened, about 3 minutes. Turn up the heat to medium-high, add the mushrooms to the pan, and sauté for an additional 5 minutes. Remove the pan from the heat and put the mushroom mixture in the bowl with the sausage. Add the bread and thyme and stir to combine.

3 In a separate bowl, whisk the eggs briefly, then add the cream, salt, and pepper and stir to combine. Fold the cream mixture into the bread, cover, and place in the refrigerator for at least 1 hour and up to 24 hours.

4 Remove the bread pudding base from the refrigerator 30 minutes before baking.

5 Heat the oven to 325°F. Grease a 9 by 13-inch baking dish.

6 Fold the vegetables confit into the bread pudding base and transfer the mixture to the baking dish.

7 Bake for 90 minutes. The top should be puffed and golden brown. Allow to sit for 15 minutes prior to serving.

Note: This can be baked ahead of time and reheated in a 300°F oven until warmed through, about 20 minutes.

Pinto Bean Hummus

By no means a traditional hummus, this is not a wild departure either. The mellow vegetables confit play nicely with the pinto beans—a nod to Texas—and the tahini and lemon juice brighten it up quite a bit.

MAKES ABOUT 2 CUPS

1 (15.5-ounce) can pinto beans, drained, 1 tablespoon liquid reserved

1 garlic clove, minced

1 tablespoon tahini

1 cup vegetables confit (page 169), roughly chopped

3 tablespoons confit oil

1 lemon, cut in half

½ teaspoon ground cumin

Salt and freshly ground black pepper

4 sprigs parsley, leaves picked and reserved

Toasted pita or crudité (page 191), for serving

1   Put the beans, reserved bean liquid, garlic, tahini, ½ cup of the confit, 2 tablespoons of the confit oil, juice of ½ lemon, and cumin into a food processor and process into a thick paste, about 1 minute.

2   Scrape down the sides, season with salt and pepper, and process for another 15 seconds. Taste and adjust the lemon juice, salt, and pepper if necessary. If the hummus is grainy, you can add a splash or two of water to help smooth it out.

3   Transfer the hummus to a shallow serving dish and use the back of a large spoon to smooth the surface. Use the spoon to create a large, shallow well in the center of the hummus.

4   Scatter the remaining ½ cup confit around the hummus. Drizzle with the remaining tablespoon confit oil and the juice of the remaining ½ lemon. Scatter the parsley leaves over the top and serve with toasted pita, cut into wedges, or crudité.

Whipped Feta Bruschetta

An excellent cocktail party snack, these little toasts are much more flavorful than they seem at first glance. Again, this recipe uses both the confit aromatic of your choice *and* its oil, paired with a feta spread. Depending on the size of the bread you use, you may have some leftover dip and confit—think of these as your treat to snack on while you clean up after your guests have left.

SERVES 6 TO 8 AS AN APPETIZER

6 (1½-inch-thick) slices Italian country-style bread (sourdough or ciabatta work well)

⅓ cup confit oil

Salt and freshly ground black pepper

Whipped Feta (recipe follows)

3 cups vegetables confit (page 169), cut into bite-size pieces if necessary

½ cup julienned fresh basil

1 Prepare a grill or heat a broiler to medium heat.

2 Brush the bread with half of the confit oil liberally on both sides. Season both sides with salt and pepper. Grill or broil the bread until lightly browned on both sides.

3 Cut each piece of bread into two bite-size pieces. Spread each with a generous amount of whipped feta and top with the vegetables confit. Sprinkle with the basil and serve.

Whipped Feta

8 ounces crumbled feta cheese

½ cup Greek yogurt

½ cup confit oil

2 tablespoons lemon juice

½ teaspoon salt

¼ teaspoon freshly ground black pepper

Put the feta and yogurt in a food processor and pulse a few times to combine. Add the confit oil, lemon juice, salt, and pepper and process until smooth.

Base Ingredient: **Meat Confit**

Maybe you got a deal on some chicken at the grocery store, but it's twelve pieces and you're not going to use all of it at once. Or there was rabbit at the farmers' market, but you don't have immediate plans to cook some rabbit. Or your uncle gifted you some of his duck hunt haul. Confit is a great way to save meat, and since it's so flavorful with the salt and the herbs and the fat, it's super versatile. It also happens to be almost impossible to screw up. And it's going to make whatever you're cooking taste better.

I know that people get scared about preserving meat, so let me explain what you're dealing with: as long as the meat is covered by the fat, it's in an anaerobic environment and it's not going to break down. In fact, I think it gets better. When using your meat confit, allow the container to come to room temperature so that the fat becomes liquid again. Use a new clean slotted spoon to remove each and every piece of meat, or wash the spoon between each retrieval. (I know, but this part is important.) Allow the fat to resettle over any remaining meat before putting it back in the refrigerator, to maintain the seal. Of course, you can use all the meat at once, too. And the flavorful fat is great to cook with once it's no longer needed for preservation.

Meat Confit

There are a range of cook times here; you'll know it's done once the bone starts to stick out a bit and the meat is truly tender. You can use store-bought schmaltz as the fat, or use grapeseed or another neutral oil.

MAKES APPROXIMATELY 3 POUNDS CONFIT, PLUS USABLE SEASONED FAT
Begin recipe the day before using.

3 pounds bone-in chicken, duck, or rabbit pieces

¼ cup (62g) salt

2 teaspoons freshly ground black pepper

Seasoning (variations follow)

5 cups rendered duck or chicken fat, or neutral oil, plus more to cover if necessary

1 Pat the meat dry with paper towels. Season all over with the salt and pepper and put in a Dutch oven large enough so that the pieces are in one layer.

2 Top the meat with the recommended seasoning (see variations on page 178). Cover and refrigerate for 12 to 24 hours.

3 Heat the oven to 225°F.

4 Add the fat to the pan and warm over medium-low heat until the fat is liquid. Add additional fat or oil until the meat is completely submerged.

5 Bake, covered, until the meat is falling off the bone and completely tender when pierced with a sharp knife, 3 to 5 hours. Remove the meat pieces from the fat using a slotted spoon and transfer to a separate pan. Do not use tongs, as the meat could fall apart. Strain the fat and save for other uses. If not using right away, completely cover the meat with the strained fat and place in the refrigerator. It can be stored like this for several weeks.

Meat Confit Variations

Chicken Thigh Confit: Use skin-on chicken thighs. Season with 12 thinly sliced garlic cloves, 4 sprigs rosemary, and 1 lemon sliced into thin rounds, seeds removed.

Duck Confit: Use skin-on duck legs. Season with 2 tablespoons juniper berries, 6 sprigs thyme, 8 thinly sliced garlic cloves, and 2 crumbled bay leaves.

Rabbit Confit: Use whole rabbit legs. Season with 2 teaspoons Sichuan peppercorns, 1 star anise pod, and 1 orange sliced into thin rounds, seeds removed.

Easy Ideas for Using Shredded Meat Confit

- Add to an omelet or scrambled eggs
- Layer into a grilled cheese (or whatever sandwich you like)
- Top rice bowls
- Fold into salads
- Add to quesadillas or tacos
- Sprinkle over fried rice
- Fold into meatloaf
- Use in soups, pastas, or braises
- Use in lasagnas, enchiladas, or other casseroles

Meat Confit with Baked Oatmeal and Agrodolce Sauce

Oatmeal is an unexpectedly lovely accompaniment to fatty meats like confits. Its sweetness counterbalances the garlicky saltiness of the meat, while the sweet-tart sauce brings everything together. You can use whatever dried fruit you like for this recipe; just make sure to chop larger fruit like prunes or apricots.

SERVES 6

6 servings meat confit (page 177)
Baked Oatmeal (recipe follows)
Agrodolce Sauce (recipe follows)
Chopped mint, for garnish

1   Use a clean slotted spoon to remove each piece of the confit from the container of fat. Clean the spoon between each retrieval. Using clean hands, wipe away as much fat as possible. Place the meat on a racked sheet pan or roasting pan and allow to sit at room temperature for 20 minutes.

2   Crisp the meat under a broiler until warmed through and golden brown. The timing on this will vary depending on your broiler setup, so keep an eye on it. It should take between 5 and 10 minutes.

3   To serve, cut the oatmeal into squares and serve warm, with the meat and the sauce. Garnish with chopped mint.

Baked Oatmeal

1 tablespoon unsalted butter
2 large eggs
1½ cups whole milk
⅓ cup honey
1 teaspoon vanilla extract
½ teaspoon salt
½ teaspoon baking powder
3 cups old-fashioned rolled oats
1½ cups oven-dried fruit (page 88), chopped into bite-size pieces if necessary

1   Grease an 8-inch square baking pan with the butter. Stir together the eggs, milk, honey, vanilla, salt, and baking powder in a mixing bowl. Stir in the oats and dried fruit.

2   Pour the batter into the pan and push the oats into the liquid. Bake until the edges turn golden brown, 50 minutes. Let rest for 10 minutes before serving.

Agrodolce Sauce

1 tablespoon extra-virgin olive oil
½ small red onion, finely diced (about ¼ cup)
¾ cup rice wine vinegar
¼ cup molasses
¼ cup oven-dried fruit (page 88), chopped
½ teaspoon red pepper flakes

Heat the olive oil in a small saucepan over medium heat. Add the onion and sauté until soft, about 4 minutes. Add the rest of the ingredients and bring to a boil. Reduce the heat and simmer until the sauce becomes syrupy, about 10 minutes. Serve warm.

Chicory Salad with Meat Confit and a Poached Egg

My take on a salade Lyonnaise. I love that it uses both the meat confit and the flavorful fat in the dressing. The other thing that makes this recipe is tons of tarragon—it's such a nice accent to the bitter greens and creamy egg.

SERVES 1

½ cup shredded meat confit (page 177)
2 tablespoons fat from the meat confit
1 teaspoon Dijon mustard
2 teaspoons sherry vinegar
Salt and freshly ground black pepper
1 cup radicchio, leaves torn into bite-size pieces
1 cup frisée, leaves torn into bite-size pieces
¼ cup whole fresh tarragon leaves
Poached Egg (recipe follows)
2 thin slices baguette, toasted crisp, for serving

1 Heat a sauté pan over medium-high heat. Add the meat and the confit fat and sauté until the meat crisps slightly, about 3 minutes.

2 Remove the pan from the heat. Stir in the mustard and vinegar; add salt and pepper to taste.

3 Toss the radicchio, frisée, and tarragon together in a large bowl. Add the warm dressing, meat, and salt and pepper to taste.

4 Serve topped with a poached egg and baguette slices.

Poached Egg

1 teaspoon white vinegar
1 teaspoon salt
1 large egg, at room temperature

1 Bring a small saucepan of water to a simmer over medium heat. Add the vinegar and salt.

2 Crack an egg into a small bowl—it's easier than trying to crack the egg directly into the water.

3 Use a slotted spoon to slowly stir the simmering water in a circle. Pour the egg into the center of the swirling water.

4 Simmer gently until the white of the egg is fully set but the yolk is still liquid, about 4 minutes. Use the slotted spoon to remove the egg from the water and serve.

Cheesy Acorn Squash Stuffed with Meat Confit, Greens, and Pomegranate

Every fall, farmers' markets put out mountains of gorgeous pumpkins and squash, but what to do with them besides roasting? I love acorn squash, but I hate trying to wedge a peeler into all its grooves. This recipe uses it as an edible serving dish for this cheesy all-in-one autumnal meal—and you can even eat the peel! This is a great dinner party main, served with a salad and a loaf of crusty bread.

SERVES 6

3 tablespoons unsalted butter, softened

3 acorn squash, halved and seeded

Salt and freshly ground black pepper

¼ cup extra-virgin olive oil

1 green onion, chopped

2 garlic cloves, minced

½ cup hazelnuts, coarsely chopped

4 cups roughly chopped, tightly packed mustard greens

½ cup chicken stock (page 51)

4 cups shredded meat confit (page 177)

½ cup pomegranate seeds

1 cup ½-inch cubes fresh mozzarella

1 Heat the oven to 375°F. Grease a baking dish or roasting pan with the butter. Sprinkle the squash halves with salt and pepper and place cut-side down in the pan. Add ½ inch of water to the pan and bake for 45 minutes.

2 Meanwhile, heat the olive oil in a large sauté pan over medium-high heat. Add the green onions and garlic and cook for 1 minute. Add the hazelnuts to the pan and cook, stirring, for 1 minute longer. Add the mustard greens and chicken stock and cook until the greens are wilted, about 2 minutes. Remove from the heat and fold in the meat, pomegranate seeds, and cheese.

3 Remove the squash from the oven and discard the water from the bottom of the pan. Turn the squash cut-side up and divide the filling evenly among all 6 halves. The filling should be slightly mounded in each.

4 Bake the stuffed squash until slightly browned on top, another 20 minutes. Let cool for 2 to 3 minutes and serve.

Cure

Curing is where it all started for me: preserving ingredients by packing them in salt. Salt pulls either a little water out of food, which improves flavor and texture, or a lot of water, which renders the ingredient inhospitable to harmful bacteria and extends its edibility. In this chapter, we'll discuss two examples of each: partially cured vegetables and brined meats, and completely cured fish and meat.

Curing can be intimidating, especially curing raw fish and meat. But I hope once you get through this chapter, you'll understand how worthwhile it can be to cure your own ingredients. Cured ingredients bring intensity to a dish, which means you don't have to use a lot of one to get a lot of flavor—think pepperoni on a pizza or ham in a pot of beans. Cured ingredients just speak louder than other ingredients.

Like most of the preservation methods in this book, curing originated as a means of survival. If you killed an animal, you had to preserve it as best you could because it was life or death. Translating that to a modern-day restaurant, the circumstances aren't so dire. But curing allows us to showcase the hard work of our farmers and ranchers and honor the beautiful meats they raise. Once we have the steaks and chops we need, we often have a lot of good leftover meat to process. We don't freeze or grind it for burgers. Nope. True to the restaurant's name, we cure hams and coppas and whole loins and salami.

As I said in the introduction, I don't expect you to make a 25-pound ham in your garage. We'll cover much simpler territory here. But a big ham was where it all started for me. When I first got into curing, there weren't a ton of books on it like there are now, and the learning curve was steep. But with that first ham, I got lucky. I had to wait for 12 months to know whether it was gonna be worth a damn. Turns out? It was one of the best hams I'd ever eaten in my life. It was exhilarating. I was hooked.

That was really the birth of Cured, the restaurant, years before we opened. I just knew what I wanted to do. And I hope this chapter will bring you a little bit of that curing magic.

Base Ingredient: Quick-Cured Vegetables

Most vegetables have a lot of water in them. You can see it bead up when you slice a cucumber or peel a butternut squash. We do a lot of vegetable curing at Cured because it gives vegetables a little bit of textural oomph by taking some of the water out. Salting vegetables prior to cooking also helps to mask bitterness, and it intensifies flavors and aromas. It's also good to salt vegetables prior to grilling, as it helps prevent sticking.

Here are two Base Recipes, because some vegetables have higher water content than others. A helpful chart for quick-curing other vegetables follows!

Quick-Cured Tomatoes

MAKES 1 POUND QUICK-CURED TOMATOES

1 pound tomatoes, cores removed

1 teaspoon (5g) salt

1 Cut the tomatoes into wedges or slices, depending on how you will use them. For example, if you're making the schnitzel (page 194), slice the tomatoes and season over a racked sheet pan. If you're making a salad, cut them into wedges and season in a colander set over a mixing bowl.

2 Let the tomatoes drain for 30 minutes before using in any applications. If you collect the juices, you can use them in Bloody Marys, vinaigrettes, or gazpachos.

Quick-Cured Cauliflower

MAKES 2 POUNDS QUICK-CURED CAULIFLOWER
Begin recipe the day before using.

2 pounds cauliflower (about 1 head)

2 teaspoons (10g) salt

1 Cut the cauliflower into florets or steaks, depending on how it will be used. Place the cauliflower on a racked sheet pan or in a colander fitted over a bowl and sprinkle evenly with salt.

2 Cover and refrigerate for 24 hours.

3 Rinse the cauliflower, pat dry with paper towels, and proceed with the recipe.

Quick-Cured Vegetable Variations

Use 1 teaspoon salt (5g) per pound of vegetable.
A colander will work best for smaller, chunky
pieces, while a racked sheet pan will work for
larger slices. Taste cured vegetables before using,
and rinse off excess salt as necessary.

Vegetable	Cut or Cure Whole?	Time on Salt
Okra	Cure whole, cut after curing if desired	4 hours
Green beans	Trim stems and cure whole, cut after curing if necessary	2 hours
Radishes	Ends cut off and quartered, or cut into ½-inch-thick slices	2 hours
Broccoli	Cut into bite-size florets or ½-inch-thick steaks	12 hours
Asparagus	Cure whole, do not peel, cut after curing if necessary	2 hours
Cucumbers	Unpeeled, cut into ¾-inch dice or sliced into ½-inch-thick half moons	1 hour
Turnips	Peeled and cut into 1-inch dice or ¾-inch-thick slices	8 hours
Root vegetables, like beets, sweet potatoes, celeriac, and rutabagas	Peeled and cut into 1-inch dice or ¾-inch-thick slices	8 hours
Endive	Quartered lengthwise	2 hours
Corn	Kernels cut from the cob	1 hour
Carrots	Peeled and cut into large sticks or ¾-inch dice	4 hours
Chiles	¼-inch-thick slices, do not remove seeds	8 hours
Bell pepper	Cut into ½-inch spears or ¾-inch bite-size chunks; remove seeds	1 hour
Eggplant	¼-inch-thick slices, or peeled and cut into 1-inch chunks	1 to 2 hours
Summer squash or zucchini	Cut lengthwise into ½-inch-thick planks, or cut into ½-inch-thick half moons	1 hour
Strawberries or stone fruit	Cut into wedges	1 hour, cured in half-salt, half-sugar mixture

Easy Ideas for Using Quick-Cured Vegetables

- Use in almost every application where you would use raw vegetables—try them in salads of all kinds
- Top pizza
- Roast them
- Grill them
- Add to sandwiches
- Build an antipasti platter
- Garnish a martini (page 32)
- Tuck into omelets

The Ultimate Crudité Spread

Crudité doesn't have to be boring! Step one: Make sure you have a good mix of in-season vegetables in a variety of colors, all cut into bite-size pieces. Step two: Quick-cure the vegetables to give them extra crunch and flavor. Step three: Take time to arrange them nicely on a platter with some tasty dips. I serve this particular spread with two vegan dips so everyone at the party can enjoy. (The romesco can be made without the nuts, if necessary.) You could also serve this with the Pinto Bean Hummus (page 173) to really splash out.

SERVES 6 TO 8 AS A PARTY SNACK

2 pounds assorted raw quick-cured vegetables (page 187)

Romesco Sauce (recipe follows)

Cashew Cheese (recipe follows)

Rosemary sprigs and/or dill fronds, for garnish (optional)

1 Plunge the salted vegetables in a bowl of ice water to remove excess salt. Drain the vegetables and put them on paper towels to remove any excess moisture.

2 Place the romesco and cashew cheese in bowls in the center of a large serving platter.

3 Beautifully arrange the assorted salted vegetables in and around the dips.

4 Place the herb sprigs (if using) with the stems buried in the vegetables and the tops out.

Romesco Sauce

¾ cup diced roasted red peppers (see Note)

¼ cup toasted hazelnuts

2 tablespoons tomato paste (or oven-dried tomatoes, page 87)

1 garlic clove, smashed

2 teaspoons sherry vinegar

½ teaspoon smoked paprika

¼ teaspoon cayenne

¼ teaspoon salt

¼ cup diced country bread (such as sourdough), crusts removed

¼ cup extra-virgin olive oil

1 Put the roasted red peppers, hazelnuts, tomato paste, garlic, vinegar, paprika, cayenne, salt, and bread in a blender or food processor. Starting on a low speed, blend the mixture, slowly turning the machine to high.

2 Once the ingredients are blended, with the machine running, slowly pour in the olive oil. When all the oil has been incorporated, taste for seasoning and refrigerate until ready to serve. This sauce can be made up to a week in advance.

Note: You can use jarred or canned roasted red peppers. If using fresh, roast the pepper over an open gas burner or under a broiler, turning with tongs until the entire pepper is charred. Put in a covered container to cool for half an hour, then peel the skin from the pepper. Discard seeds and stem, then dice.

Cashew Cheese

1 cup raw cashews

2 tablespoons nutritional yeast

Juice of 1 lemon

1 garlic clove

Salt and freshly ground black pepper

1   Place the raw cashews in a bowl with cold water to cover. Let sit at room temperature for 2 hours. Drain and rinse under cold water.

2   Add the drained nuts, nutritional yeast, lemon juice, garlic, and ½ cup water to a blender or food processor and blend until smooth. It may take a couple of minutes of processing for the cashew cheese to become fully smooth. Season with salt and pepper. Refrigerate until ready to use. This dip tastes better after 24 hours; it will keep for about a week.

Any Vegetable "en Vaso" Style

This dish takes inspiration from San Antonio's ubiquitous snack shops and their classic treat, elote en vaso, or corn in a cup (also called esquites). This is excellent with corn, of course, but try it with other vegetables—cauliflower, zucchini, or okra work great—or a combination of vegetables. The recipe calls to serve this family-style in a serving bowl or platter, but don't let me stop you from serving it SATX style, in individual cups.

SERVES 6 AS A SIDE

½ cup mayonnaise

1 cup Mexican crema or sour cream

2 tablespoons vegetable oil

6 cups diced quick-cured vegetables (page 187)

¼ cup (½ stick) unsalted butter

Salt and freshly ground black pepper

½ cup crumbled cotija cheese

2 tablespoons chili powder

¼ cup cilantro leaves, chopped

1 lime, cut into wedges, for serving

1   Whisk together the mayonnaise and crema in a small bowl and set aside.

2   Heat the vegetable oil in a large skillet over medium-high heat. Add the vegetables and sauté until cooked through—the exact timing will depend on what vegetable you use, but about

5 to 8 minutes. Remove from the heat and add the butter. Stir to combine. Season with salt and pepper, but remember the cheese may be quite salty.

3 Spoon half your vegetables into a serving dish. Dollop evenly with half the crema mixture, and sprinkle with half the cheese. Repeat with the remaining vegetables, crema mixture, and cheese.

4 Sprinkle with the chili powder and cilantro leaves. Serve warm, with lime wedges on the side.

Any-Vegetable Schnitzel

This works best with bigger vegetables—eggplants, squash, cauliflower, broccoli, root vegetables—that can be cut into ½-inch-thick steaks. By salting the vegetables first and drawing out the water, you help the batter stick during frying. Otherwise you might end up with a soggy, mushy mess! You can serve these with Remoulade (page 21), and if you really want to dress things up, add a few Pickled Shrimp (page 16).

SERVES 6

Vegetable or peanut oil, for frying

3 large eggs

2 tablespoons whole milk

3 cups unseasoned panko bread crumbs

2 pounds quick-cured vegetables (pages 187–188), such as tomato, eggplant, summer squash, cauliflower, or root vegetables, cut into large slices

Salt

1 lemon, cut into 6 wedges, for serving

1 Heat 1 inch of oil in a large cast-iron skillet over medium-high heat until an instant-read thermometer reads 330°F. (If you don't have an instant-read thermometer, wait until the surface of the oil looks hazy, then carefully flick a couple of drops of water into it. They should sizzle dramatically.)

2 Meanwhile, in a shallow dish or pie plate, whisk the eggs with the milk. Put the bread crumbs in a separate, similar shallow dish.

3 Pat the vegetables dry with a paper towel. One at a time, dip the slices in the egg mixture and then in the bread crumbs. Shake off any excess bread crumbs and set aside on a racked sheet pan.

4 Line a dish big enough to hold all your schnitzels with paper towels.

5 Fry the vegetables until the bread crumbs are golden, flipping carefully with a slotted spoon or spatula halfway through. You may need to fry in batches so as not to crowd the pan. The exact cooking time will depend on which vegetable you use, but roughly 2 to 3 minutes per side. Transfer the finished schnitzels to the paper towel–lined dish and season with a good sprinkle of salt.

6 Serve immediately with lemon wedges on the side.

Note: Sturdier vegetables such as cauliflower, broccoli, or root vegetables may be held in a 275°F oven while you finish frying the batches. Vegetables with higher water content, such as tomatoes, may get soggy if held, though.

Cast-Iron-Charred Vegetables with Capers and Raisins

We don't char vegetables enough, and most would benefit from a little charring! Presalting the vegetables here helps you get that color on them. The combination of capers, raisins, and cheese is a classic one from the Mediterranean and gives this dish a sweet-salty-tart flavor oomph. Make sure you have all your ingredients prepped and ready to go before you start cooking the vegetables because this comes together quickly!

SERVES 4

¼ cup plus 1 tablespoon extra-virgin olive oil

2 pounds quick-cured vegetables, such as eggplant, zucchini, or yellow squash or a combination (page 188), cut into bite-size pieces

2 tablespoons drained capers

¼ cup golden raisins

¼ cup shaved ricotta salata or a dry, crumbly feta

2 sprigs basil, leaves removed and torn

½ teaspoon freshly ground black pepper

1 Heat 1 tablespoon of the olive oil in a 12-inch cast-iron pan or skillet over medium-high heat until hot.

2 Cook half the vegetables until slightly charred, 5 to 8 minutes. Flip the vegetables over periodically to make sure all sides are evenly charred. Use a slotted spoon to transfer the vegetables to a serving dish. (Don't worry too much about keeping them hot; this dish is great warm or at room temperature.) Repeat this process with the remaining vegetables.

3 Drizzle the vegetables with the remaining ¼ cup olive oil. Add the capers, raisins, cheese, and basil, season with black pepper, and toss gently. Serve.

Base Ingredient: **Meat Brines**

Meat brines are another technique that uses the principles of curing to improve texture and flavor without fully curing the ingredient at hand. I brine proteins to season them from the inside out, but in doing so, also ensure the meat retains moisture during the cooking process. In recent years, brining has become a popular method for preparing Thanksgiving turkeys and roasted chickens, but you can brine almost any piece of meat.

At Cured, our simplest house brine is an 8 percent saline solution. Water and salt, that's it. The brines start to get a bit more complex depending on how it will be used: for example, we sometimes add sugar because it improves flavor and helps any skin crisp up nice and brown. Roughly speaking, you'll want 2 cups of brine per pound of meat (and 1 quart for 2 pounds, and 2 quarts for 4 pounds, like the recipe below). Various factors, including the thickness of the cut (4 pounds of chops will brine faster than a 4-pound roast), surface area, and whether it has bones, will impact timing. Refer to the chart on the following page for timing by cut.

Basic Meat Brine

In addition to seasoning, brines also impart flavor. Here, I've added fennel and coriander seeds, bay leaves, and black peppercorns for a nice all-purpose brine, but you can play around with other whole spices and dried herbs. Caraway seeds might be nice in a pork brine, for example, and dried chiles would be great with beef or game.

**MAKES 2 QUARTS, ENOUGH FOR
4 POUNDS OF MEAT**

1 tablespoon fennel seeds

1½ teaspoons coriander seeds

½ cup plus 2 tablespoons (155g) salt

¼ cup packed light brown sugar

2 bay leaves

1½ teaspoons black peppercorns

1 Toast the fennel and coriander seeds in a large pot over medium heat until fragrant, about 3 minutes.

2 Add the salt, brown sugar, bay leaves, and peppercorns to the pot along with 8 cups water and bring to a boil, stirring periodically, until the salt and sugar have dissolved. Cool the brine to room temperature.

3 You can use this brine for a variety of meats, but make enough brine so the meat is completely submerged in the liquid, doubling or halving the recipe as needed. Always cover and refrigerate meat as it brines. Resealable plastic bags work well for brining and may reduce how much brine you need to make. When you're done brining, always rinse the meat and pat dry with paper towels.

How to Brine (Most) Kinds of Meat

Type of Meat	Time in Brine
Large pork cuts, boneless	6 hours per pound
Large pork cuts, bone-in	8 hours per pound
Pork chops, boneless	1 hour total
Pork chops, bone-in	2 hours total
Large cuts beef, lamb, or large game, boneless	3 hours per pound
Large cuts beef, lamb, or large game, bone-in	4 hours per pound
Small lamb or game cuts, boneless*	4 hours total
Small lamb or game cuts, bone-in*	6 hours total
Whole duck	24 hours total
Duck breasts	8 hours total
Whole chicken	45 minutes per pound
Boneless chicken cuts	1 hour total
Bone-in chicken cuts	1 hour 15 minutes total
Whole turkey	1 hour per pound
Shell-on large shrimp (16/20s, adjust timing up or down depending on size)	30 minutes total
Fish fillets such as salmon, tuna, swordfish, halibut	15 minutes total

* I do not typically recommend you brine steaks. Buy good-quality steaks and let their natural flavor shine through (preferably with a nice bordelaise sauce, page 54!).

Brined Roast Chicken

Chefs love roasting chickens! I think it's because it's one of the few dishes that is almost always better made at home than in a restaurant, and we see it as a challenge to serve a good roast chicken. Luckily, you won't have that problem at home, especially since brining chicken prior to roasting makes it so much more forgiving. No dry birds here! Serve with the roasted potatoes on page 101, a salad, and plenty of bread for mopping up the drippings.

SERVES 2 TO 4

1 whole chicken, about 4 pounds (if you use a larger or smaller bird, adjust brine time accordingly)

1 recipe meat brine (page 197)

2 tablespoons freshly ground black pepper

¼ cup (½ stick) unsalted butter, softened

2 tablespoons extra-virgin olive oil

¼ cup chopped fresh herbs (marjoram, parsley, basil, tarragon, and chives all work well)

2 garlic cloves, minced

1   Remove any package of giblets or plastic trussing from the chicken. Place the chicken in a container large enough to hold it and the brine. Pour the brine over the bird, cover the container, and refrigerate for 3 hours (or 45 minutes per pound).

2   Remove the chicken and discard the brine. Rinse it under cold water and pat dry with paper towels. Refrigerate the chicken on a roasting pan fitted with a rack for at least 2 and up to 12 hours, in order to let the skin dry out. This will help you get crispier skin.

3   Heat the oven to 375°F. Take the chicken out of the refrigerator and let it sit at room temperature for 20 minutes.

4   Combine the pepper, butter, olive oil, herbs, and garlic in a bowl, mashing with a fork until completely incorporated. Using clean hands, rub the butter mixture all over the chicken, both inside and out.

5   Place the chicken on the racked roasting pan breast-side up and roast until an instant-read thermometer inserted into the area where the thigh meets the breast reaches 160°F, about 90 minutes. The juices should run clean at this point. Let the chicken rest 10 minutes before serving.

Grilled Ribs

Not well practiced at grilling? Try your hands at these forgiving brined ribs. (Are you starting to notice a trend? Brined meats = forgiving meats.) This recipe has you brine the ribs first for seasoning and moisture, and then coat them in a rub for additional flavor and a caramelized crust. The brine time here varies from the chart because ribs aren't quite a large bone-in pork cut like the Big Holiday Pork Roast (page 203), but they're also not bone-in pork chops. They're somewhere in between.

SERVES 6
Begin recipe the day before serving.

2 racks baby back ribs (5 to 6 pounds total)

1½ recipes (3 quarts) meat brine (page 197)

2 tablespoons mustard powder

2 tablespoons paprika

¼ cup packed light brown sugar

2½ teaspoons onion powder

2½ teaspoons garlic powder

2 cups pecan wood or applewood chips or chunks, soaked in water for a minimum of 2 hours (optional)

1 Refrigerate the ribs in the brine, covered, for 12 hours.

2 Remove the ribs and discard the brine. Rinse them under cold water and pat dry with paper towels.

3 Combine the mustard powder, paprika, brown sugar, onion powder, and garlic powder in a small mixing bowl. Rub the spice mixture all over the ribs, both front and back, and refrigerate, covered, on a sheet pan or roasting pan, for at least 2 hours and up to 8 hours. Pull the ribs from the refrigerator and let rest at room temperature for 2 more hours.

4 Meanwhile, heat a grill to 300°F. Drain the wood chips (if using) and sprinkle a few over the coals. Place the ribs directly on the grill, as far from the coals as possible, and cook with the cover on and the vents open for 3 hours. Sprinkle more chips over the coals every hour. The temperature of the grill will drop over the course of several hours. Do not let it drop below 225°F. If this happens, toss in a handful of charcoal to bring the temperature back up. The ribs are done when they flop over when held by a pair of tongs, or reach an internal temperature of about 190°F. Let rest for 10 minutes, cut into individual ribs, and serve.

Big Holiday Pork Roast

Skip the turkey this year and make a giant pork roast for the holidays instead. Juicy, flavorful, forgiving, and relatively affordable, a pork loin roast makes a dramatic centerpiece to your meal. What's not to love? Pork loin roasts are a Christmas tradition in many parts of the world, and you'll start to see them at your butcher counter more during that time of year. A good butcher should be able to cut one of these for you as a custom order, though. And don't worry if you can only find a skinless roast—the method will work the same; you'll just miss out on the delightfully crispy cracklings.

Serve this with a jammy fruit sauce: heat equal parts water or wine with jam (page 131) in a saucepan until warm and syrupy.

SERVES 6 TO 8
Begin recipe 48 hours before serving.

1 (5- to 6-pound) bone-in center-cut pork loin roast
1½ recipes (3 quarts) meat brine (page 197)
¼ cup extra-virgin olive oil
2 tablespoons freshly ground black pepper

1   Place the loin on a cutting board and use a very sharp knife to score the skin in a crosshatch pattern, creating ½-inch squares. You want to cut through the skin and just barely into the fat; do not cut all the way down to the meat. (If you can convince your butcher to do this, it will save you a bit of time.)

2   Refrigerate the pork loin in the brine for 48 hours. It should fit nicely in a 2-gallon resealable plastic bag; a pot with a lid will work as well, so long as the meat is submerged and covered.

3   One hour before roasting, remove the loin and discard the brine. Rinse it thoroughly under cold water and pat dry with paper towels. Place it skin-side up in a roasting pan with a rack and allow it to come to room temperature.

4   Whisk the olive oil and pepper together in a small bowl. Brush the mixture over the entire pork loin.

5   Heat the oven to 450°F and roast the pork for 25 minutes. This helps crisp the skin and renders a bit of the fat. Reduce the heat to 325°F and cook until an instant-read thermometer inserted in the center of the loin reads 145°F, about 1 hour and 30 minutes. The skin should be crispy. If not, place the roast under the broiler for a minute or two until the skin gets nice and bubbly.

6   Let rest for 10 minutes before carving. To serve, cut into chops between the bones.

Cast-Iron-Seared Lamb Chops with Charred Brussels Sprouts

Look, lamb chops can be pricey. So make sure they taste as good as they possibly can by brining them ahead of time. The brine will also help remove some of lamb's gamey flavor, in case you have some picky eaters on your hands. The Brussels sprouts here serve to pick up any caramelized meaty bits that stick to the pan. And the sweet, sharp, citrusy glaze, well, the glaze is just tasty.

SERVES 6, WITH 2 CHOPS PER PERSON

12 bone-in lamb loin chops (about 4 pounds total), ½ to ¾ inch thick

½ recipe (1 quart) meat brine (page 197)

Freshly ground black pepper

6 tablespoons extra-virgin olive oil

2 pounds Brussels sprouts, trimmed and halved lengthwise

½ teaspoon salt

Juice of ½ lemon

2 tablespoons chopped fresh mint

Orange Glaze (recipe follows)

1   Refrigerate the lamb chops in the brine for 6 hours.

2   Heat the oven to 200°F.

3   Remove the chops and discard the brine. Rinse them thoroughly under cold water and pat dry with paper towels. Generously season on both sides with pepper.

4   Heat 2 tablespoons of the olive oil in a 12-inch cast-iron pan over medium-high heat. Sear the chops until golden brown, about 4 minutes per side. Remove from the pan and keep warm in the oven.

5   Add 2 tablespoons of olive oil to the pan and add half the Brussels sprouts, cut-side down. After 5 minutes, add ¼ teaspoon salt and sauté for an additional 4 minutes. When the sprouts are browned and cooked through, transfer to an oven-safe bowl and keep warm in the oven. Repeat this process for the remaining Brussels sprouts. Add additional olive oil if needed so that the sprouts do not stick and burn.

6   Juice the lemon over the sprouts and sprinkle with mint; stir to combine.

7   Serve the chops alongside the sprouts, with the orange glaze on the side.

Orange Glaze

1 cup orange marmalade (page 138)

2 tablespoons honey

⅛ teaspoon ground ginger

1 star anise pod

Combine ⅓ cup water with the orange marmalade, honey, ginger, and star anise pod in a small saucepan and bring to a simmer. Lower the heat and reduce for 5 minutes to thicken. Remove star anise and set aside. Serve at room temperature.

Base Ingredient: **Preserved Citrus**

When life gives you lemons? You know, you can only drink so much lemonade.

In South Texas, farmers grow grapefruit, oranges, kumquats, and more. And in fact, I do occasionally find myself in a situation where life has given me an overabundance of citrus. I like to preserve these in salt, a technique that originated in northern Africa. It's a good way to make use of the local harvest and couldn't be simpler to make at home.

Preserving lemons and other citrus this way almost calms the flavor. It's more rounded, less harsh. When fresh, the flavor of a lemon is very aggressive, and that brilliant acid is useful in so many dishes. But preserved, the fruitiness comes out with a natural kind of sweetness. There's so much you can do with lemons once they've had a chance to mellow a bit in salt. I sometimes even use the juice from my preserved lemons in recipes that call for fresh lemon juice, just to change things up.

Preserved Citrus

There are two key factors to successfully preserving lemons. First, the fruit must be completely submerged in liquid—this prevents mold. I find using a jar with "shoulders" (as opposed to a wide-mouth jar) allows you to wedge the fruit below the surface of the liquid. (You could also use fermentation weights, see page 240.) Second, that liquid must be rather acidic. Lemon, lime, and grapefruit all work well with their own juices, but sweeter citrus like oranges should be covered in lemon juice.

MAKES 1 QUART
Begin recipe 30 days before using.

4 to 6 whole citrus, depending on size
½ cup (124g) salt
Juice of 4 to 6 lemons, to cover

1 Clean and dry a quart canning jar. It should be totally dry, no water droplets.

2 Cut an X in each citrus that goes almost, but not all the way, through the fruit. Leave about ½ inch uncut. (If you're using larger citrus like grapefruit and they don't fit in the jar, you may cut them completely in half or even quarters.)

3 Sprinkle a good amount of salt into each cut citrus and pack them into the jar. Cover the citrus completely with juice, and top with any leftover salt.

4 Loosely screw the lid on the jar—you want air to come in contact with the surface of the lemon juice to allow any gasses to escape. Store in a dark place for about 30 days. After that, the preserved citrus will be ready to use and can be stored in the refrigerator for several months.

Preserved Citrus Variations

Proceed with the recipe as written, using lemons, limes, grapefruit, Meyer lemons, oranges, clementines, tangerines, kumquats, blood oranges—you name it. If using extremely acidic citrus like limes or grapefruit, you may cover the fruit in lime juice or grapefruit juice. When using sweeter citrus like oranges or tangerines, use lemon juice to cover.

Thin-skinned citrus like Meyer lemons and clementines may fall apart a bit after preservation, so these are best used in pureed applications like the Preserved Lemon Chicken Soup on page 215.

You may also flavor your preserved lemons by adding the following to the jar along with the citrus:

- A sprig of thyme
- A sprig of lavender (use a light touch; it can be overpowering)
- A sprig of rosemary
- A 1-inch piece of ginger, peeled and thinly sliced
- A teaspoon of red pepper flakes
- A few peeled garlic cloves (use only for savory applications)

Easy Ideas for Using Preserved Citrus

- Blend with olive oil for a two-ingredient salad dressing
- Chop and add to grains while cooking
- Slice thin and slip under the skin of a chicken before roasting
- Smash a wedge of preserved citrus in the bottom of a glass and top with ice and soda water (and a splash of gin, if you like)
- Use wherever you want lemon or lemon juice (just remember that it's salty)

Preserved Citrus Ceviche

When it comes to seafood, sustainability is very important to me—we serve only seafood that has been caught or farmed in environmentally responsible ways. Thankfully, the Gulf is close enough to San Antonio that we have access to a variety of high-quality seafood. I went with snapper as a sustainable option for this ceviche because it's easy to get—it's so abundant, it's not harmful to fish. Other fish could be easily substituted: you want a flaky fish with a bit of tooth to it like sea bass or halibut, especially if you can get them locally.

SERVES 6 AS AN APPETIZER, 4 AS A LIGHT LUNCH

1 pound red snapper (or other firm white fish) fillets, skin removed, cut into ½-inch dice

½ cup preserved citrus (page 209, about ½ preserved lemon), pith and flesh removed, rind finely chopped

Juice of 1 lime

½ teaspoon salt

2 tablespoons extra-virgin olive oil

1 cup cilantro leaves, roughly chopped

2 serrano peppers, thinly sliced (optional)

1 large shallot, thinly sliced into rings

1 cup finely diced tomato

1   Combine the snapper, preserved citrus, lime juice, salt, and olive oil in a medium mixing bowl and combine gently with a rubber spatula. Spread the ceviche on a nonmetal plate (so the acid doesn't react with the metal and create an off metallic taste), cover with plastic wrap, and refrigerate for at least 2 hours, and no more than 6 hours.

2   Remove the fish from the refrigerator and top with the cilantro, serranos (if using), shallot, and tomatoes.

3   Enjoy with tortilla chips or crusty bread. And a cold beer.

Note: You can buy fish with the skin removed or ask the fish counter to do it for you. Otherwise, set the fillet skin-side down on a cutting board. Moving away from your body, slip a sharp knife between the skin and the fillet, keeping the blade flat against the cutting board as you cut.

Israeli Couscous with Preserved Lemon, Bacon, and Greens

Here, the mellow preserved lemon plays against the smoky, fatty bacon and the bitterness of the greens. Toasting the Israeli couscous gives it a great nutty texture. This is fantastic as a side with fish or grilled chicken, or as an entrée served with a poached egg (see page 180). To make it vegetarian, swap the bacon for 6 tablespoons olive oil and the chicken stock for vegetable stock.

SERVES 4 AS A MAIN, 6 AS A SIDE

4 strips thick-cut bacon, cut into ¼-inch wide pieces (about 1 cup)

3 garlic cloves, thinly sliced

1½ cups Israeli couscous or fregola

2 cups chicken stock (page 51)

2 tablespoons extra-virgin olive oil

1 teaspoon freshly ground black pepper

½ teaspoon red pepper flakes

1 teaspoon chopped fresh oregano

¼ cup grated Parmesan

1 large bunch dandelion greens, woody stems removed and leaves roughly chopped, or 2 cups baby arugula

½ teaspoon salt

¼ cup roughly chopped preserved lemon (page 209), seeds removed

1 In a large skillet that has a lid, cook the bacon, uncovered, over medium heat until crisp, about 8 minutes. Add the garlic and sauté for 1 minute. Add the couscous and continue to sauté, stirring constantly, to coat the couscous and bring out its toasty aroma, about 4 minutes.

2 Add 1 cup water and the chicken stock to the pan and bring to a boil. Reduce the heat to a simmer, cover, and cook for 8 minutes. Drain and return the couscous to the pot.

3 While the couscous is warm, add the olive oil, black pepper, red pepper flakes, oregano, Parmesan, greens, salt, and preserved lemon. Stir until the greens are half-wilted and serve.

Preserved Lemon Chicken Soup

You can't have a cookbook called *Cured* without a recipe for the original penicillin. This version is finished by adding pureed preserved citrus, which really gives it a bright pick-me-up quality. I also add a bit of chopped cilantro at the end—this is South Texas, after all.

SERVES 6

1 small whole chicken (about 2½ pounds), cut into quarters (or the equivalent in bone-in, skin-on pieces)

8 cups chicken stock (page 51)

1-inch piece ginger, peeled and smashed

1 bunch cilantro, leaves picked and roughly chopped (about ½ cup), stems reserved

1 star anise pod

Salt

3 tablespoons extra-virgin olive oil

1 medium onion, finely diced

1 carrot, peeled and finely diced

2 stalks celery, finely diced

2 tablespoons white wine (optional)

1½ cups sugar snap peas, ends trimmed and cut into ½-inch pieces

1 bunch Swiss chard, stems removed, leaves chopped (4 to 5 cups)

½ cup preserved citrus (about ½ preserved lemon), seeds removed, pureed in a blender or food processor (page 209, see Note)

Freshly ground black pepper

1   Put the chicken, chicken stock, ginger, reserved cilantro stems, star anise, and 1 teaspoon salt in a large pot. Bring to a boil, then reduce to a simmer. Simmer for 35 minutes.

2   Use tongs to remove the chicken and set aside to cool. Use a slotted spoon to discard the ginger, cilantro stems, and star anise. Set the chicken stock aside and keep warm.

3   While the chicken is cooling, heat the olive oil in a clean soup pot over medium-high heat. Add the onion, carrot, celery, and a pinch of salt and sauté until soft, about 5 minutes. Add the wine (if using) and stir until the liquid has evaporated.

4   Add the reserved chicken stock, bring to a boil, then reduce to a simmer. Simmer, covered, over medium-low heat for 30 minutes.

5   When the chicken is cool enough to handle, pick the meat and dice it into bite-size pieces. Discard the skin and bones.

6   Add the chicken, peas, and chard to the pot and simmer for 5 minutes. Stir in the preserved lemon puree. Season with black pepper to taste.

7   Divide the soup among six bowls and garnish with chopped cilantro.

Note: If the lemon proves difficult to puree, you can add a couple of ladles of the chicken stock to help everything blend smoothly.

Brown Butter
Lemonade Blondies

Hear me out on this one. I'm always thinking about how to balance sweet and acid and salt in savory dishes, but that concept doesn't always get applied to baked goods. I love the idea of using preserved citrus, with its salt and acid, to balance something that could otherwise be overly sweet. A blondie can be a sugar bomb, but this one is tempered with preserved citrus for a salty-sweet-tart treat.

MAKES ONE 8-INCH SQUARE PAN OF BLONDIES

½ cup (1 stick) unsalted butter

1½ cups packed light brown sugar

3 large eggs

1½ teaspoons vanilla extract

½ cup preserved citrus (about ½ preserved lemon), seeds removed, pureed in a blender or food processor (page 209, see Note)

2 cups all-purpose flour

1 cup bittersweet chocolate chips

1 Heat the oven to 375°F. Grease an 8-inch square baking dish with butter.

2 Melt the butter in a small sauté pan over medium heat. Simmer the butter until it begins to brown, stirring occasionally with a rubber spatula. (I find it also helps to swirl the pan.) Continue until all foaming has subsided and the butter is golden and fragrant, about 6 minutes. Remove from the heat.

3 Using a stand mixer fitted with the paddle attachment, beat the brown sugar, eggs, vanilla, and preserved lemon puree on medium-high speed until the mixture has thickened, about 6 minutes.

4 Reduce the speed to low and add the browned butter. Mix briefly to combine.

5 Add the flour in three batches, mixing briefly to combine after each addition.

6 Use a rubber spatula to scrape down the sides of the bowl and fold the chocolate chips into the batter.

7 Pour the batter into the prepared pan and smooth the top with an offset spatula.

8 Bake until the top of the blondies has started to crack, 25 to 30 minutes.

9 Let the blondies cool completely, cut into squares, and serve.

Note: If the lemon proves difficult to puree, you can mince it with a knife, but it will impact the texture.

Base Ingredient: **Cured Fish**

Cured fish is a more flexible ingredient than you might think. So long as you don't overcure it, you're in good shape. You can cure fillets for an hour and then toss them on the grill, or completely cure a side of salmon for 3 hours for the centerpiece of a cocktail party buffet. You can cure many different kinds of fish, like tuna, mackerel, trout, and cod. Meatier fish tends to be easier to deal with and gives you something to slice when you're done. Just make sure any bones (including pin bones) have been removed prior to curing.

If using store-bought cured fish in the Application Recipes in this section, it's fine to use cured and smoked fish. Cured fish that has not been smoked can be tricky to find commercially.

Citrus-Cured Fish

The base cure here has a ton of citrus zest in it, but I've also provided versions flavored with miso, soy, gin, or beets. Make sure you pay attention to the thickness of the fillet you're curing; thinner cuts will cure much, much faster than the recipe below outlines.

MAKES 1 POUND CURED FISH

1 pound fish (such as tuna or salmon),
skin removed and trimmed

½ cup (124g) salt

6 tablespoons sugar

Zest of 2 lemons

Zest of 2 oranges

Zest of 2 limes

2 tablespoons coriander seeds,
toasted and cracked

2 tablespoons ground black pepper
(preground is fine)

¼ cup chopped cilantro (optional)

1 Cut the fish into 2-inch-thick pieces. The shape will vary depending on the type of fish you use, but thickness is important. Evenly space them in a shallow container big enough to hold the pieces without touching.

2 Combine the salt, sugar, citrus zest, coriander, pepper, and cilantro in a small mixing bowl. Completely cover the fish with the curing mix, picking up all the pieces and patting the mixture into each side of the fish. Cover and refrigerate in an airtight container for 1 to 3 hours, depending on use.

3 Remove the fish from the cure and rinse thoroughly under cold water. Place the fish on a racked sheet pan and place back in the refrigerator for 2 hours to air-dry slightly. Store wrapped in plastic in the refrigerator for up to 4 days.

Note: Juice all the citrus when you're done zesting, and freeze the juice for later!

Cured Fish Variations

Variations all call for 1 pound of fish.

Beet-Cured Salmon: For the cure, combine ½ cup packed dark brown sugar, ½ cup (124g) salt, 1 tablespoon crushed black peppercorns, 1 cup roughly chopped fresh dill, zest of 1 lemon, and 2 cups peeled and grated red beets (about 2 medium beets).

Miso- and Soy-Cured Fish: For the cure, combine ¾ cup soy sauce, ½ cup brown miso, 1¼ cups packed light brown sugar, 2 tablespoons grated fresh ginger, ½ cup (124g) salt, and 2 teaspoons freshly ground black pepper.

Gin-Cured Fish: For the cure, toast and crack ¼ cup fennel seeds, 1 tablespoon whole white peppercorns, and 2 tablespoons juniper berries. Combine these with ¼ cup sugar, ¼ cup packed light brown sugar, ½ cup (124g) salt, and ¼ cup gin.

Easy Ideas for Using Cured Fish

- Eat on a bagel
- Serve as a cocktail appetizer on toasts
- Top avocado toast
- Fold into omelets
- Add to scrambled eggs
- Add to pastas
- Use as a pizza topping (after baking)
- Add to a rice bowl
- Top deviled eggs

Cured Fish, Melon, Cucumber, and Green Onion Salad

Melon salads can be so one-dimensional—a little mint here, a little goat cheese there—but the fish in this recipe counterbalances the supersweetness of in-season melons with its fatty saltiness. Use a mix of melon varieties, if you can, and don't forget to save your rinds for pickles (page 31)!

SERVES 6

1 pound melon, rind and seeds removed, cut into 1-inch pieces

1 English (seedless) cucumber, peeled and cut into ¾-inch dice

2 tablespoons red wine vinegar

Salt and freshly ground black pepper

8 ounces cured fish (page 219), thinly sliced against the grain

1 jalapeño (optional)

¼ cup extra-virgin olive oil

2 green onions, chopped (green and light green parts only)

1 Put the melon in a large mixing bowl with the cucumber, vinegar, and a large pinch each of salt and pepper. Gently stir to coat the melon with the vinegar.

2 Use a slotted spoon to plate the melon mixture on a large platter, leaving the liquid behind. Top with the slices of cured fish.

3 If using, cut the jalapeño into quarters lengthwise and remove the seeds and any pith. Thinly slice the quarters crosswise into short matchsticks and sprinkle over the salad.

4 Finish the salad by drizzling the olive oil over the top and sprinkling with the chopped green onions.

Cured Fish and Tapenade Baguette Sandwich

This is my take on a Niçoise salad—with its hard-boiled eggs, olives, and fish—as a sandwich. It's sturdy and makes for a great packed lunch; just make sure you wrap it tightly so it doesn't come apart.

MAKES 1 SANDWICH

1 (8-inch) section baguette (approximately one-third of a standard baguette), split in half horizontally

1 tablespoon extra-virgin olive oil

¼ cup Tapenade (recipe follows)

2 tablespoons mayonnaise

2 large eggs, hard-boiled and sliced (see Note, page 22)

3 ounces cured fish (page 219), thinly sliced against the grain

2 tablespoons thinly sliced radish (1 to 2 radishes)

⅓ cup baby arugula

1   Heat the broiler on low.

2   Brush the baguette with olive oil on its cut sides and place on a sheet pan under the broiler. Toast until golden, 1 to 3 minutes. (You could also do this in a toaster oven.)

3   Spread the tapenade on the toasted bottom of the bread, and spread the mayonnaise on the toasted top of the bread.

4   Lay the sliced eggs on top of the tapenade, then lay the fish slices over the eggs, and finally top the sandwiches with the sliced radish and arugula. Finish with the top of the baguette.

Tapenade

½ cup pitted Kalamata olives

½ cup pimento-stuffed green olives

3 garlic cloves

2 anchovy fillets (optional)

Juice of 1 lemon

2 teaspoons capers, drained

¼ cup extra-virgin olive oil

1   Pulse the olives, garlic, anchovy fillets (if using), lemon juice, and capers in a food processor until they are coarsely ground but not pureed.

2   Scrape the olive mixture into a mixing bowl and fold in the olive oil.

Cured Fish Noodle Casserole with Everything Bagel Topping

This casserole takes inspiration from an everything bagel with cured fish, cream cheese, and all the fixings.

MAKES ONE 9 BY 13-INCH CASSEROLE

2 tablespoons extra-virgin olive oil

1 medium red onion, finely diced (about ½ cup)

4 garlic cloves, minced

½ teaspoon red pepper flakes

1 (28-ounce) can crushed tomatoes

¾ cup pitted Castelvetrano olives, roughly chopped

2 tablespoons capers, drained

Salt

1 pound wide egg noodles

1 pound cured fish (page 219), cut against the grain into bite-size pieces

½ cup parsley leaves, finely chopped

½ cup whole milk

½ cup (1 stick) unsalted butter, melted

1 (8-ounce) package cream cheese

Everything Bagel Bread Crumbs (recipe follows)

1　Heat the oven to 400°F. Grease a 9 by 13-inch casserole (or other 3-quart casserole).

2　Heat a medium pot over medium heat. Add the olive oil and onion and sauté for about 2 minutes. Add the garlic and sauté for an additional minute. Stir in the red pepper flakes, and then add the crushed tomatoes, olives, capers, and a large pinch of salt. Fill the tomato can with water and add that to the pot as well. Bring to a simmer, reduce the heat slightly, and simmer for 10 minutes. Remove from the heat.

3　While the sauce is cooking, bring a large pot of salted water to a boil. Boil the egg noodles for 4 minutes less than the package instructions indicate. Drain.

4　Put the noodles in a large mixing bowl. Add the sauce, cured fish, and parsley. Stir to combine. Taste and adjust the seasoning.

5　Whisk the milk, ¼ cup of the melted butter, and cream cheese in a small saucepan over medium-low heat until smooth.

6　Combine the remaining ¼ cup melted butter with the bread crumbs in a small bowl; stir until the bread crumbs are evenly coated.

7　Add half the noodle mixture to the casserole. Dollop the cream cheese mixture over the noodles, then top with the rest of the noodle mixture. Finally, sprinkle the bread crumbs over the top.

8　Bake until the bread crumbs are golden and the sauce is bubbling, about 40 minutes. Let cool 10 minutes and serve.

Everything Bagel Bread Crumbs

1 cup unseasoned panko bread crumbs

2 tablespoons sesame seeds

1 tablespoon dried minced onion

1 tablespoon dried minced garlic

1 tablespoon poppy seeds

1 teaspoon caraway seeds

1 teaspoon salt

1 teaspoon freshly ground black pepper

Add all the ingredients to a small bowl and stir to combine.

Base Ingredient: **Cured Meat**

You've made it! It's time to cure some meat. Curing a piece of meat entirely, so that it's edible without cooking, may seem complicated and easy to mess up. But I assure you, so long as you follow these recipes, it's quite the opposite. Simple and (here's that word again!) forgiving.

Would you believe the process described in this section is the same one used to cure those 25-pound hams I keep talking about, just on a smaller and simpler scale? It's a two-step process: First, you pack a cut of meat in salt and allow the salt to permeate to the center, drawing out liquid and changing the cell structures of the meat. Then, you remove the meat from the cure and dry it in the refrigerator, which continues the process of pulling moisture from the meat. Some cured meats, such as the two hams in the chart on page 231, are also smoked.

In this section, you'll learn how to cure bresaola (an Italian dried beef), duck breast, pork tenderloin, and pork shoulder. I promise, each of these recipes are within your reach so long as you use good-quality ingredients, measure your salt accurately, use clean equipment, and make sure the cured item has good airflow around it in your refrigerator while drying. That's it!

But . . . if you don't believe me, here's how to tell whether your cured meat has gone off: you will know. You will see mold; you will smell spoilage. It will have black, blue, or green mold on it. It will smell terrible. This is not a trick question; you are built to know if food has gone bad. Trust yourself. And if you are still not convinced, you can make the Application Recipes in this chapter with just about any store-bought cured meat (including bacon!).

Bresaola

Bresaola is an Italian air-dried beef that typically would cure for a few days and then dry for months. My version is a bit faster than that. Note: Never use previously frozen meat for cured meats, as they don't take on the salt properly.

MAKES JUST UNDER 2 POUNDS OF BRESAOLA
Begin recipe about a week before using.

2 pounds center-cut beef tenderloin or top round, trimmed of any connective tissue and fat

½ cup (124g) salt

2 sprigs rosemary, leaves stripped from stems and roughly chopped

2 bay leaves, crushed

¼ cup packed light brown sugar

1 garlic clove, crushed

1 tablespoon black peppercorns, cracked

Zest of 1 orange

1 tablespoon red pepper flakes

1 Slice the beef in half lengthwise so that you have two pieces about 2 to 3 inches thick.

2 Make the cure by combining the salt, rosemary, bay leaves, brown sugar, garlic, cracked black peppercorns, orange zest, and red pepper flakes in a mixing bowl.

3 Put the beef and the cure in a resealable plastic bag. Turn the beef several times in the cure, pressing it into all sides and making sure some of the cure is under the meat.

4 Refrigerate for 4 days. Every day, move the meat around in the bag, rubbing the cure into all sides. You should notice that it is starting to pull moisture from the muscle—this is a good thing.

5 Remove the beef from the cure and use clean or gloved hands to wipe off any cure sticking to the meat. Next rinse the beef and pat dry with a paper towel.

6 Place the beef on a racked sheet pan and place back in the refrigerator, uncovered, for 2 to 6 days longer to dry. The outside will harden, but the inside will stay smooth, and when you squeeze the meat, it should have a slight give to it—it should not be rock hard.

7 Slice the beef very thinly across the grain to serve. If not eating immediately, wrap tightly in plastic wrap and store in an airtight container for up to 2 weeks.

Easy Ideas for Using Cured Meats

- Use pretty much anywhere you'd use bacon or ham
- Layer into sandwiches
- Top a pizza
- Substitute for the ham in eggs Benedict
- Crisp in the oven (see Broccoli Salad with Crisped Cured Meat, page 234) and crumble over sautéed vegetables or salads
- Serve with fresh fruit

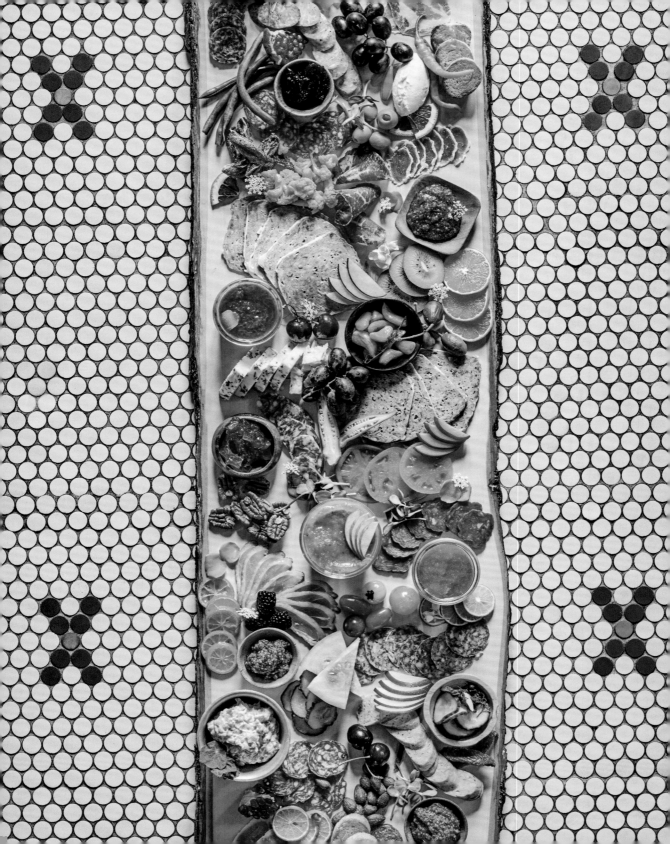

Cured Meat Variations

	Meat Prep	Cure	Time on Cure	Smoke or Dry
Cured pork tenderloin	2 pork tenderloins (about 1 pound each), silver skin and fat removed (you can ask your butcher to do this); trim 2 inches from the thin end of each tenderloin and save these for another use	1 cup (248g) salt, ¼ cup packed light brown sugar, 2 tablespoons toasted and cracked coriander seeds	2 days	Rub the tenderloins with 2 tablespoons dry white wine and 2 tablespoons herbes de Provence, then wrap in cheesecloth (this helps keep the herbs on the meat). Refrigerate on a racked sheet pan for 3 weeks. Remove the cheesecloth and slice thinly to serve.
Cured tasso ham	2 pounds boneless pork shoulder butt, cut into 1-inch-thick slices and patted dry with paper towels	1 tablespoon plus 1 teaspoon (20g) salt, 2 teaspoons cayenne, 1½ tablespoons paprika, 1 tablespoon minced fresh garlic, 2 teaspoons freshly ground black pepper, 2 teaspoons light brown sugar	Cure on a racked sheet pan in the refrigerator, uncovered, for 3 days.	*Heat a smoker to 200°F and smoke until ham reaches an internal temperature of 150°F. Cool completely before serving in thin slices.
Smoked duck ham	1 skin-on breast, about 8 ounces	½ cup (124g) salt, 3 tablespoons light brown sugar, 1 tablespoon juniper berries, 1 tablespoon Sichuan peppercorns, 4 bay leaves	12 hours	*Smoke at 225°F until the duck's internal temperature is 145°F. Cool completely before serving in thin slices.

*If you do not want to smoke these, you can cook them in the oven instead. In that case, use smoked paprika instead of plain. For more on smoking, see the Smoke chapter.

Cured Meat Served Carpaccio-Style

This is just a very fun way to start a meal. Carpaccio, which according to legend was invented in the mid-twentieth century at Harry's Bar in Venice, is traditionally served as thin slices of raw meat dressed with lemon juice, olive oil, and Parmesan. A cured meat (or a combination of cured meats!) really dresses things up. Make sure your knife is sharp so you get the thinnest slices possible.

SERVES 4 TO 6 AS AN APPETIZER

8 ounces cured meat, thinly sliced (page 228 or use store-bought)

Salt and freshly ground black pepper

3 tablespoons extra-virgin olive oil

1 lemon

1 ounce Parmesan

Handful of arugula leaves, for garnish

1 Fan out the sliced meat on a serving dish. Sprinkle the meat with a large pinch of salt and several twists of pepper, and then drizzle with the olive oil.

2 Zest the lemon over the meat, and then cut the lemon in half. Squeeze one-half of the lemon over the meat.

3 Use a grater or Microplane to grate the Parmesan over the meat (it'll be about ½ cup of cheese) and finish with a scattering of arugula.

Broccoli Salad with Crisped Cured Meat

My take on a classic summer picnic salad that you might take to a cookout or a potluck. I omitted the standard mayonnaise-based dressing, though—this way, the taste of the cured meat really shines through.

SERVES 6 AS A SIDE

10 to 12 slices (about 2 ounces) cured meat (page 228)

2 pounds broccoli florets, cut into bite-size pieces (you can save the stalks for another use)

¼ cup pine nuts, lightly toasted in a dry sauté pan

¼ cup diced red onion (about ½ onion)

¼ cup golden raisins (dried cranberries or cherries work as well)

2 tablespoons extra-virgin olive oil

3 tablespoons sherry vinegar

2 tablespoons stone-ground mustard

1 tablespoon honey

Salt and freshly ground black pepper

1 Heat the oven to 400°F. Line a sheet pan with aluminum foil or parchment paper.

2 Lay the cured meat slices on the prepared pan, making sure they don't touch. Bake for 10 to 15 minutes. Keep a close eye on it, as cured meats will bake at different times based on the fat content. You want the edges to crisp and lift slightly, creating a shallow curve.

3 Remove the meat from the oven and let cool completely. The slices will continue to crisp as they cool.

4 Meanwhile, put the broccoli, pine nuts, onion, and raisins in a large mixing bowl.

5 In a small bowl, combine the olive oil, vinegar, mustard, and honey to create the dressing. Add the dressing to the broccoli salad and stir until coated. Season with salt and pepper.

6 Break the crisp cured meat into small pieces and sprinkle over the salad.

Beer Can Mussels with Cured Meat

I love to work with mussels. For the most part they're inexpensive, and they have this magical ability to pair with just about anything. Seriously, just about any spice, liquid, herb, meat, or vegetable you can think of will work well with mussels. This dish was on the menu at Cured when we opened and has never left. Mussels sometimes need to be cleaned and debearded before cooking, although the vast majority of fish markets will do this for you. If not, here's what to do: First, go through all the mussels and discard any that are cracked or open. Scrub any debris off the mussels with a brush or sponge. Finally, locate a small brown stringy bit sticking out from between the shells; this is the "beard." Tug on it to remove it. It's possible that not all the mussels will have beards, so don't worry if some don't.

SERVES 4 AS A MAIN, 6 AS AN APPETIZER

3 tablespoons extra-virgin olive oil

½ cup diced cured meat (page 228)

3 green onions, sliced, white and green parts separated

2 tablespoons minced garlic (about 4 cloves)

4 pounds fresh mussels

1 (12-ounce) can lager

½ teaspoon salt

½ teaspoon freshly ground black pepper

¼ cup (½ stick) unsalted butter, diced

½ cup diced tomatoes

1 rustic country loaf, sliced and toasted, for serving

1 In a large pot with a lid, heat the olive oil over medium-high heat. Add the cured meat and sauté to open up the flavors and caramelize it slightly, about 3 minutes.

2 Add the white parts of the green onions and the garlic and sauté 1 additional minute. Add the mussels and stir to coat them with the oil.

3 Add the beer, salt, and pepper and cover with the lid. After 2 minutes, open the pot and stir the mussels. Simmer, covered, stirring every 2 minutes or so, until all the mussels have opened, about 6 minutes total. Keep a close eye on it, as you don't want them to overcook. Add the butter; when the butter has melted, remove the pot from the heat.

4 Serve the mussels along with their broth, and top each bowl with some diced tomatoes and reserved green onions. Serve with the bread.

Ferment

Fermentation is the process of letting an ingredient start to break down on purpose. There are different ways to achieve this, which involve exposing an ingredient to yeast, bacteria, and other organisms in a controlled setting that allows fermentation to occur safely. Thankfully, such controlled settings are easy to reproduce in a home kitchen, and you likely already have the things you need to do so.

First, though, let's talk about *why* you might want to ferment foods. Years ago, one of my farmers showed up at the back door of the restaurant where I was working in New Orleans with a ton of cabbage, and the only answer was to make sauerkraut. The primary reason you ferment something is to prolong its edibility, and there was no way the restaurant was going through that much cabbage quickly. So sauerkraut it was. I loved how simple it was to make: just cabbage and salt and time was all it took for this epic transformation to happen.

I didn't get truly serious about fermentation, though, until I got sick. When I was first diagnosed, I just sort of ate whatever I wanted. I was trying to keep weight on, you know? But eventually I needed to get my nutrition in order, and that's when I started researching the digestive benefits of fermented foods. By the time I was out of treatment and planning Cured, I was truly hooked. I wanted the restaurant to ferment all kinds of things, and we do, from shrubs to hot sauce to kimchi to, yes, sauerkraut. And not just any sauerkraut: at Cured, we make fennel sauerkraut and collards sauerkraut and much more.

Fermentation changes the taste and texture of the ingredient—I like to say it takes an ingredient's flavor from two dimensions to three. Ferments taste a little funky and a little sour; their flavor is slightly more intense than the raw ingredient before fermentation, but also segmented. You can clearly taste notes of a fermented vegetable that are barely perceivable in the same ingredient prior to fermentation; different elements become more prominent while others recede to the background. Take fermented hot sauce, for example: fermenting the chiles takes them from this blindly hot, crunchy vegetable to something that's mellower, with a little citrus and a little smoke to it. Fermentation allows you to taste beyond the heat of the chiles and unlocks their true flavor potential, and it does the same for just about any fruit or vegetable.

So don't be intimidated. With the right equipment and a little know-how, fermentation is an incredibly simple process that yields huge transformations.

Fermentation Equipment

A fermentation vessel needs to do a few things: It needs to expose the ferment to yeasts and bacteria in the air. It needs to prevent the food from breaking down in harmful ways; this often means fermentation vessels block out light, but if you're using a transparent vessel, just make sure you keep it in a cool, dark place. It also needs to let any gas that forms during the fermentation process escape. And finally, it needs to be made from nonporous food-grade materials: glass, nonporous ceramics, and food-grade plastic are most common.

Glass Jar with Plastic Bag This is the simplest vessel I know of that produces fairly consistent results. Sanitize your jar, fill it with the ferment, and then half fill a resealable plastic bag with water. Stuff the bag in the top of the jar; this will keep the ferment safely under the surface of the fermenting liquid while still allowing gas to bubble up around the edges of the bag.

Glass Jar with Airlock Special Fermentation lids with airlocks are fairly cheap to buy online. These lids have a special plastic piece that fits into a hole in the lid. When you add water to the airlock, it allows gas out of the fermentation vessel but doesn't let anything in. It's a great, simple way to prevent your ferments from spoiling.

Fermentation Crocks Ceramic Fermentation crocks come in a wide variety of colors and sizes, and you can easily find them online or in Korean grocery stores, where they are sold to make kimchi. These will often have a lip on top of the crock that can be filled with water; with the crock's lid in place, it performs the same function as the airlock in letting the fermentation gasses out and letting nothing bad in.

Fermentation Weights One of the surest ways to spoil a ferment is to have some of the fermenting ingredient sticking up out of the fermenting liquid. You can buy glass and ceramic fermentation weights online that will weigh down the ferment below the surface of the liquid to help with this. The above resealable plastic bag vessel also functions nicely as a fermentation weight. If any ingredients float above the fermentation weight, I recommend spooning them out so they don't impact your final product.

Note: If you use unglazed ceramic fermentation weights, such as those that often come with crocks, you will need to clean them before storing. After your fermentation is complete, cover the weights with water in a saucepan and bring to a boil. Boil for 20 minutes to kill off any potential molds or bacteria, then let cool. Allow the weights to dry for a full 24 hours before storing.

Salt I used Morton kosher salt to test the recipes in this book. If you are using a different kind of salt, I recommend you measure by weight. This is particularly important in this chapter, where the amount of salt used will make or break your ferment. For more information on salt, see page 5.

Fermentation Methods

Sanitization It's very important to sanitize any equipment you'll use when prepping your ferments. This includes the fermentation vessel itself, but also any equipment you use to prepare the fermentation, including knives, cutting boards, spoons, tongs, food processors, and/or mandolines. I also recommend washing your hands more carefully and thoroughly than usual when fermenting. To sanitize, wash equipment in hot, soapy water, rinse with very hot water, and let air-dry. You may also use equipment that's come straight out of a hot dishwasher. Do not touch the inside of any vessels after they've been sanitized.

Saltwater Solution You may discover that you need additional liquid to cover your ferments. If this happens, dissolve 1 teaspoon (5g) Morton kosher salt in 1 cup boiling water, add a couple of ice cubes to cool, and pour over the top of your ferment. Repeat as needed until the ferment is submerged.

How to Know if a Ferment Has Spoiled For the most part, you'll be able to tell when a ferment has spoiled beyond safe consumption. Any ferments that grow mold or develop a *distinctively* bad, rancid smell need to be trashed. (I am not talking about the funky smell sauerkraut and other vegetables develop as they ferment. You'll know these smells when you encounter them, trust me.)

Base Ingredient: **Sauerkraut**

Fermented greens in various forms are a dietary staple around the world, and sauerkraut is one of the simplest: shredded cabbage combined with salt and fermented. But that's just the beginning of where you can take sauerkraut. Depending on what you have on hand, just about any type of cabbage or sturdy greens, like collards, will work, and fennel makes a shockingly pleasant kraut.

Green Cabbage Sauerkraut

This recipe calls for a nice medium-size head of cabbage, one that weighs roughly 2 pounds. If you end up with a different quantity one way or the other, you can always adjust the salt up or down slightly. As with all ferments, make sure all your equipment has been properly sanitized and dried before beginning (see page 241). This recipe asks you to shred the cabbage; this is important so that you have as much surface area as possible in contact with the salt to create your brine.

MAKES ABOUT 6 CUPS
Begin recipe 2 weeks before using.

1 head cabbage (2 pounds)
3 tablespoons (47g) salt

1   Peel away any large, dirty, or fibrous leaves from the outside of the cabbage. Cut the cabbage through its center into quarters, and cut the cores from each quarter.

2   Next, finely shred the cabbage: If you have a mandoline, use it to provide a uniform, fine shred that will ferment evenly. Otherwise, set the cabbage quarters flat-side down on a cutting board and use a long, sharp knife to slice the cabbage into fine shreds from end to end (see Note, page 244).

3   Place the shredded cabbage in a large mixing bowl and use clean hands to massage the salt into the cabbage for 5 full minutes. As you work, you will begin to see liquid that the salt is pulling from the cabbage. This will create the brine necessary for fermenting.

4   Spoon the cabbage into a 2-quart fermentation vessel and pour any remaining brine from the bowl over the top.

5   Put fermentation weights on top of the cabbage to help weigh it down under the surface of the brine. Make sure the cabbage is completely submerged under the brine; if not, add additional weight (see Fermentation Equipment, page 240). You may also add more brine (see Saltwater Solution, page 241). Spoon out any floating shreds of cabbage.

6   Put the lid on your fermentation vessel and place it in a cool, dark corner. Ferment the sauerkraut for roughly 2 weeks. The first week, you should see lots of bubbles from the fermentation process. If your kitchen runs a bit warm, fermentation will take less time. Don't be afraid to smell and even taste your

kraut to check the flavor and texture! Just use a clean fork when you do.

7 Throughout the process, skim off any foam that collects on the surface and discard. If you notice any mold forming around the edges, scrape it away with a knife. As long as your cabbage remains under the surface of the brine, all is well.

8 Once fermentation is complete, transfer the kraut to a clean, airtight container and place in the refrigerator. The kraut will keep for 6 months.

Note: I do not recommend using a food processor to shred the cabbage, tempting though it may be. In my experience, the processor produces an uneven shred that results in an equally uneven ferment. Besides, this is a good opportunity to practice those knife skills!

Sauerkraut Variations

All variations call for 2 pounds of vegetables and 3 tablespoons (47g) salt.

Red Cabbage Sauerkraut: Add 2 to 4 teaspoons peeled and grated fresh ginger after the cabbage has been salted and massaged.

Collards Sauerkraut: Cut the collard greens into ½-inch-wide strips across the ribs. (I like to roll up a stack of collard leaves to make the cutting easier.) After salting and massaging the collards, add 3 crushed garlic cloves and 1 jalapeño, seeded and chopped.

Fennel Kraut: Cut out the cores and thinly shred the fennel using a mandoline or knife. After salting and massaging, add 1 teaspoon caraway seeds and 1 teaspoon black peppercorns.

Easy Ideas for Using Sauerkraut

- Add to sandwiches (especially hot ones!)
- Top burgers and hot dogs
- Fold into sautéed greens
- Add to soups
- Use the brine as a marinade
- Add to meatballs prior to cooking

Sauerkraut Hash Browns

A lot of hash brown recipes ask you to soak the shredded potato in water to help remove starch. This recipe skips that step because you want the potato to stick to the sauerkraut. You can make these as individual servings, as outlined below, or as a large, full-pan hash brown that you cut into wedges. (With the larger pancake, cook for 5 minutes on each side.) Serve for breakfast with eggs and bacon or as an unexpected side dish for roast pork or sausages.

SERVES 4 TO 6

4 medium russet potatoes (3½ to 4 pounds), peeled

2 cups drained sauerkraut (page 243)

1½ teaspoons salt

½ teaspoon freshly ground black pepper

1 teaspoon onion powder

5 tablespoons vegetable oil, plus more as needed

1   Grate the potatoes on a box grater over a bowl. Stir in the sauerkraut and dump the mixture onto a clean kitchen towel. Twist up the ends of the cloth and squeeze over the sink, twisting to force out as much liquid as you can. Put the potatoes and sauerkraut back in the bowl.

2   Add the salt, pepper, and onion powder to the potato mixture and stir to combine.

3   Heat the vegetable oil in a large cast-iron or nonstick pan over medium-high heat. Place roughly ⅓ cup of the potato mixture in the pan to form an individual serving of hash browns and press down with a spatula. Add as many hash browns as you can fit in the pan without touching. Add more oil if the pan looks dry. Cook until nicely browned, using a spatula to gently check the underside of the hash browns, about 5 minutes. Flip and continue to cook until the second side is golden brown, 2 to 3 more minutes. Place on a rack when finished so that they stay crisp.

4   Repeat with the remaining potato mixture until all hash browns are cooked, and serve.

Sauerkraut with Sausage

A one-pot version of the classic (and classically labor-intensive) Alsatian dish choucroute garnie, which literally translates to "garnished sauerkraut." Traditionally these garnishes are pork, including ham hocks, ribs, salt pork, sausages, and more. Here we call for bacon and Wisconsin's favorite sausage—bratwurst—but you can use any uncooked pork sausage with flavors that lean French or German. Serve this with mustard and potatoes on the side, like the Crispy, Herby Smashed Potatoes on page 101.

SERVES 6

2 tablespoons vegetable oil

2 pounds bratwurst (about 8 links, depending on size)

8 ounces thick-cut bacon, diced

2 yellow onions, halved and cut into ¼-inch-wide slices

1 cup Riesling or other dry white wine (optional)

2 tablespoons honey

2 quarts sauerkraut (page 243), drained, brine reserved (up to 1 cup)

2 teaspoons caraway seeds

1 bay leaf

1 quart chicken stock (page 51)

1   Heat the oil in a heavy pot or Dutch oven over medium-high heat. Add the sausages and brown, turning with tongs, about 3 minutes per side. Remove the sausages and set aside.

2   Add the bacon to the pot and cook, stirring frequently, until browned, about 8 minutes. Use a slotted spoon to transfer the bacon to a paper towel–lined plate, leaving the fat in the pot.

3   Reduce the heat to medium-low. Add the onions and cook, stirring frequently, until well caramelized, about 45 minutes.

4   Whisk together the wine and honey in a small bowl. Add this to the pot along with the reserved brine and use a wooden spoon to scrape any browned bits that have stuck to the bottom. Increase the heat to medium-high and cook until reduced to a syrup, about 15 minutes.

5   Add the bacon, drained sauerkraut, caraway seeds, bay leaf, and chicken stock. Stir to combine, then layer the sausages on top. Increase the heat to high and bring to a boil. Reduce the heat to medium-low and simmer, uncovered, for 20 minutes. Serve.

Oven-Roasted Cauliflower with Sweet and Sauer Sauce

Sweet and sauer sauce was developed out of a necessity to use up leftover kraut. The finished texture of the sauce should be similar to applesauce, which is why this feels right at home with roasted or grilled pork.

SERVES 6

1 medium cauliflower (2 to 2½ pounds), cut into bite-size florets

¼ cup plus 2 tablespoons extra-virgin olive oil

1 teaspoon salt

½ teaspoon freshly ground black pepper

2 teaspoons smoked paprika

Sweet and Sauer Sauce (recipe follows)

1 large sprig mint, leaves torn into pieces

1   Heat the oven to 425°F.

2   Put the cauliflower in a large mixing bowl and drizzle with ¼ cup of the olive oil. Season with the salt, pepper, and smoked paprika and stir to coat.

3   Distribute the cauliflower evenly on a sheet pan and roast for 20 minutes. Stir the cauliflower two or three times during cooking. The cauliflower should be nicely browned and tender when pierced with a knife.

4   Spoon the sweet and sauer sauce onto the bottom of a serving dish. Arrange the roasted cauliflower on top of the sauce, drizzle with the remaining 2 tablespoons olive oil, and sprinkle with mint.

Sweet and Sauer Sauce

½ cup extra-virgin olive oil

2 pounds (about 6 cups) sauerkraut (page 243), drained, with ¼ cup brine reserved

2 cups dry white wine

4 garlic cloves, sliced

1 cup maple syrup

1 bay leaf

Juice of 1 lemon

Salt and freshly ground black pepper

1   Heat ¼ cup of the olive oil in a large cast-iron pan or Dutch oven over medium-low heat. Add the sauerkraut and cook for about 15 minutes, stirring frequently, until golden brown and caramelized.

2   Add the wine, garlic, maple syrup, and bay leaf and continue to cook until the liquid has almost entirely disappeared and a deep mahogany color is achieved, another 30 to 40 minutes. Stir periodically, scraping the bottom, with increasing frequency as the liquid reduces.

3   Remove from the heat and let the mixture cool slightly, 5 minutes. Remove the bay leaf.

4   Scoop the mixture into a food processor and, while the machine is running, add the lemon juice, ¼ cup reserved sauerkraut liquid, and the remaining ¼ cup olive oil.

5   Season with salt and pepper and serve warm.

Miso Mushroom Vegetarian Reuben

This recipe brings sauerkraut together with another fermented ingredient I love to work with: miso, a paste made from soybeans. The miso mushrooms are great on their own, but it's worth the effort to make the whole sandwich. The recipe calls for brown miso, but you could easily substitute red miso.

MAKES 1 SANDWICH

2 tablespoons unsalted butter, softened

2 slices seeded rye bread

2 tablespoons Thousand Island Dressing (recipe follows)

½ cup Miso Mushrooms (recipe follows)

¼ cup sauerkraut (page 243)

1½ teaspoons chopped fresh dill

2 slices Swiss cheese

1   Warm a skillet over medium heat.

2   Lightly butter one side of each slice of bread and place one of them butter-side down in the skillet. Smear the dressing on the unbuttered side of each slice. Top one slice on the dressing side with the mushrooms, sauerkraut, dill, and cheese, in that order.

3   Top with the second slice, butter-side up. Cook over medium heat until the bread is golden and cheese has melted, 4 to 5 minutes per side.

Thousand Island Dressing

½ cup mayonnaise

2½ tablespoons ketchup

2 tablespoons sweet pickle relish

1 tablespoon rice wine vinegar

2 tablespoons diced onions

½ teaspoon smoked paprika

¼ teaspoon hot sauce (page 262)

Pinch of salt

Whisk all the ingredients together in a bowl and refrigerate until ready to use.

Miso Mushrooms

½ cup brown miso paste

2 tablespoons light brown sugar

1 teaspoon yellow mustard seeds

⅛ teaspoon ground coriander

Pinch of ground allspice

Pinch of ground ginger

¼ cup lemon juice

Zest of 1 lemon

10 to 12 portobello mushroom caps, stems removed

Salt and freshly ground black pepper

1 Combine the miso paste, brown sugar, mustard seeds, coriander, allspice, ginger, ½ cup water, lemon juice, and lemon zest in a small saucepan over medium heat. Stir until the sugar dissolves, about 3 minutes.

2 Line a sheet pan with aluminum foil or parchment paper. (The marinade has sugar in it and can be difficult to clean off pans.) Put the mushroom caps in a single layer on the prepared sheet pan. Brush the marinade on both sides of the caps and refrigerate, covered, for at least 1 hour and up to 12 hours. The longer the mushrooms marinate, the deeper the flavor will be.

3 Heat the oven to 400°F. While the oven is warming, remove the pan from the refrigerator and remove the cover from the pan.

4 Bake the mushrooms for 20 minutes. Use a spatula to turn them, then bake for an additional 5 minutes.

5 Transfer the mushrooms to a cutting board and allow to cool for a few minutes, until easily handled. Cut the mushrooms into ¼-inch slices. Season with salt and pepper.

Base Ingredient: Kimchi

After the simple fermentation of sauerkraut, the next logical step is kimchi, a flavored ferment from Korea. Kimchis range from super simple to elaborate, complex creations and can be made from so many more ingredients than cabbage! I encourage you to go to your local Korean market to check out all the kimchis on offer and try them in the recipes in this section.

Basic Kimchi

This very simple kimchi ferments fairly quickly. If you like making this and want to dig deeper into kimchi methods and variations, check out *Smoke & Pickles* by Ed Lee or *The Kimchi Cookbook* by Lauryn Chun.

MAKES 2 QUARTS
Begin recipe 1 week before using.

1 head napa cabbage (2 to 2½ pounds)

1 cup shredded carrots

1 cup chopped green onions

3 tablespoons (47g) salt

3 garlic cloves, minced

1 teaspoon grated fresh ginger

1 cup gochujang

1 Thinly shred the napa cabbage using a knife or mandoline and put it in a large mixing bowl. Add the carrots and green onions. Sprinkle with the salt and stir the vegetables for about 3 minutes to help release moisture and create the brine.

2 Let the mixture sit for 20 minutes at room temperature.

3 Add the garlic, ginger, and gochujang to the cabbage and massage with gloved hands until well combined.

4 Transfer the kimchi and any collected brine to a 2-quart fermentation vessel and tamp it down with a pestle or wooden spoon. Top the kimchi with crock weights or a small plate, making sure the vegetables are below the brine. Add more weight or saltwater solution if necessary (see page 241). Spoon out any vegetables that float.

5 Cover and place the jar in a cool, dark corner. Ferment for 5 to 7 days. Taste the kimchi after 5 days to see if it is to your liking. You want to make sure your kimchi still has a bit of crunch.

6 When finished fermenting, put the kimchi in an airtight container and refrigerate for up to 6 months.

Kimchi Variations

Apple Kimchi: Substitute shredded apples for the carrots. Apples with high sugar content, like Fuji or Honeycrisp, will really round out the flavor of this kimchi.

Green Onion Kimchi: Substitute 2 pounds trimmed green onions for the cabbage and omit the carrots and additional green onions. Ferment for 3 days.

Turnip Kimchi: Substitute 2 pounds of turnips with their leaves for the cabbage, and omit the carrots and green onions. Peel the turnips, leaving the greens attached, then spread the gochujang mixture all over the whole roots and leaves alike. Roll the leaves around the turnips to make tight little balls, and pack them into your fermenting vessel. Ferment for 3 days.

Easy Ideas for Using Kimchi

- Use in place of sauerkraut
- Put on top of a burger
- Add to fried rice
- Fold into sautéed greens
- Add to scrambled eggs
- Use in soups and stews

Kimchi Pancake

This makes a great starter or side dish. Sweet rice flour is pretty common in most supermarkets and will make for a super-light, crispy pancake. The tangy, funky, spicy kimchi cuts through the salt and fat of the pancake, and the dipping sauce brings sweetness and umami. You can use all-purpose flour, but it will yield a denser pancake.

SERVES 6

3 tablespoons soy sauce

3 tablespoons rice wine vinegar

½ teaspoon sugar

Pinch of freshly ground black pepper

1 large egg

1½ cups drained kimchi (page 253), chopped if necessary, with ¼ cup brine reserved

1 cup cold water

1¼ cups sweet rice flour

3 green onions, thinly sliced

Up to 5 tablespoons vegetable oil, as needed

1   To make the sauce, whisk together the soy sauce, rice wine vinegar, sugar, and pepper in a small bowl. Set aside.

2   In a large mixing bowl, whisk together the egg, kimchi brine, and water. Slowly add the flour, a few tablespoons at a time, whisking between each addition until combined. Fold in the kimchi and half the green onions.

3   Heat 1 tablespoon of the oil in a large nonstick skillet or cast-iron pan over medium

heat. Scoop half the batter into the skillet and use a spatula to press it down into a pancake with a 10-inch diameter. Cook until golden brown, 4 to 6 minutes. (Use a spatula to check.) Flip the pancake over—sliding it onto a plate might help—and cook for an additional 2 to 3 minutes. Remove from the pan and place on a paper towel–lined plate to rest. Repeat with the remaining batter, adding oil if the pan looks dry. Cut the pancakes into six portions each.

4 Serve the sauce alongside the pancakes, and sprinkle the remaining green onions over the top.

Kimchi Bloody Mary

For me a Bloody Mary should be all about the drink itself—I'm not one for all the crazy garnishes that adorn some Bloodys. If you do want to top this bad boy off, though, I suggest the Pickled Shrimp on page 16. The addition of the kimchi really takes this drink to a fun place and can help cure an aggressive hangover (so I'm told). If you're not making drinks for a crowd, the base of this—the mixture before you add the vodka—will freeze nicely.

MAKES 1 PITCHER, ABOUT 6 DRINKS

4 cups tomato juice, chilled
1 cup kimchi, with its brine (page 253), chilled
½ teaspoon celery salt
Juice of ½ lime
9 ounces vodka, chilled
Lime wedges, for garnish

1 Chill six cocktail glasses in the freezer while you prepare the drink.

2 Puree the tomato juice, kimchi, celery salt, and lime juice in a blender until smooth.

3 Put the Bloody Mary mixture into a pitcher and stir in the vodka.

4 Divide the drinks among the six frozen glasses. Squeeze a lime wedge over the top of each Bloody Mary and enjoy.

Kimchi Meatloaf

I teach a lot of classes on charcuterie, and students are often hung up on terrines and pâtés. But when it comes down to it, pâté is just a fancy meatloaf! The biggest difference is that with a pâté, terrine, or even a sausage, you use a mixer with a paddle attachment to mix the meat, which makes the proteins tacky and the end result tight. With meatloaf, you work everything with your hands, barely mixing the ingredients together so that it does not become too dense.

This particular meatloaf is one of my favorites; deceptively simple, it is definitely more than the sum of its parts. Something about having the kimchi in the mix produces a really tender, flavorful meatloaf. This can be baked in a greased 9 by 5-inch loaf pan, or you can shape it freeform on a lined sheet pan. This will pair nicely with the Hominy Puree with Gravy (page 55).

SERVES 6

½ cup ketchup

¼ cup gochujang

2 tablespoons light brown sugar

2 tablespoons rice wine vinegar

1½ pounds ground chuck

1½ cups unseasoned panko bread crumbs

1 cup drained kimchi (page 253), chopped if using store-bought

1 bunch green onions, chopped (about ⅔ cup)

2 large eggs, lightly beaten

1 teaspoon salt

1 Heat the oven to 350°F. Line a sheet pan with aluminum foil or parchment paper.

2 Next, make the sauce: Whisk together the ketchup, gochujang, brown sugar, and rice wine vinegar in a small saucepan. Bring the mixture to a simmer over medium heat and stir until the sugar dissolves, about 2 minutes. Remove from the heat and set aside while you prepare the rest of the meatloaf.

3 Using clean hands, mix the ground chuck, bread crumbs, kimchi, green onions, eggs, and salt together in a bowl until everything is just combined.

4 Transfer the meat mixture to the prepared pan and form it into a rectangular loaf about 3 inches tall and 5 inches wide. Spoon the sauce over the top.

5 Place the pan on the center rack of the oven and bake until an instant-read thermometer inserted into the center reads 160°F, about 1 hour.

6 Allow it to rest for 10 to 15 minutes before serving in thick slices.

Cheesy Kimchi and Summer Squash Gratin

Here we have taken a classic "Sunday supper" staple and made ferments the star of the show. This dish really lends itself to other types of kimchi as well—green onion kimchi and turnip kimchi would both fit in nicely here. Serve as a side for grilled chicken or on its own with rice.

SERVES 6

2 tablespoons extra-virgin olive oil

1 white onion, halved and thinly sliced lengthwise (about 1½ cups)

3 garlic cloves, minced

1½ pounds zucchini, cut into ¼-inch-thick half moons

1½ pounds yellow squash, cut into ¼-inch-thick half moons

1½ teaspoons salt

1 teaspoon freshly ground black pepper

2 cups drained kimchi (page 253), chopped

1 cup heavy cream

2 cups shredded cheddar

1 Heat the oven to 375°F. Grease a 9 by 13-inch pan (or other 3-quart casserole).

2 Heat the olive oil in a wide pot or Dutch oven over medium heat. Add the onions and sauté until soft, about 5 minutes. Add the garlic and sauté 1 minute more. Add the squash, 1 teaspoon of the salt, and ½ teaspoon of the pepper. Cook, stirring, until softened, about 10 minutes. Add the kimchi, sauté for 3 minutes more, and remove from the heat.

3 Add the cream, the remaining ½ teaspoon salt, and the remaining ½ teaspoon pepper to the vegetables. Use a rubber spatula to combine until evenly coated.

4 Add half the squash mixture to the prepared pan, then add roughly two-thirds of the cheese. Add the rest of the squash mixture, and use the rubber spatula to scrape any remaining sauce into the casserole. Cover with the last third of the cheese.

5 Bake until the liquid is bubbling and the topping has browned, about 45 minutes. Let rest 10 minutes and serve.

Base Ingredient: **Hot Sauce**

For me, a great hot sauce has some heat but not so much you can't taste the other flavors the chile has to offer. Cooking with hot sauce is all about adding flavor and, believe it or not, roundness to a dish. For example, a small amount of a good hot sauce can tie together the flavors of a soup or a big pot of beans without you even noticing it's there.

To achieve that balance, to accentuate the flavors of chiles beyond heat, you have to ferment your hot sauce. And while New Orleans and Louisiana are famed for their fermented hot sauces, it wasn't until my friend and Houston chef Hugo Ortega served me an amazing dish of whole grilled fish drizzled with habanero hot sauce that I got it. I was amazed at the natural fruitiness of the chiles and how well it paired with the smokiness of the grill. Hugo told me the key was fermenting the chiles—it tames a bit of the heat and allows other flavors to shine. I've been fermenting my hot sauces ever since.

Habanero Hot Sauce

You can swap the habaneros here for any other kind of spicy chile, such as jalapeños and serranos. You could also use a combination. Just make sure you wear gloves when handling the chiles!

MAKES 1 QUART
Begin recipe 7 to 10 days before using.

2½ tablespoons (38g) salt, plus more to taste

1 pound habaneros, stemmed and halved (roughly 55 to 60 peppers)

The following ingredients will not be needed until after fermentation:

¼ cup extra-virgin olive oil

3 red bell peppers, stemmed, seeded, and thinly sliced

½ yellow onion, thinly sliced

5 garlic cloves, minced

1½ cups distilled white vinegar

1 Combine the salt and 1 quart water in a pot over medium heat. Heat until the salt dissolves, about 2 minutes. Let cool completely. This is your brine.

2 Put the habaneros in a fermentation vessel and add the cooled brine. Place a weight over the peppers and cover. (See Fermentation Equipment, page 240.)

3 Put the jar in a cool, dark corner and allow it to ferment for 7 to 10 days. While it's fermenting, check on it every other day, skimming off any white scum that forms on the top of the brine. When it's ready, the liquid will be cloudy and have a prominent funk, and the chiles will have softened.

4 Strain the brine through a fine-mesh strainer. (The brine may be reserved for other uses, see Note.)

5 Heat the olive oil in a sauté pan over medium-high heat. Add the bell peppers, onion, and garlic and sauté until soft, about 6 minutes. Let cool slightly.

6 Place the habaneros and sautéed vegetables in a blender and blend while slowly adding the vinegar.

7 Taste for seasoning and add salt, if desired.

Note: Don't throw that fermentation liquid away! It's useful for all kinds of things: as the acid in a vinaigrette (page 11) or marinade, to flavor gravies, or even as the liquid element in bread. Store in a glass or ceramic airtight container in the refrigerator.

Hot Sauce Variations

Mango Hot Sauce: Substitute 8 ounces Hungarian wax peppers and 8 ounces mango, peeled and roughly chopped, for the habaneros. Use yellow bell peppers in place of red.

Green Hot Sauce: Substitute 8 ounces jalapeños and 8 ounces serranos for the habaneros, and use green bell peppers for the red.

Thai Chili Sauce: Use red Thai chiles, or if you can't find them, try red jalapeños. Add the garlic to the chiles while they ferment. Make a simple syrup by combining ⅔ cup coconut sugar and ⅓ cup water; bring to a simmer and stir until the sugar is dissolved. Let the syrup cool completely and add to the chiles when blending the hot sauce.

Easy Ideas for Using Hot Sauce

- Add to a soup or a pot of beans
- Perk up dressings, dips, and mayonnaise-based sauces
- Add to macaroni and cheese before baking
- Mix into marinades and vinaigrettes
- Shake sparingly over popcorn
- Top eggs
- Serve over ice cream (trust me!)
- Top raw or grilled oysters
- Serve alongside pizza
- Make a fantastic gift to friends and family

Michelada

San Antonio is a michelada town, and you can get them any which way you like at bars and restaurants across the city. I like mine simple, especially if you're going to the trouble of using homemade hot sauce in it! Really, though, you can use whatever hot sauce you like here. Add some lime juice, some soy sauce, and your favorite Mexican lager or any other crisp, light beer. My personal favorites for micheladas are Buenaveza from Stone Brewing in San Diego (which has salt and lime in it, so it's halfway to being a michelada anyhow) and Adiós Pantalones from Rahr & Sons in Fort Worth. I also like to mix things up sometimes and use a German rauchbier for the smoky flavor.

MAKES 1 COCKTAIL

1 lime, halved
2 tablespoons chile lime salt, such as Tajín
2 tablespoons kosher salt
1 tablespoon hot sauce (page 262)
1 teaspoon soy sauce
1 (12-ounce) can Mexican lager

1 Wet the rim of a pint glass with one of the lime halves. Add the chile lime salt and kosher salt to a saucer and roll the edge of the glass in it. Fill the glass with ice.

2 Squeeze both lime halves into the glass and add the hot sauce and soy sauce. Stir to combine. Top with beer; if there's any beer left in the can, serve it on the side for topping off the drink.

Twice-Baked Firecracker Saltines

These are the crackers you didn't even realize you needed—just about anywhere you would plop down a sleeve of saltines, you're gonna want these instead (pictured on page 35). Serve them alongside raw oysters, big bowls of chili, ceviches, or on a cheese tray with some pickles.

SERVES 6

1 sleeve saltines (about 3 dozen, or 4 ounces)
1 tablespoon unsalted butter
2 tablespoons hot sauce (page 262)

1 Heat the oven to 400°F. Line a sheet pan with parchment paper.

2 Arrange the saltines on the prepared pan so they do not touch.

3 Heat the butter and hot sauce in a small saucepan over medium-low heat until the butter has melted.

4 Use a pastry brush to brush the saltines on their salty side with the hot sauce mixture.

5 Bake until fragrant and toasted, 5 minutes. Let cool completely.

Hot Sauce–Brined Fried Chicken

The secret to amazing fried chicken is brining the chicken. The buttermilk and hot sauce in this brine team up to tenderize the meat and add tons of flavor; the salt seasons everything beautifully. (For more on brines, see page 197.) It's important to cook pieces separately based on their size, as the cooking time varies. Using the bacon is optional, but I find chicken fries better in slightly "dirty" oil (sullied with a bit of bacon). It breaks down the oil slightly, so that when you add the juicy chicken to the pot, it's not quite so volatile. Plus it's nice to have some crispy bacon to snack on while you fry the chicken.

SERVES 6
Begin recipe 12 to 24 hours before serving.

5 pounds chicken, either 1 whole chicken cut into 10 pieces (2 thighs, 2 legs, 2 wings, 4 breast pieces) or the equivalent weight of your preferred cuts (all dark meat, all white meat, all wings, etc.)

2 tablespoons (31g) salt, plus additional for final seasoning

3 cups buttermilk

¼ cup hot sauce (page 262)

4 cups all-purpose flour

2 tablespoons cayenne

2 teaspoons garlic powder

2 teaspoons onion powder

1 tablespoon celery salt

Vegetable or peanut oil, for frying

½ cup diced bacon (optional)

Freshly ground black pepper

1   Put the chicken in a large container and season with the salt. Stir to evenly distribute the salt among the pieces and let sit at room temperature for 20 minutes.

2   In a gallon-size resealable plastic bag, combine the buttermilk and hot sauce. Add the chicken and seal. Squish the chicken around in the bag to make sure it is covered with the brine. Refrigerate the chicken for at least 12 hours, and up to 24 hours.

3   Combine the flour, cayenne, garlic powder, onion powder, and celery salt in a shallow dish.

4   Drain the chicken in a colander, but do not wash off the brine. Dredge the chicken in the flour and place it on a rack. Let rest for 10 minutes.

5   While the chicken is resting, heat 1 to 1½ inches of oil and the bacon in a high-sided cast-iron pan until an instant-read thermometer reads 300°F. When the bacon has cooked completely, use a skimmer to remove the pieces. It will likely be done before the oil has reached temperature, so keep a close eye on it.

6   Working in batches, fry similar cuts together: breasts and thighs will take roughly 15 minutes, while wings and legs will take about 8 minutes. Regardless of cut, fry all pieces until the coating is golden brown. Turn the chicken over and continue to fry until completely browned on all sides. Make sure you let the oil come back up to 300°F between batches. You can also use an instant-read thermometer to check for doneness: you want dark meat cooked to 160°F and white meat to 170°F.

7   Let the chicken rest on a clean rack for about 5 minutes before enjoying, as this allows the juices to redistribute. If you are frying quite a bit of chicken, you can keep batches warm in a 200°F oven until everything is cooked. Season with salt and pepper before serving.

Blue Cheese Ravioli with Hot Sauce and Quick-Pickled Celery

The classic Buffalo wings flavor combination works surprisingly well as a pasta! You can use square store-bought wonton wrappers for this recipe if you don't have a pasta machine.

SERVES 4 TO 6

For the quick-pickled celery:

½ cup red wine vinegar

2 tablespoons sugar

2 tablespoons salt

1 serrano pepper, stemmed and halved lengthwise

2 stalks celery, cut into ¼-inch-thick slices, celery leaves reserved for garnish

For the pasta dough:

1½ cups all-purpose flour, plus more for dusting the work surface

½ teaspoon salt

2 large eggs

1 teaspoon extra-virgin olive oil

For the ravioli filling:

1 cup ricotta

1 cup blue cheese crumbles

¼ teaspoon salt

¼ teaspoon freshly ground black pepper

1 large egg, separated, egg white lightly beaten

For the hot sauce:

¼ cup (½ stick) unsalted butter

¼ cup hot sauce (page 262)

2 teaspoons honey

1 First, pickle the celery: Combine ½ cup water, the vinegar, sugar, salt, and serrano in a small saucepan over medium heat. Bring to a simmer and stir to dissolve the sugar and salt.

2 Pour the hot pickling liquid over the celery in a glass jar and let sit for at least 2 hours, and up to 2 weeks refrigerated.

3 Next, make the pasta: Using a stand mixer fitted with the paddle attachment, combine the flour and salt on low speed. Stop the mixer and use a spoon to form a divot in the center of the flour. Add the eggs and olive oil and mix on low speed until a dough forms. (If the dough isn't coming together, add a splash or two of water until it does.)

4 Swap the paddle attachment for the dough hook. Knead on medium-low speed for 8 minutes, or until the dough becomes smooth and elastic. Wrap the dough tightly in plastic wrap and refrigerate for 30 minutes.

5 While the dough is resting, make the ravioli filling: Combine the ricotta, blue cheese, salt, black pepper, and egg yolk in a bowl. Stir until fully combined.

6 Next, make the hot sauce: Melt the butter on low heat in a sauté pan or small saucepan. Once melted, whisk in the hot sauce and honey. Keep warm.

7 Line a sheet pan with plastic wrap.

8 Remove the dough from the refrigerator and divide it into four equal portions. Work with one piece at a time, covering the remaining dough with plastic wrap or a kitchen towel to prevent it from drying out.

9 Flatten one of the portions into a small rectangle. Then roll it through a manual or electric pasta roller, starting with the widest setting and repeating, moving one setting thinner with each pass, until you reach the thinnest setting. Lay the dough onto a cutting board and cut into 3-inch squares.

10 Brush the outer edges of the squares with the egg white and place 1 teaspoon of the filling in the center of each. Fold the opposite corners together to form a triangle and seal tightly with your fingers. Place the ravioli on the prepared

sheet pan and repeat steps 9 and 10 until all the dough has been used up.

11 Bring a large pot of salted water to a boil. (You do not want to overcrowd the pasta, so if your pot is not very large, you may have to cook the ravioli in two batches.) Boil the ravioli until they're tender and float to the surface, about 3 minutes. Transfer them with a slotted spoon to a large bowl and cover with the sauce. Gently stir the pasta until it is coated.

12 Sprinkle pickled celery and the celery leaves over each serving and enjoy.

Base Ingredient: **Chow-Chow**

A staple of the southern preservation canon, chow-chow is a condiment or relish comprised of chopped and fermented vegetables, often including cabbage, red or green tomatoes, onions, peppers, and more. I love chow-chow because you can basically add any in-season vegetable to the mix. I love experimenting with carrots, garlic, eggplant, squash, cauliflower, sweet chiles, cooked black-eyed peas and other crowder peas, collards and other sturdy greens, and more.

The uses for chow-chow are as limitless as the ingredients you can put into it; you can use it pretty much anywhere you'd use a pickle relish. Or, for the true fans, just eat it on its own, straight out of the jar. It's that good.

Chow-Chow

A pretty classic chow-chow made from summer produce. My best tip for cutting corn off the cob is to put a cutting board inside a sheet or roasting pan and cut down the sides vertically. This will keep the kernels contained as they fall off.

MAKES 2 QUARTS
Begin recipe 3 days before using.

2 tablespoons salt

2 teaspoons sugar

½ red onion, diced

¾ teaspoon freshly ground black pepper

4 cups corn kernels (from about 4 ears; thawed frozen kernels also work)

1 medium green tomato, diced

1 zucchini, diced

2 garlic cloves, smashed

1 jalapeño, stemmed and halved lengthwise

1 tablespoon dill seeds

1½ tablespoons yellow mustard seeds

1 Combine 1½ cups water, the salt, and sugar in a small saucepan over medium heat. Bring to a simmer and stir to dissolve the sugar and salt. Remove the brine from the heat and let cool to room temperature.

2 Combine the red onion, pepper, corn, green tomato, zucchini, garlic, jalapeño, dill seeds, and mustard seeds in a large mixing bowl, and stir to combine. Spoon the chow-chow mixture into a 2-quart fermenting vessel.

3 Pour the cooled brine over the vegetables. Top the vegetables with fermenting weights. Don't worry if the vegetables aren't covered in liquid immediately; wait an hour and they'll have released enough liquid to cover. If not, try adding extra weights or saltwater solution (see page 241).

4 Ferment the chow-chow in a cool, dark area for 3 days.

5 Store the fermented chow-chow in an airtight container in the refrigerator for up to 3 months.

Chow-Chow Variations

Ratatouille Chow-Chow: Increase the sugar in the brine to 2 tablespoons. Omit the corn, green tomato, jalapeño, dill, and mustard seeds. Substitute 3 cups diced eggplant; 2 diced red tomatoes; 1 diced yellow squash; 1 teaspoon each minced fresh thyme, fresh rosemary, and fresh parsley; and 1 tablespoon red pepper flakes.

Autumn Chow-Chow: Increase the sugar in the brine to 2 tablespoons. Omit all vegetables and seasonings. Substitute 2 cups butternut squash, peeled and cut into ½-inch dice; 2 cups finely diced cauliflower; 1 diced small yellow onion; 1 pear, peeled, cored, and diced; ½ cup raisins; 1 teaspoon turmeric; ½ teaspoon curry powder; a pinch of ground cloves; and 1 star anise pod. (Swap the raisins for dried cranberries and serve this one at Thanksgiving!)

Easy Ideas for Using Chow-Chow

• Serve as a condiment for grilled meats
• Fold into an omelet
• Top a hot dog
• Put a scoop on a bowl of beans
• Add to tuna salad

Chow-Chow Succotash

Traditional succotash, with its sweet corn and stewed lima beans, can be a little cloying, as a lot of sugar comes from the vegetables. The sourness of the chow-chow helps cut through all of that, bringing vibrancy and texture.

SERVES 6 AS A SIDE DISH

2 cups fresh southern peas, such as crowder, pink lady, black-eyed, or purple hull (see Note)

1 teaspoon salt

1 bay leaf

1 onion, halved

2 sprigs thyme

2 tablespoons extra-virgin olive oil

2 ears fresh corn, husked and cut from the cob, or about 1 cup thawed frozen corn kernels

2 tomatoes, seeded and diced

8 fresh basil leaves, torn

2 tablespoons chopped fresh chives

2 tablespoons chopped fresh parsley

¾ cup chow-chow (page 270)

Salt and freshly ground black pepper

1 Put the peas, salt, bay leaf, one-half of the onion, and thyme sprigs in a medium pot and cover with cold water. Bring to a boil and then turn down to a simmer. Simmer until the peas are fully cooked through, about 40 minutes. Skim off any foam that forms on the surface of the water. Check the peas for doneness. All peas have slightly different cooking times; they should be creamy, not chalky or mushy.

2 Remove ¼ cup of the bean cooking liquid and set aside. Drain the beans and discard the onion, bay leaf, and thyme.

3 Dice the remaining half onion. Heat the olive oil in a sauté pan over medium-high heat. Add the onion and sauté for 3 minutes. Add the corn and cook for an additional 2 minutes. Next, add the diced tomato and reserved bean cooking liquid and cook for 1 minute to soften.

4 Remove the pan from the heat and fold in the cooked peas along with the herbs and chow-chow.

5 Season with salt and pepper and serve.

Note: Frozen southern peas will also work. If they are not precooked, proceed with recipe as written. If they are precooked, skip step 1. Use ¼ cup water or stock in place of the bean-cooking liquid in step 3.

Cornmeal-Breaded Catfish with Chow-Chow Tartar Sauce

Fried catfish would taste great with regular old chow-chow, but I encourage you to make this chow-chow tartar sauce. The fermented vegetables, with their funky personality and lots of texture, really take it to the next level.

SERVES 6

6 catfish fillets (about 8 ounces each)

1 cup buttermilk

2 tablespoons hot sauce (page 262)

2 tablespoons yellow mustard

1 tablespoon dried thyme

¼ teaspoon garlic powder

½ teaspoon salt

¼ teaspoon freshly ground black pepper

Vegetable or peanut oil, for frying

3 cups cornmeal

Chow-Chow Tartar Sauce (recipe follows)

1 lemon, cut into 6 wedges, for serving

1 Cut each catfish fillet in half lengthwise and pat with paper towels to remove any excess moisture.

2 Whisk together the buttermilk, hot sauce, mustard, thyme, garlic powder, salt, and pepper in a medium bowl. Put the fish in a shallow dish or large resealable bag and add the marinade. Make sure the fish is coated with the marinade on all sides and let sit at room temperature for 15 minutes.

3 While the fish is marinating, heat ½ inch of oil in a large cast-iron pan over medium heat until an instant-read thermometer reads between 325° and 350°F. If you don't have an instant-read thermometer, sprinkle a few crumbs of cornmeal in the oil to check the temperature; the oil will sizzle when it's ready.

4 Place the cornmeal in another shallow dish. One at a time, use clean hands to remove any excess marinade from each fillet. Press each piece of fish into the cornmeal, ensuring it sticks to all sides. Repeat with the remaining fillets.

5 Line a plate with paper towels.

6 Fry the catfish in the oil in batches, making sure not to overcrowd the pan. Cook the fillets for 2 to 3 minutes on the first side without moving them. Use a pair of tongs to carefully turn the fillets and cook on the opposite side for an additional 2 minutes. The cornmeal crust should be golden brown on both sides. Transfer the fillets to the plate and repeat the frying process with the remaining fillets.

7 Serve with the tartar sauce and lemon wedges.

Chow-Chow Tartar Sauce

2 cups mayonnaise

½ cup chow-chow (page 270), plus 1 tablespoon chow-chow brine

¼ teaspoon onion powder

¼ teaspoon garlic powder

Pinch of cayenne

1 teaspoon Worcestershire sauce

⅛ teaspoon white pepper

¼ teaspoon salt

Combine all the ingredients together in a mixing bowl and refrigerate until ready to serve.

Chow-Chow Quiche

A jar of chow-chow can be a great shortcut, letting you skip much of the chopping required for a dish. In the case of this quiche, chow-chow is what gets a lovely breakfast or brunch on the table in no time.

SERVES 6

1½ tablespoons extra-virgin olive oil

1 tablespoon minced garlic

2 cups packed fresh baby spinach

1 cup drained chow-chow (page 270), with 1 tablespoon brine reserved

3 large eggs

½ cup heavy cream

½ cup whole milk

½ teaspoon salt

½ teaspoon freshly ground black pepper

1 pie crust (page 118)

½ cup goat cheese

1   Heat the oven to 375°F.

2   Heat the olive oil in a sauté pan over medium-high heat. Add the garlic and sauté for 1 minute, stirring. Add the spinach and sauté for an additional minute. Add the brine to help steam the spinach and cook for an additional minute. Remove the spinach from the pan and let it cool. Once cool, roughly chop the spinach.

3   Whisk together the eggs, cream, milk, salt, and pepper in a medium mixing bowl.

4   Spread the chopped spinach evenly on the bottom of the pie shell and then do the same with the chow-chow.

5   Pour the egg mixture over the vegetables. Dot the goat cheese over the top of the quiche.

6   Bake until the cheese is browned but the center of the quiche is still slightly jiggly, about 45 minutes. Remove from the oven and let rest for 10 minutes before serving.

Base Ingredient: **Fruit Shrubs**

Today people typically think of shrubs as a cocktail ingredient, but they were originally invented as a way to preserve fruit. And while they do make an excellent cocktail (see the Day Drinker, page 279), you can do so much more with these sharply flavorful ferments. I love to use shrubs in smoothies, in desserts, even to glaze vegetables. They add a sweetly acidic note to any dish and can be used most places you'd use a flavorful vinegar, or even as a substitute for orange juice.

Blackberry Shrub

Blackberries make a lovely deep purple, almost black shrub. This is not something you want to make while wearing a white shirt, trust me. Just about any berry can be substituted for the blackberries—try substituting 1-inch cubes of watermelon or kiwi for the blackberries, or whatever fruit you like.

It's important to use *unpasteurized* apple cider vinegar in this recipe. These will often have a sticker on the bottle declaring the vinegar comes "with the mother," a "good" bacterial colony that aids in fermentation. Pasteurization kills this bacteria.

Finally, I recommend using one of the two jar-based fermentation vessels (see page 240). This is because you need to seal the jar and swirl it periodically during the fermentation process.

MAKES 4½ TO 5 CUPS
Begin recipe 18 days before using.

3 cups fresh blackberries

3 star anise pods

2½ cups unpasteurized apple cider vinegar

The following ingredients will not be needed until after fermentation:

4 sprigs mint

1 cup sugar

1 cup lime juice

1 In a 2-quart fermentation vessel, use a cocktail muddler, pestle, or wooden spoon to mash up the berries and release their juices.

2 Add the star anise to the berries and cover with the vinegar. Make sure the fruit is completely submerged in the vinegar—fermentation weights may help (see page 240). Cover the fermentation vessel.

3 Place the jar in a cool, dark place to ferment for 24 hours. After 24 hours, remove the cover and fermentation weights (if using), secure a lid on the vessel, and shake vigorously. Remove the lid and replace with the fermentation vessel cover. Repeat this process once a day for the next 3 days.

4 After a total of 4 days fermenting, remove the fermentation vessel cover and replace with an airtight lid. Refrigerate the shrub for 4 more days, swirling the jar daily.

5 After 4 days, strain the shrub through a fine-mesh strainer into a clean jar, pressing the fruit with a rubber spatula to get all the juice out. Discard the pulp. Add the mint, sugar, and lime juice to the jar. Shake vigorously to combine everything.

6 Secure the lid on the jar and refrigerate for another 10 days, swirling the contents daily. After 10 days, strain your shrub through a fine-mesh strainer into a clean jar. It is now ready for use.

Fruit Shrub Variations

Apple Caraway Shrub: Substitute 3 apples, peeled and grated, for the blackberries. Skip the star anise, mint, and lime juice. Add 1 tablespoon crushed caraway seeds in step 5.

Stone Fruit Shrub: Substitute 3 cups diced stone fruit (peaches, cherries, apricots, plums, etc.) for the berries. Omit the star anise and apple cider vinegar and substitute 1 cinnamon stick and rice wine vinegar.

Fig Shrub: Substitute 3 cups figs for the berries, and swap half the apple cider vinegar for balsamic vinegar.

Easy Ideas for Using Fruit Shrubs

- Add a splash to soda water, iced tea, or lemonade and serve over ice
- Simmer to reduce by half and swirl into cheesecake before baking
- Use in cocktails, combined with gin, whiskey, or tequila
- Add a splash to just about any sautéed vegetable
- Finish a pot of greens

The Day Drinker

My wife, Sylvia, who is a partner in our restaurants, was a bartender in New Orleans for many years. She still creates most of the cocktails for the restaurants, and she created this gem when I asked her to come up with something that uses a fruit shrub. You could substitute Aperol or Cocchi Americano for the Cappelletti here, and while any good gin will work, I really love the peppered gin from Green House Spirits.

MAKES 1 COCKTAIL

2 ounces gin

1 ounce Cappelletti Aperitivo

½ ounce fruit shrub (page 277)

1 teaspoon honey

⅓ cup Topo Chico or other unflavored sparkling water

Fresh fruit, for garnish (use the same fruit used in the shrub)

1   Combine the gin, Cappelletti, shrub, and honey in a cocktail shaker or glass and stir briskly to combine.

2   Pour into a collins glass filled with ice, and top with Topo Chico. Garnish with fresh fruit.

Note: This makes a delightful nonalcoholic refreshment if you leave out the gin and Cappelletti. Simply combine the shrub and honey as written, pour over ice, and top with Topo Chico.

Berry Shrub Smoothie

This one's a real eye-opener, sweet and tart and packed with fruit! If you have any chia seeds left over, I like to sprinkle some on top right before serving.

MAKES 1 PITCHER OF SMOOTHIES

6 tablespoons chia seeds

1½ cups fruit shrub (page 277)

3 cups assorted berries (fresh or frozen strawberries, raspberries, or blackberries all work great)

2 bananas

1 cup unsweetened Greek yogurt

¼ cup honey

1 Add the chia seeds and fruit shrub to a small bowl and stir to combine. Refrigerate for at least 20 minutes or overnight.

2 Put the soaked seeds and shrub in a blender with the berries, bananas, yogurt, and honey and blend until smooth. Serve. Leftovers will last in the fridge for 2 days.

Shrub-Glazed Turnips

I love turnips. But if you've got people in your family who don't, try these—depending on what shrub you use, they turn out delightfully colorful, and they taste like turnip candy.

SERVES 4 TO 6 AS A SIDE

3 tablespoons vegetable oil

4 to 5 medium turnips, peeled and cut into 1-inch pieces (about 6 cups total)

½ cup chicken or vegetable stock (page 51)

½ cup fruit shrub (page 277)

2 teaspoons sugar

3 tablespoons unsalted butter

Salt and freshly ground black pepper

2 tablespoons chopped parsley

1 Heat the olive oil in a medium heavy saucepan over medium-high heat. Add the turnips and stir a few times as they begin to soften and brown slightly, about 8 minutes.

2 Add the chicken stock and fruit shrub to the pan, scraping up any browned bits on the bottom of the pan with a wooden spoon. Add the sugar, reduce the heat to medium, and cook, stirring frequently, until the liquid has become syrupy and starts to coat the turnips, 8 to 10 minutes.

3 Remove from the heat, add the butter, and stir to coat. Season the turnips with salt and pepper and toss with the parsley. Serve warm.

Berry Shrub Pie

My riff on a Depression-era vinegar pie, when vinegar was used to flavor pies during tough times, gets a fruit-flavored update with the addition of a shrub. Alas, the vibrant color of the shrub fades during baking, but you can bring it back into the equation by making the optional sauce to serve with the pie.

MAKES ONE 9-INCH PIE

4 large eggs

5 tablespoons whole milk

1½ cups sugar

¼ cup (½ stick) unsalted butter, melted

½ teaspoon salt

2 tablespoons cornmeal

1 tablespoon all-purpose flour

3 tablespoons fruit shrub (page 277)

1 pie crust (page 118)

Quick and Easy Shrub Sauce, for serving (optional; recipe follows)

1 Heat the oven to 375°F.

2 Using a stand mixer fitted with the whisk attachment, combine the eggs and milk on medium-low speed for 30 seconds.

3 While the mixer is still on medium-low, slowly pour in the sugar until fully incorporated.

4 Add the butter, salt, cornmeal, flour, and shrub and mix on low speed until combined. You may need to stop the mixer and scrape down the sides once or twice.

5 Pour the mixture into the prepared pie crust and bake until a toothpick inserted in the center of the pie comes out clean, 1 hour. Allow to cool completely before enjoying.

Quick and Easy Shrub Sauce

1½ cups jam (page 131, preferably the same flavor as your shrub)

Juice of 1 lemon

2 tablespoons fruit shrub (page 277)

1 Heat the jam, lemon juice, and shrub in a small saucepan over medium heat until the jam has melted.

2 Strain if desired and keep warm. Serve with the shrub pie.

Smoke

Historically, smoking was often combined with dehydration as a preservation method—the smoke would raise the temperature around the food slightly during the dehydration process and also helped keep insects away. Smoke itself has some preservation characteristics, and while smoked pork shoulder will keep ever-so-slightly longer than fresh, it's not going to keep as long as, say, a fully dehydrated smoked fish. But you just can't have a book on preservation from a Texas chef without talking about smoke! So here we are.

This chapter will cover two types of smoking: cold and hot. Cold smoking is anything you want to infuse with smoky flavor but do not want to cook, like nuts or cheese. (Imagine smoking a wheel of cheese at a high temperature!) You can cold smoke pretty much anything on a regular grill; you don't use heat but instead trap the smoke and try to draw it over your ingredient, raising the temperature only slightly. I like to use a smoking tube, which is a 12-inch-long perforated metal tube you stuff full of wood chips or pellets and then light on fire on one end. It smolders for quite a while and fills the grill chamber with smoky goodness for long enough to smoke your cheese or nuts. You can get one for pretty cheap anywhere you get barbecue and grilling supplies. (I ordered mine online.)

Hot smoking, on the other hand, is perhaps the most complicated technique in this book, as you're trying to do two things at once. Hot smoking occurs when the ingredient is smoked and cooked at the same time, and here we apply that technique to seafood, fish, and meat. It's a low-and-slow process, which is why you'll often see the same cuts used for braises—pork shoulder, brisket—in smoked recipes.

Managing a smoker, particularly an offset smoker like we use in Texas, takes practice. Making sure you maintain a consistent temperature, keeping the smoke thin and flavorful and not cloudy and ashy: these are skills that are hard won. Others have written excellent technical guides to this process (most famously, perhaps, Austin pitmaster Aaron Franklin), and I will not entirely duplicate their efforts here.

That said, the two basic components to keeping a hot smoker going are coals to maintain temperature and wood to maintain smoke. If the temperature dips, add more coals. If the smoke burns off, add more wood. Whatever type of smoker you use for these recipes, whether it's an offset or an automated pellet smoker, make sure you follow the manufacturer's instructions for smoking. You can also smoke in a regular kettle grill by sprinkling soaked wood chips over the coals. If you get into smoking and really want to perfect your craft, I recommend keeping a notebook to track each smoke. What works? What doesn't? Soon, you'll be a pro.

With all that in mind, this is the chapter where I expect you might use the most store-bought ingredients for the Application Recipes. Smoked fish and seafood, whether canned, vacuum-sealed, or from the deli, are abundantly available these days and come in many flavors. Maybe you get big tins of smoked nuts every Christmas from a client and you have no idea what to do with them. Or perhaps you just like smoked Gouda. This chapter has ideas for all of these, and if you live in a barbecue-loving state like Texas, you might even be able to get smoked meat at your supermarket or corner barbecue joint. (If not, those recipes will also work with regular grocery store rotisserie chicken.)

When used in recipes, smoked ingredients hold up to strong flavors: a chile relleno, for example, or a chocolate tart. That smoked flavor just seems to get along with everybody: you see it in desserts, soups, and entrées. It can steal the show if you let it, but with a subtle hand, its distinctiveness hangs out in the background and accentuates other flavors.

Base Ingredient: Smoked Nuts

Smoke is drawn to fat, which is why I toss nuts in melted butter before smoking them. You could use a neutral oil like grapeseed for a dairy-free version, if you like. I think smoked nuts work particularly well with apple, pecan, or cherry wood chips, but feel free to play around with other types of wood. The base recipe in this section is for neutral smoked nuts, which you can use in sweet and savory recipes alike. The variations, though, feature several seasoning options—check out the dried spice mixes on page 105 for more ideas.

Smoked Nuts

MAKES 1 POUND SMOKED NUTS

Apple, pecan, or cherry wood chips soaked in water for at least 2 to 24 hours

1 pound shelled nuts of your choice (pieces or whole nuts will work)

2 tablespoons unsalted butter, melted

1 teaspoon (5g) salt

1 Heat a smoker or charcoal grill to 225°F. If using a charcoal grill, build the fire to one side of the grill and add wood chips to the coals once the temperature has been reached.

2 Toss the nuts with the melted butter in a mixing bowl until coated. Add the salt and toss again to coat.

3 Put the nuts in a smoking basket or a small pan or pie dish and place on the grill grates on the opposite side of the grill from the heat.

4 Smoke the nuts for 2 hours, with the lid on and vents open, stirring every 30 minutes.

5 Remove the nuts from the grill and let cool before serving. These will last 2 weeks in an airtight container at room temperature, and 1 month refrigerated.

Smoked Nut Variations

Everything-Spiced Smoked Nuts: After tossing the nuts in the melted butter, season with 4 teaspoons white sesame seeds, 1 tablespoon poppy seeds, 1 tablespoon dried minced garlic, 1 tablespoon dried minced onion, and 2 teaspoons salt. Stir until the seasonings are evenly distributed. Proceed with the recipe as written. (Works best with cashews, peanuts, pistachios, walnuts, pine nuts, and hickory nuts.)

Warm-Spiced Smoked Nuts: After tossing the nuts in the melted butter, season with 1 tablespoon light brown sugar, ¼ teaspoon ground ginger, ¼ teaspoon allspice, ¾ teaspoon cinnamon, and a pinch of salt. Stir until the seasonings are evenly distributed. Proceed with the recipe as written. (Works best with almonds, pecans, macadamia nuts, Brazil nuts, hazelnuts, and chestnuts.)

Easy Ideas for Using Smoked Nuts

- Sprinkle on salads
- Add to pesto (page 60)
- Add to cookies, brownies, and other baked goods.
- Garnish vegetables
- Add to granola (page 111)
- Add to ice cream or the Ice Cream Terrine (page 80)

Smoked Nuts Old-Fashioned

The old-fashioned is the quintessential cocktail and doesn't need much tweaking. This variation on the classic infuses a bourbon of your choice with subtle smoky flavor. You don't want to use a fancy, expensive bourbon for this, though—in fact, this is a great way to dress up budget bourbons. Depending on what nut you use for this, your drink may start to turn cloudy as the ice melts. Don't worry, that's supposed to happen!

MAKES 1 COCKTAIL

1 teaspoon light brown sugar

2 to 3 dashes Angostura bitters

1 dash orange bitters

2 ounces Smoked Nut–Infused Bourbon (recipe follows)

1 orange twist, for garnish (see Note)

2 smoked nuts (page 288), for garnish

1 In an old-fashioned glass, muddle the brown sugar, ½ ounce water, and both bitters together for about 1 minute.

2 Fill the glass with ice cubes and top with the bourbon. Stir to combine using a cocktail spoon.

3 Garnish the top of the cocktail with the orange twist and smoked nuts.

Note: To create an orange twist, use a peeler to cut a thin strip of peel, taking care to remove only the orange-colored peel and none of the bitter white pith.

Smoked Nut–Infused Bourbon

Begin recipe 3 days before serving.

1 cup smoked nuts (page 288)

1 (750ml) bottle bourbon

1 With a knife or food processor, coarsely chop the nuts and spoon them into the bottom of a 1-quart jar. Add the bourbon. Screw the lid onto the jar and shake to mix.

2 Let the jar sit at room temperature for 3 days.

3 Strain the bourbon through a fine-mesh strainer and use a funnel to pour it back into the original bottle.

Watermelon Wedge Salad with Smoked Nuts

It occurred to me a few years ago to cut watermelon into wedges for a summery riff on the steakhouse classic. In a typical wedge, you've got iceberg lettuce doused in tomato, blue cheese, bacon, and red onion. The nuts here act like the bacon, with their smoky fattiness. We swap the blue cheese in favor of summery feta. The basil, the mint, the arugula, the jalapeño: all of these flavors really bring it into the season, too.

SERVES 6

6 (1-inch-thick) wedge-shaped slices watermelon, rind attached

Salt and fresh ground black pepper

1 cup fresh basil leaves

¾ cup fresh mint leaves

2 cups arugula leaves

1 to 2 jalapeños (depending on size and spice tolerance), sliced into ¼-inch-thick rings, seeded

1 cup crumbled feta cheese

1 cup smoked nuts (see page 288), cut into bite-size pieces

Poppy Seed Dressing (recipe follows)

1   Put the watermelon wedges on individual plates (or a serving dish) and season with a large pinch of salt and pepper. Distribute the herbs and arugula on top of each wedge of watermelon, and then top the herbs with a couple of jalapeño rings. Sprinkle with the feta and smoked nuts.

2   Drizzle 2 to 3 tablespoons of the dressing to one side of each salad and enjoy.

Poppy Seed Dressing

3 tablespoons mayonnaise

¾ cup extra-virgin olive oil

¼ cup white balsamic vinegar

1½ teaspoons Dijon mustard

1 tablespoon honey

Pinch of salt

1 tablespoon poppy seeds

Whisk together all the ingredients in a small bowl to combine.

Snapper Crusted with Smoked Nuts

The nuts in this preparation add a ton of texture to the fish, and it also happens to be very forgiving, thanks to the butter. As a bonus, the smoked nuts are kind of a cheat code for adding smoky flavor to a dish when the weather doesn't encourage grilling.

SERVES 6

1 cup smoked nuts (page 288)

½ cup unseasoned panko bread crumbs

½ cup all-purpose flour (see Note)

Salt

¾ cup (1½ sticks) unsalted butter, softened

6 snapper fillets (about 5 ounces each), skin removed

Freshly ground black pepper

1 Heat the oven to 350°F. Line a sheet pan with parchment paper.

2 Pulse the smoked nuts in a food processor several times until finely chopped. (Be careful not to overprocess, though, or you'll get nut butter.)

3 Combine the nuts, bread crumbs, flour, and a large pinch of salt together in a bowl. Use a rubber spatula to fold in the softened butter until thoroughly combined.

4 Put the snapper fillets on the prepared pan and season both sides with salt and pepper.

5 Spread a ¼-inch-thick coating of the smoked nut mixture evenly over the fish with an offset spatula or butter knife.

6 Bake until the fish fillets are opaque throughout, 15 to 20 minutes. The cooking time will depend on the thickness of the fish. A small paring knife should not meet any resistance when inserted into the flesh of the fish. The top should be slightly browned as well. (If not, you can broil it briefly to brown.) Serve immediately.

Note: Nut flours can be substituted to reflect the smoked nut being used; for example, use almond flour with smoked almonds, and so on.

Smoked Nuts Chocolate Tart

Heat is your enemy when working with tart dough, so really stick to the refrigeration times in the recipe below. Beyond the shell, though, this recipe could not be simpler, and it brings intense, rich flavor to the table.

MAKES ONE 9-INCH TART
Begin recipe 1 day before serving.

1½ cups chopped smoked nuts (page 288)
Chocolate Tart Shell (recipe follows)
12 ounces milk chocolate, finely chopped, or 1 (12-ounce) bag chocolate chips
¼ cup (½ stick) unsalted butter, diced
1 cup heavy cream

1   Put the nuts in the bottom of the prepared tart shell and jiggle the shell until they are evenly dispersed.

2   Put the chocolate and butter in a medium mixing bowl.

3   Heat the cream in a small saucepan over medium heat just to a simmer and pour it over the chocolate and butter. Let sit for 1 minute.

4   Whisk the chocolate mixture until smooth. Pour it over the nuts and refrigerate for at least 2 hours until set.

5   Slice the tart with a warm knife.

Chocolate Tart Shell

½ cup powdered sugar
1 cup all-purpose flour
¼ cup cocoa powder
Pinch of salt
½ cup (1 stick) cold unsalted butter, diced
1 large egg

1   Put the powdered sugar, flour, cocoa powder, and salt in a food processor and pulse to combine.

2   Add the butter and pulse six to eight more times, until the mixture resembles coarse sand.

3   Add the egg while continuing to pulse several times until a dough forms. (It may help to crack the egg into a bowl first and then pour it in, to avoid getting shell in your dough.)

4   Put the dough on a sheet of plastic wrap and flatten it into a small disk. Wrap the dough in plastic and refrigerate for a minimum of 2 hours.

5   Remove the dough from the refrigerator and let it sit for 10 minutes at room temperature to make rolling a bit easier.

6   Lay a piece of parchment paper or plastic wrap larger than your 9-inch tart pan on a work surface. Flour the parchment and place the dough on top. Flour the dough and top with another piece of parchment or plastic wrap.

This will make the dough easier to roll and prevent it from sticking. Roll the dough to an ⅛-inch-thick circle, about 11 inches in diameter. Keep the dough between the sheets of parchment or plastic and refrigerate for 20 minutes. (To move the dough without cracking, it may help to slip it onto a sheet pan or to use the removable bottom from the tart pan.)

7 Remove the dough from the refrigerator and peel away the top layer of parchment. Invert the dough onto a 9-inch tart pan with a removable bottom and remove the other piece of parchment. Tuck the dough into the sides of the pan and remove the excess dough by rolling the rolling pin over the top of the pan.

8 Refrigerate the tart shell for 1 hour.

9 Heat the oven to 325°F. Line the tart shell with parchment paper and fill with dried beans, uncooked rice, or pie weights.

10 Bake for 25 minutes. Remove the tart from the oven and remove the weights and the parchment. Bake for 10 minutes longer. Let cool before filling.

Base Ingredient: Smoked Cheese

When smoking cheese, you want a mild wood that leaves a subtler smoke: from fruit trees, pecans, maples, or alders. This way, smoked cheddar still tastes like cheddar, and smoked Gouda still tastes like Gouda. You're not masking any of that; you're simply improving upon it.

Smoked Cheese

Cheese is best smoked during cooler months, as you want the grill temperature below 80°F. It's tricky but doable during the summer; you can place a pan of ice inside the smoking chamber to keep it cool. Or buy your smoked cheese. There are some really amazing options out there!

MAKES 8 OUNCES SMOKED CHEESE
Begin recipe the day before using.

8 ounces fresh mozzarella, cheddar, provolone, Gouda, or brie, at room temperature

Apple, pecan, or cherry wood chips soaked in water for at least 2 to 24 hours

1 If the cheese is wet, pat it dry with paper towels.

2 Fill the smoking tube with wood chips or pellets. Place the tube on the lower level of the grill, on the opposite side from any vents in the lid. This ensures the smoke will travel up and around the cheese.

3 Use a long lighter to light 2 inches of pellets toward one end of the tube. Let the flame burn for about 5 minutes and then blow it out.

4 Place the cheese on a small rack or grill basket and place on the grill directly under the vents.

Open the vents completely. (If your grill has multiple vents on top, just open the one directly above the cheese.)

5 Keep an eye on the temperature of your grill, keeping it between 65° and 80°F. If it gets above 80°F, add a pan of ice to help lower the temperature.

6 Smoke the cheese for 2 hours, turning it over every 30 minutes to ensure an even smoke.

7 Wrap the cheese in parchment paper and place in the refrigerator for 24 hours. This will allow the cheese to breathe slightly. Wrap tightly in plastic wrap after 24 hours. The cheese will get better as it sits over 1 to 2 weeks and will last in the refrigerator for up to 6 months.

Easy Ideas for Using Smoked Cheese

- Shred and fold into mashed potatoes or grits
- Swap for the cheese in your favorite mac and cheese recipe
- Use in grilled cheese
- Upgrade almost any cheesy breakfast food
- Use in quesadillas
- Top cheeseburgers
- Use in fondue, either on its own or as part of a medley of cheeses

Smoked Cheese Waldorf Salad Sandwich

A traditional Waldorf salad is a combination of fruit and nuts dressed in mayonnaise, but the addition of smoked cheese here transforms it into something akin to a vegetarian chicken salad. So I put it on a sandwich!

MAKES 1 SANDWICH

2 butter lettuce leaves

2 slices tomato

1 large croissant, cut in half horizontally

¾ cup Smoked Cheese Waldorf Salad (recipe follows)

Place the lettuce and tomatoes on the bottom half of the croissant and top with the Waldorf salad filling. Finish with the top half of the croissant.

Smoked Cheese Waldorf Salad

8 ounces smoked cheese (page 299), diced

1 cup diced celery

1 Granny Smith apple, peeled and diced

1 cup halved seedless red grapes

1 cup walnuts, chopped

2 tablespoons chopped chives

1 cup mayonnaise

1½ tablespoons whole-grain mustard (page 19)

1 tablespoon prepared horseradish

Add all the ingredients to a mixing bowl and stir to combine.

Note: A smaller dice on the salad ingredients makes it easier to pile into the croissant.

Grilled Little Gem Salad with Smoked Cheese, Avocado, and Soft Herbs

For this salad, you'll want to get your grill very hot and grill the lettuce briefly, just long enough to change its flavor and texture slightly. In doing so, you bring out lovely flavors in the lettuce itself, which are then emphasized by the smoke in the shredded cheese. Make sure your grill is super clean, too, or else the lettuce will stick to it.

SERVES 6

1 ripe avocado

½ cup yogurt

½ teaspoon salt, plus more to taste

½ teaspoon freshly ground black pepper, plus more to taste

6 Little Gem lettuce hearts, or 3 romaine hearts, halved lengthwise

1 teaspoon ground coriander

1 teaspoon ground cumin

2 tablespoons extra-virgin olive oil

Juice of 1 lemon

½ cup roasted peanuts, roughly chopped

¾ cup shredded smoked cheese (page 299)

½ cup fresh herbs, such as basil, tarragon, parsley, and chives

1 First, make the dressing: Blend half of the avocado and all of the yogurt in a small food processor or single-serving blender. Season to taste with ½ teaspoon salt and pepper. You can also mash the avocado into the yogurt with a fork or pastry cutter. Dice the other half of the avocado and set aside.

2 Heat a grill to a high temperature. When you can only hold your hand above the grill grate for 5 seconds or less, your coals are ready.

3 Place the lettuce hearts on a tray cut-side up and sprinkle with the salt, pepper, coriander, and cumin. Drizzle the hearts with the olive oil and allow to sit for 2 minutes so the oil seeps down in between the layers.

4 Place the lettuce hearts cut-side down on the grill and cook for 1 minute. Rotate the lettuce hearts one-quarter turn without flipping and cook for 1 minute longer. (This gives you nice, crisscrossed grill marks.)

5 Place the lettuce hearts grilled-side up on a large platter and drizzle with the lemon juice. Place a dollop of the avocado-yogurt mixture on each half and then sprinkle with the diced avocado, peanuts, and cheese. Scatter the herbs to finish.

Apple Crisp with Smoked Cheese

Cheese-and-apple pie is a Midwestern thing, or at least it certainly was in my house growing up. My mom used to say, "Apple pie without the cheese is like a hug without the squeeze." I call for Granny Smiths here, but you can use any tart baking apple, and while cheddar is traditional, you can use pretty much any smoked hard cheese.

MAKES ONE 10-INCH ROUND OR 8-INCH SQUARE APPLE CRISP

1 tablespoon cornstarch

Juice of 1 lemon

5 Granny Smith apples (2½ to 3 pounds), peeled, cored, and thinly sliced

½ cup plus 5 tablespoons light brown sugar

1 teaspoon cinnamon

½ cup (1 stick) unsalted butter, softened

¾ cup all-purpose flour

½ teaspoon salt

1 cup old-fashioned rolled oats

1 cup lightly packed finely shredded smoked cheese (page 299)

Vanilla ice cream, for serving

1 Heat the oven to 350°F.

2 Whisk together the cornstarch and lemon juice in a large mixing bowl until completely smooth. Add the apples, 5 tablespoons of the brown sugar, and the cinnamon. Stir until the apples are evenly coated.

3 Transfer the apples to a 10-inch cast-iron pan or an 8-inch square baking pan and spread in an even layer.

4 Combine the butter, flour, salt, remaining ½ cup brown sugar, and oats in a separate medium mixing bowl and use a fork or a pastry cutter to distribute the butter evenly through the dry ingredients. Gently fold in the shredded cheese, breaking up any clumps as you go.

5 Crumble the topping over the apples, making sure to cover the entire surface evenly.

6 Bake until the filling is bubbling and the top is golden brown, 45 to 50 minutes.

7 Serve warm with a scoop of vanilla ice cream.

Smoked Cheese Scones

Scones have a reputation for being boring and dry, but the addition of smoked cheese solves both of those problems nicely.

MAKES 8 SCONES

2½ cups all-purpose flour

1 tablespoon baking powder

¼ teaspoon salt

½ cup (1 stick) cold unsalted butter, diced

1 cup shredded smoked cheese (page 299)

2 teaspoons chopped fresh chives

2 large eggs

¾ cup whole milk, plus more for brushing scones

1 Heat the oven to 400°F. Line a sheet pan with parchment paper.

2 Pulse the flour, baking powder, and salt in a food processor to combine. Add the butter and pulse several times until the mixture looks like fine crumbs. Pour this mixture into a medium mixing bowl and add the smoked cheese and chives. Stir to combine.

3 In a small bowl, whisk together the eggs and milk. Add to the flour mixture and stir just until a dough forms.

4 Place the dough on a floured work surface and knead the dough with the heel of your hand, folding it over onto itself about six times. Do this quickly so the dough does not warm up too much. Form the dough into a round and use a rolling pin to roll it out into a 1-inch-thick circle.

5 Cut the dough into eight wedges and place them on the prepared sheet pan about 1 inch apart. Brush the tops with a bit of milk.

6 Bake until golden brown, about 20 minutes.

7 Let cool slightly before serving.

Base Ingredient: Smoked Fish and Seafood

Smoke is such a great flavor to match with briny seafood, and in turn smoked seafood brings fantastic umami flavor to all kinds of dishes. Cans of smoked fish and seafood are readily available in stores, but I think a lot of the time people don't know what to do with them. If you're not the type to crack open a can of smoked sardines or clams and start snacking, there's still a lot you can achieve with these tiny tins, as you'll see in the following pages.

Smoked Oysters

I smoke fish and seafood at a lower temperature than meat, but this is still considered a hot smoking technique. Do note that for many different kinds of smoked seafood—bivalves in particular—you'll lose a lot of volume during smoking thanks to water that gets cooked out. So make sure you buy more raw seafood than you think you'll need—better to have leftovers than not enough!

MAKES ABOUT ½ CUP

1 pound shucked oysters, drained

½ teaspoon salt

½ teaspoon freshly ground black pepper

¼ teaspoon soy sauce

¼ teaspoon light brown sugar

Apple, pecan, or cherry wood chips soaked in water for at least 2 to 24 hours

2 tablespoons extra-virgin olive oil

Zest of ½ lemon

1   Combine the oysters in a medium mixing bowl with the salt, pepper, soy sauce, and brown sugar. Refrigerate for 1 hour.

2   Meanwhile, heat the smoker or charcoal grill to 200°F. When the temperature is achieved, add the wood chips.

3   Put the oysters in a perforated smoking pan on the opposite side of the grill from the heat source. Close the grill's bottom dampers and open the top vent halfway. Smoke the oysters until they lose their gloss, 1½ to 2 hours. They will shrink quite a bit. Add more chips throughout the process as needed.

4   While the oysters are smoking, combine the olive oil with the lemon zest.

5   Remove the oysters from the grill and let them cool slightly. Toss the oysters with the olive oil mixture. Oysters can be kept in the olive oil in the refrigerator for 1 week.

Smoked Seafood Variations

Smoked Mussels: Unlike oysters, mussels are not sold preshucked, so steam them before smoking. Bring ½ cup dry white wine (or water) to a simmer over medium-high heat in a medium pot and add 2 pounds mussels. Cover the pot and steam the mussels for 5 to 6 minutes. Remove open mussels with tongs and let cool completely. Remove the top shell from each mussel and discard; drizzle 2 tablespoons olive oil over the mussels and sprinkle them with 1 teaspoon salt. Smoke the mussels directly on the grate at 200°F for 30 minutes. Drizzle with the juice of ½ lemon, let cool completely, and refrigerate up to 1 week.

Smoked Trout: Sprinkle 6 skin-on trout fillets (about 2½ pounds total) with 1½ teaspoons salt and refrigerate for 45 minutes. Rinse the fillets with water and pat dry with clean towels. Smoke skin-side down in a smoker heated to 275°F for 45 minutes. Let cool completely and refrigerate for up to 1 week.

Easy Ideas for Using Smoked Fish and Seafood

- Serve as party snacks, wrapped with bacon and stuck through with a toothpick, or on a cracker
- Fry them up tempura-style
- Stir into pasta
- Top salads
- Garnish a Bloody Mary
- Swap in anywhere you'd use anchovies—soups, stews, salad dressings

Note: Make sure the grill of your smoker is very clean or the trout skin will stick to it.

Smoked Seafood Dip

I love an easy dip you can make ahead for having people over. This smoky, creamy number works great hot or cold, depending on the season, and is friends with beer, wine, or cocktails.

MAKES ABOUT 2 CUPS

6 ounces smoked seafood (page 307), diced (fish works best)

1 (8-ounce) package cream cheese, softened

Zest of 1 lemon

¼ teaspoon garlic powder

1 teaspoon paprika

¼ teaspoon cayenne

1 teaspoon Worcestershire sauce

¼ teaspoon hot sauce (page 262 or store-bought)

2 teaspoons chopped fresh dill

Salt and freshly ground black pepper

Crackers, for serving (the Twice-Baked Firecracker Saltines on page 264 are fantastic with this)

Combine all the ingredients in a medium mixing bowl. Taste for seasoning and serve.

Note: You can also bake this for a hot, cheesy dip. To the above, add ¼ cup unseasoned panko bread crumbs, ¼ cup sour cream, ¼ cup mayonnaise, and 1 cup grated cheddar cheese. Spoon into a greased baking dish and bake at 350°F for 20 to 25 minutes. Let cool for 10 minutes before enjoying.

Smoked Seafood Caesar Salad

A nice, smoky riff on a classic Caesar salad, this manages to taste distinct without going too crazy. Traditionally, this would have anchovies in it, but smoked oysters, mussels, clams, trout, or sardines totally transform the salad. You can make this a full meal by adding extra smoked seafood on top.

SERVES 6

2 pounds romaine lettuce (about 2 heads), outer leaves removed

Smoked Seafood Caesar Dressing (recipe follows)

Croutons (page 25)

¼ cup shredded Parmesan

6 ounces smoked seafood (page 307), left whole

Freshly ground black pepper

1 Cut the lettuce crosswise into 1-inch-wide strips. Stop about 2 inches before the root end; discard the end. Wash and dry the lettuce, and place it in a large mixing bowl.

2 Toss the lettuce with the dressing until well combined.

3 Portion the salad among six bowls and finish with croutons, Parmesan, smoked seafood, and pepper.

Smoked Seafood Caesar Dressing

1 egg yolk

2 teaspoons lemon juice

⅓ cup extra-virgin olive oil

1 tablespoon Dijon mustard

1 tablespoon red wine vinegar

2 tablespoons finely chopped smoked seafood (page 307)

1 garlic clove, minced

½ teaspoon Worcestershire sauce

Dash of hot sauce (page 262 or store-bought)

1 tablespoon grated Parmesan

Salt and freshly ground black pepper

1 Find a small mixing bowl that will fit snugly in a small pot. Place a wet towel over the pot and place the bowl over the towel. This will keep the bowl from moving around while making the dressing.

2 Put the egg yolk in the bowl and whisk with the lemon juice.

3 Slowly drizzle the olive oil into the egg yolk mixture while continuing to whisk until all the oil has been incorporated. Whisk in the Dijon, vinegar, seafood, garlic, Worcestershire sauce, hot sauce, and Parmesan. Adjust the seasoning with salt and pepper. This dressing will keep refrigerated for 2 weeks.

Smoked Seafood Spaghetti

If you're going to go to all the trouble of smoking your own seafood, you're going to want a dish that showcases your hard work! This pasta does just that, with a simple sauce flavored with garlic, red pepper flakes, parsley, lemon, and Parmesan.

SERVES 6

1 pound spaghetti

⅓ cup extra-virgin olive oil

3 garlic cloves, sliced

¼ teaspoon red pepper flakes

Juice of 1 lemon

12 ounces smoked seafood, diced (page 307), (about 1½ cups)

¼ cup (½ stick) unsalted butter

3 tablespoons chopped fresh parsley

½ cup grated Parmesan

1   Bring a large pot of generously salted water to a boil. Cook the pasta according to the package instructions, stirring periodically to prevent sticking.

2   Just before the pasta is finished, scoop out ¼ cup of the pasta water and set aside. Drain the pasta, then put the pasta and the reserved pasta water into a large serving bowl.

3   While the pasta is cooking, heat the olive oil in a sauté pan over medium heat. Add the garlic and sauté for 45 seconds. Remove from the heat and add the red pepper flakes, lemon juice, and smoked seafood, and stir to combine.

4   Pour the sauce over the noodles and use tongs to combine.

5   Fold in the butter, parsley, and cheese. Serve warm.

Creamy Smoked Seafood, Parsnip, and Celery Root Soup

Smoked seafood plays the role of both seafood and bacon in this chowder, which also makes good use of some underappreciated root vegetables, like parsnips and celery root.

SERVES 4 TO 6, WITH LEFTOVERS

2 tablespoons unsalted butter

1 yellow onion, diced

Salt

2 stalks celery, diced, leaves reserved for garnish

4 garlic cloves, minced

2 quarts fish, chicken, or vegetable stock (page 53)

2 parsnips, peeled and diced (about 1½ cups)

1 small celery root, peeled and diced (about 1½ cups)

1 russet potato (about 12 ounces), peeled and diced (about 1½ cups)

1 pound smoked seafood (page 307), cut into bite-size pieces, (about 2 cups)

1 cup heavy cream

Freshly ground black pepper

1 thick slice rustic country sourdough per person, toasted, for serving

Fresh chives, parsley, and reserved celery leaves, chopped, for garnish

1 Melt the butter in a large, heavy soup pot over medium heat. Add the onion along with a big pinch of salt and sauté until translucent, about 8 minutes. Add the celery and sauté 3 minutes more. Add the garlic and sauté 1 minute more.

2 Add the stock and bring to a boil. Reduce the heat to medium-low and wait for the broth to fall to a vigorous simmer. Add the parsnips and celery root and simmer for about 20 minutes. Add the potatoes and simmer until the potatoes are tender but not falling apart, another 8 minutes.

3 Add the smoked seafood and simmer for another 3 minutes, just until it is warmed through.

4 Add the cream and add salt and pepper to taste.

5 Serve in bowls with a slice of toasted bread and a sprinkling of herbs.

Base Ingredient: Smoked Meat

Brisket is the king of smoked meats in Texas, but it can be a tricky cut to smoke, particularly for beginners. That's why I'm starting you off with smoked pork shoulder—it's just so difficult to mess up. There's so much fat within the cut that it's really hard to dry out or overcook. Get comfortable cooking a few pork shoulders, and you'll get to brisket soon enough.

For our purposes, smoked pork is also very versatile in dishes. That smoky pork flavor goes well with so many things, from a simple pot of beans to an intricate gumbo. I got my start in New Orleans, after all, and I wasn't planning on letting you out of here without a killer gumbo recipe!

Smoked Pork Shoulder

This recipe calls for you to cook the pork shoulder to an internal temperature of 190°F, which is on the lower end of the temperature range for pork and works better if you're looking for more of a firmer, chunked consistency with your finished product. If you prefer your pork pulled or shredded, you can take it 5 to 8 degrees higher.

SERVES 6
Begin recipe 2 days before serving.

4 pounds boneless pork shoulder

⅓ cup equal parts salt and ground black pepper (preground works fine here), about 2 tablespoons plus 2 teaspoons of each

⅓ cup pork herbs (optional, page 97)

⅓ cup extra-virgin olive oil

Oak, hickory, or mesquite wood chips, soaked in water for at least 2 hours and up to 24 hours before smoking

1 Pat the pork shoulder dry with paper towels.

2 Combine the seasonings and olive oil in a small bowl. Put the pork in a larger bowl and rub the seasoning all over it. Cover the pork with plastic wrap and place it in the refrigerator for 24 hours.

3 Heat a smoker or charcoal grill to 275°F. If using a charcoal grill, pile the coals on one side of the grill, on the opposite side of any vents in the lid. Add a handful of wood chips on top of the hot coals and continue to add them throughout the cooking process as needed.

4 Unwrap the pork shoulder and rub it with any seasoning that may have collected in the bottom of the bowl.

5 Put the pork shoulder in the smoker, or on the grill on the opposite side from the coals. Close the lid and keep the temperature of the grill between 225°F and 275°F. Smoke the shoulder for 4 hours, or until the pork's internal temperature reaches 190°F. Remove the pork from the smoker or grill and let sit for 15 minutes before serving, to allow the juices to redistribute within the meat.

Smoked Meat Variations

Smoked Sausage: Raw Italian and Polish sausage and bratwurst work well for this. You'll want links that are about 8 ounces each. Smoke at 250°F for 1 hour, or until the internal temperature of the sausages is 160°F. If eating immediately, move the sausages directly over the heat source for 2 minutes per side for a nice, crisp casing.

Smoked Chicken: Pat a 4-pound chicken dry with paper towels. Rub with 2 tablespoons extra-virgin olive oil, and then season all over with 2 teaspoons salt and 1 teaspoon freshly ground black pepper. Smoke at 250°F for 2½ to 3 hours, or until an instant-read thermometer inserted where the thigh meats the breast reads 160°F and the juices run clear. After 1½ hours of smoking, rotate the chicken and drizzle with an additional 2 tablespoons olive oil.

Smoked Brisket: Trim a 12- to 14-pound packer cut brisket of any silver skin, and trim its fat to about ¼-inch thickness all around. Rub all over with ¼ cup yellow mustard and season with ⅓ cup salt and ⅓ cup ground black pepper. (Be heavy-handed with the seasoning. Some may fall off, but that's how you get a good bark on the surface of your brisket.) Place the meat directly on the grate, fat-side up, with the fattiest end closest to the heat source, in a 265°F smoker. Smoke for 6 hours. After 6 hours, remove the brisket from the smoker and place it on a 3 by 3-foot square of unwaxed butcher paper (or aluminum foil). Roll the paper twice around the brisket so the fat side is back on top, and tuck the ends under the brisket. Smoke for another 2 hours, or until a thermometer inserted into the thickest part of the meat reads 210°F. Allow to rest, still wrapped, for 1 hour before serving.

Easy Ideas for Using Smoked Meat

• Serve in a taco
• Use in place of bacon for a similar flavor but different texture
• Layer into sandwiches
• Stir into soups
• Add to beans
• Add to pasta sauces
• Use in fried rice
• Use as a ravioli filling
• Add to mac and cheese
• Use in a quesadilla
• Serve with barbecue sauce (page 41)

Gigante Beans with Smoked Meat

Beans have a flavor of their own, but they also take on flavors nicely. You could make this recipe with any kind of bean and any kind of smoked meat, and you'll end up with a different flavor combination every time.

SERVES 6

3 tablespoons extra-virgin olive oil

1 onion, diced

2 stalks celery, diced

2 carrots, peeled and diced

2 garlic cloves, minced

¼ cup dry white wine

2 sprigs thyme

2 bay leaves

2 cups gigante beans, soaked overnight, then drained

2 quarts chicken stock (page 51)

8 ounces smoked meat, diced (page 317)

Salt and freshly ground black pepper

1   Heat the olive oil in a large Dutch oven over medium heat. Add the onions and sauté until translucent, about 6 minutes. Add the celery and carrots and sauté for an additional 8 minutes. Finally add the garlic and sauté 1 more minute. Stir in the wine, scraping the bottom of the pot with a wooden spoon to loosen the good browned bits.

2   Add the thyme and bay leaves to the pot and stir to combine. Next add the beans and the chicken stock and bring to a boil.

3   Lower the heat to a simmer and add the smoked meat. Continue to simmer the beans, uncovered, until cooked completely through, 1 to 2 hours. You may need to add more stock to keep the beans covered. Discard the thyme stems and bay leaves, and season the finished beans with salt and pepper.

Grilled Chile Relleno

This spicy, creamy, smoky centerpiece is simpler to put together than it seems. It's great for a dinner party: you can make the stuffed chiles and sauce up to 5 days ahead of time. Then simply heat the sauce, grill the chiles, and enjoy good company!

SERVES 6

6 large poblano peppers

2 cups fresh cilantro leaves

2 large tomatoes, diced

½ red onion, thinly sliced

Juice of ½ lime

2 tablespoons extra-virgin olive oil

Salt and freshly ground black pepper

1 pound smoked meat (page 317), shredded (about 2 packed cups)

2 cups shredded Monterey Jack cheese (about 8 ounces)

8 garlic cloves, minced

1 cup Mexican crema (or sour cream)

Relleno Sauce (recipe follows)

1 Build a charcoal fire in a grill and allow it to burn until the coals are white and hot. Set the poblanos over the heat and cook until blackened on all sides. Flip the chiles constantly, as they will get too soft if left too long.

2 Transfer the chiles to a large mixing bowl and cover (plastic wrap or a pot lid work well) until cool enough to handle, about 15 minutes.

3 Combine the cilantro, tomatoes, onion, lime juice, and olive oil in a medium mixing bowl and mix to combine. Season with salt and pepper and refrigerate until ready to use.

4 Peel the burned skin from the chiles and slice them open lengthwise on one side. Remove the seeds and stems.

5 In a large mixing bowl, combine the shredded meat, cheese, garlic, and Mexican crema. Stuff the chiles with the mixture; larger chiles will use more filling than smaller ones. Fold over the sides of the chiles, reforming the original shape, and use toothpicks to seal up the seam. Refrigerate the chiles for at least 20 minutes and up to 5 days in advance for the mixture to stiffen up. This will make grilling easier.

6 Grill the chiles over the hot coals until heated all the way through, 3 to 5 minutes per side, but the exact cooking time will depend on the size of each chile. You are looking for a chile that is fully cooked; it will have char marks on both sides and be slightly slumped due to the cheese melting on the inside. You may also see some cheese start to ooze out of the seam.

7 Carefully remove the toothpicks from the chiles. Spoon some of the warm sauce onto the plates, place a relleno in the middle, and top with a handful of the cilantro salad.

Relleno Sauce

3 tablespoons extra-virgin olive oil

½ cup diced white onion

2 garlic cloves, minced

1 (14.5-ounce) can diced tomatoes, including the juice

2 chipotle peppers in adobo sauce

1 teaspoon smoked paprika

½ teaspoon dried oregano

¼ teaspoon salt

¼ teaspoon freshly ground black pepper

1 teaspoon cumin powder

1 teaspoon white wine vinegar

1   Heat the olive oil in a medium saucepan over medium-high heat. Add the onion and sauté for 5 minutes. Add the garlic and sauté for 1 minute longer.

2   Next, add the tomatoes, chipotle peppers, smoked paprika, dried oregano, salt, pepper, and cumin along with 1 cup of water. Bring to a simmer and simmer for 10 minutes.

3   Remove from the heat. Add the contents to a blender and blend until smooth. Add the vinegar and taste to adjust seasoning. Keep warm until ready to serve.

Cured's Famous Poutine

This dish has been on Cured's menu since day one. At the restaurant we make our own fries, of course, but you can get pretty close with frozen fries (or use tater tots!). This recipe was inspired by my early days as a chef in New Orleans, when I'd throw a scoop of gumbo on French fries for lunch. And the cheese curds are, of course, a nod to growing up in Wisconsin.

SERVES 6

1 (32-ounce) bag frozen French fries or tater tots, prepared according to the package instructions

8 ounces smoked meat, shredded (page 317)

1½ cups cheese curds

Gravy (recipe follows)

1 bunch green onions, chopped

1 cup pickled cauliflower (page 31; optional)

1   Heat your oven's broiler on high.

2   Spread the cooked fries or tots in a 12-inch cast-iron pan (a small sheet pan or lasagna pan will also work in a pinch).

3   Sprinkle the smoked meat and cheese curds over the fries. Place the pan on the rack below the broiler until the pork is warmed through and the curds are melted.

4   Remove from the oven and ladle the gravy over the top. Garnish with the chopped green onions and pickled cauliflower (if using).

Gravy

2 tablespoons (¼ stick) unsalted butter

1 shallot, diced

½ stalk celery, diced

¼ cup diced green bell pepper

1 garlic clove, minced

2 teaspoons minced jalapeño

2 tablespoons all-purpose flour

2 cups beef stock (page 53 or store-bought)

2 teaspoons Worcestershire sauce

½ teaspoon hot sauce (page 262 or store-bought)

Pinch of garlic powder

Pinch of onion powder

Pinch of celery salt

Salt and freshly ground black pepper

2 teaspoons lemon juice

1   Heat the butter in a medium heavy pot over medium heat. Add the shallot and sauté for 4 minutes. Add the celery, bell pepper, garlic, and jalapeño and sauté for 4 more minutes.

2   Add the flour and stir with a wooden spoon until combined. Cook for 5 minutes, stirring frequently. It should be very blond. Add the stock and bring to a boil. Reduce the heat to medium-low and simmer for 10 minutes.

3   Add the Worcestershire sauce, hot sauce, garlic powder, onion powder, celery salt, and salt and black pepper to taste, and stir to combine. Continue to cook until the gravy has thickened and the flour taste has disappeared, about 10 more minutes. Add the lemon juice and taste for seasoning. Keep warm until ready to serve.

Smoked Meat and Sausage Gumbo

Seems like anyone who has spent time in New Orleans has a gumbo trick up their sleeve, and I'm no different. My trick is using a wooden spoon. When you're doing this kind of long-simmering pot cooking, some things might get a little burned, and those bits tend to stick to the bottom of the pot. And the great thing about wooden spoons is they'll pick up everything that *isn't* stuck, unlike a metal spoon, which will pull up everything into the soup. So, you can avoid a lot of headache just by using a wooden spoon.

I'll be honest: this recipe makes a lot of gumbo. About 5 quarts, to be exact. But gumbo is a lot of work, and if you're going to go to the effort, you might as well make a lot of it! The good news is it freezes nicely.

MAKES ABOUT 5 QUARTS

1 cup vegetable oil

1½ cups all-purpose flour

2 large onions, diced

4 stalks celery, diced

2 green bell peppers, diced

6 garlic cloves, minced

1 pound smoked sausage, halved lengthwise and then sliced into ½-inch-thick half moons (page 318)

4 pounds bone-in smoked meat, such as turkey or chicken, shredded with skin and bones discarded (page 318), or 2½ pounds boneless smoked meat, such as pork shoulder (page 317), shredded

3 quarts chicken stock (page 51)

2 cups ½-inch coins okra, tops discarded if woody

3 bay leaves

1 tablespoon minced fresh thyme leaves

½ teaspoon cayenne

1 tablespoon Worcestershire sauce

2 tablespoons Creole seasoning

1 teaspoon filé powder (optional)

1 teaspoon hot sauce (page 262 or store-bought), plus more for serving

1 teaspoon each salt and freshly ground black pepper, plus more to taste

6 cups cooked white rice, for serving

1 bunch green onions, chopped, for serving

1 Heat the oil in a 2-gallon stockpot over medium heat. Whisk in the flour, stirring constantly for 20 minutes, or until the roux reaches a dark mahogany color. It may smoke some at the end, but as long as the roux is brown and not black, you should be okay.

2 Add the onions to the pot and sauté for 10 minutes. Add the celery, bell peppers, and garlic and sauté for 2 minutes longer.

3 Next add the sausage to the pot and sauté for 15 minutes. Add the smoked meat, chicken stock, okra, and bay leaves and bring to a boil, then reduce to a simmer for 1 hour. Use a ladle to skim off any fat that rises to the top.

4 After 1 hour, stir in the thyme, cayenne, Worcestershire sauce, Creole seasoning, file powder (if using), hot sauce, 1 teaspoon salt, and 1 teaspoon pepper and simmer for an additional hour until the meat is tender and falling apart. Taste and adjust the seasoning.

5 Serve the gumbo in bowls topped with cooked rice, hot sauce, and diced green onions.

Note: If you plan on making a ton of gumbo, it's probably easier to make a double batch of roux in the oven. Heat the oven to 300°F. Combine 2 cups vegetable oil and 3 cups all-purpose flour in a large, round shallow pot or Dutch oven. Whisk the roux every 15 minutes until you achieve that dark mahogany color, 1 to 1½ hours.

Charcuterie Boards

If my specialty is preserving foods, charcuterie boards are my masterpieces. But you don't have to be a professional chef to put one together! You can serve an amazing spread composed entirely of store-bought ingredients or a combination of homemade and store-bought. The key is taking the time to arrange them beautifully on a nice board or serving tray.

Charcuterie and cheese boards are not only great for entertaining, they're also the perfect showcase for everything you've learned in this cookbook. Plenty of these recipes, from pickles to ferments to mustards to jams, work splendidly on a charcuterie board and add flair to store-bought salami or homemade chicken liver mousse. How much of the board is homemade is up to you, but here are some basic tips on how I balance flavors and style boards to get you started.

First of all, everyone likes different things. Build your charcuterie board from foods you like. There are no rules that say you *have to* put olives on a charcuterie board or that you can't do an all-salumi board.

I love a good mix of cured items (salumi, cured hams, bresaola, etc.) and forcemeats (pâtés and sausages), because you get a lot of texture differences. Pickles, jams, and mustards provide complementary flavors to your charcuterie and can be a really fun way to add color to your board. Some flavor pairings I love include chicken liver mousse with jam and serving smoky items with a spicy condiment—like smoked sausage with a good hot mustard. And don't forget the serving accompaniment! A nicely spiced, salted cracker, or slices of baguette that have been drizzled with a little olive oil and just barely toasted, will really take your board to the next level.

When it comes to actually putting all your ingredients on the board, get creative. I like to fan out sliced items. This is a great opportunity to get out any tiny bowls or dishes you might have and fill them with your various pickles, mustards, and jams; they will add a little bit of vertical interest and definition to the board (as opposed to plating everything directly on the board itself). Tinned fish can go straight onto the board in the tin, and you can sprinkle it with fresh chopped herbs to chef it up just a little. Pay attention to texture, and add elements that crunch, like spiced nuts, alongside softer elements, like cheeses. And above all have fun with it! This shouldn't be a daunting task. It's just fancy snacks.

Recipes from this Book

Store-Bought Ideas

Store-bought versions of any of the above, plus:

Capers or caperberries

Charcuterie

Cheeses

Cornichons

Dried fruit

Fresh fruit

Honey

Olives

Pretzels

Canning

Wherever there are pickles and jams, there will be canning jars. The preservation methods in this book help delay spoilage to some extent, but for longer-term storage, you're going to want to can your preserves. Here are some simple guidelines for how to water-bath can some of the recipes in this book, but if you get serious about canning, you will need more. There are tons of resources available online—I'm partial to the National Center for Home Food Preservation at the University of Georgia (https://nchfp.uga.edu); you can also check your local university extension website for regionally specific resources.

Use a Tested Recipe

In canned preserves, we're looking for a pH lower than 4.6, which prevents the deadly *Clostridium botulinum* (the bacterium that causes botulism) from forming. Using quality, tested recipes like the ones in this book means you shouldn't need to test the pH, but if it would make you feel more comfortable, testing pH in your canned preserves is pretty easy. You can buy tester strips for relatively cheap online and digital pH meters for not much more. The sweet spot for pickles in particular is between 3.0 and 3.4, while something like tomato sauce or jam might be slightly higher. So as long as you're under 4.6, you should be okay.

Use Good Equipment

At the restaurant, we use fancy Victorian square jars we order online. But widely available brands like Ball and Kerr make reliable canning jars with two-part metal lids. Prior to canning, inspect your jars to make sure the opening is smooth and has no chips. The jars and the bands are reusable; you'll need to use a new lid each time you can.

Sanitize Your Jars

This can either be done by boiling them for a couple of minutes or running them through the dishwasher. Either way, you'll want the jars hot when you fill them. This helps prevent the glass from breaking during the canning process.

Fill the Jars, Put the Lids On, and Boil Them

If the ingredient you are canning needs to be canned hot, heat the ingredient. (See table on the following page.) Fill the jars, leaving ½ inch of room at the top. Wipe the rim of the jar clean with a fresh paper towel. Cover it with the flat lid, and then screw on the band. Then wipe any debris off the outside of the jar to keep your canning water clean. Use a pair of canning tongs (tongs with rounded rubber-coated ends that grip the jar securely) and carefully lower the jars into a stockpot full of boiling water. You need the water to cover the jar by a couple of inches. Boil for the length of time recommended by the chart, and use the tongs to remove the jars from the water. Allow to cool on the counter.

Did It Seal?

You'll know your canning worked when the dimple in the center of the lid is depressed—this means the jar has vacuum sealed. You may hear a popping noise when this happens as the jars cool. If you can press the dimple down, your jar has not sealed properly.

Storage

Use a permanent marker to label the lid with the jar's contents and the date. Remove the band for storage. Do not store filled canning jars on top of one another—they're not designed for it and may topple. Ideally you want to store filled jars at a temperature lower than 70°F, but living in Texas, I know that's not always possible. Definitely do not store your jars in temperatures over 80°F, and do not allow jars to freeze. No garages! Enjoy your canned preserves within a year.

Recipe	Page	Can Hot or Cold	Boiling Time
Pickles	29	Cold	10 minutes for pints, 15 minutes for quarts
Mustard	19	Cold	10 minutes for pints or half pints
Tomato sauce	39	Hot; add the juice of ½ lemon to each jar before canning.	35 minutes for pints, 40 minutes for quarts
Sauerkraut	243	Cold	20 minutes for pints, 25 minutes for quarts
Kimchi	253	Cold	20 minutes for pints, 25 minutes for quarts
Hot sauce	262	Cold	10 minutes for pints or half pints
Chow-chow	270	Cold	20 minutes for pints, 25 minutes for quarts
Fruit shrubs	277	Cold	10 minutes for pints and half pints, 15 minutes for quarts
Jams	31	Hot	10 minutes for pints and half pints
Marmalades	138	Hot	10 minutes for pints and half pints

Note: Water-bath canning times are for elevations of 1,000 feet or lower. If you are at elevation, please consult your local university extension for canning times.

Recipes by Dish or Occasion

Snacks

For Holidays

For Weeknight Dinners

For Sunday Suppers

For Picnics

Further Reading

Now that you've learned the hows and whys of basic techniques, perhaps you've caught the preservation bug. Here are a few of my favorite guides for further reading.

- *Pickles, Pigs & Whiskey* by John Currence
- *The Art of Preserving* by Rick Field, Lisa Atwood, and Rebecca Courchesne
- *The Preservation Kitchen* by Paul Virant with Kate Leahy
- *Smoke & Pickles* by Edward Lee
- *Cooking by Hand* by Paul Bertolli
- *The Farmhouse Culture Guide to Fermenting* by Kathryn Lukas and Shane Peterson
- *The Art of Fermentation* by Sandor Ellix Katz
- *Preserving the Japanese Way* by Nancy Singleton Hachisu
- *Six Seasons* by Joshua McFadden with Martha Holmberg
- *Salted and Cured* by Jeffrey P. Roberts
- *Charcuterie* by Michael Ruhlman and Brian Polcyn
- *The River Cottage Curing and Smoking Handbook* by Steven Lamb
- *Mes Confitures* by Christine Ferber
- *The Kimchi Cookbook* by Lauryn Chun
- *Franklin Barbecue* by Aaron Franklin and Jordan Mackay
- *The Noma Guide to Fermentation* by René Redzepi and David Zilber

Acknowledgments

_____

Steve McHugh

When we opened Cured, we created a place to support local ranchers and farmers. That means buying in bulk and finding ways to preserve the harvest. In other words, we created a restaurant based on the methods shared in this book. None of this would be possible without those farmers and ranchers, the community of San Antonio, and the (too many to name) regulars of Cured.

Thank you, Paula, my fellow cookbook nerd, for walking this path with me and for the many hours of hand-holding while I learned to find my voice. You made this experience extremely fruitful, and I am forever grateful for your patience and, more importantly, your friendship.

Thanks to David Black of the Black Agency for all you have done fighting for me to tell this story. And thank you to John T. Edge of the Southern Foodways Alliance for encouraging me to team up with David, because you believed I had a story to tell.

Thanks to Kelly Snowden, Emma Campion, and the team at Ten Speed Press for trusting us and encouraging us to dive deeper. What started out as a book on preservation turned into a manual on how your home kitchen can be as efficient and creative as the one I run at Cured.

Huge thanks to Denny Culbert for the gorgeous photographs. It was amazing watching you turn this story into art. Thanks to Joe Vidrine for assisting, and Elizabeth Pearson and Alicia Mendez for styling help. And thanks to Randy Smith for providing such a beautiful space for shooting some of the photography.

None of this would be possible without our army of volunteer recipe testers. Thank you for your invaluable feedback and insights.

To the entire team at Cured, thank you for the many hours of hard work building this book. Extra hugs to chefs Larkin and Latoya for the months of prepping for the photo shoot. Thank you, Bob, Veronica, and Winnie, for putting our restaurants on your shoulders. I am in awe of you every day. And thanks to the teams at Luminaire, Las Bis, and Landrace for your patience while I worked on this dream.

Big hugs to Simone, Misi, and the team at SimoneInk. From day one, you said I would write a book and I always said you were crazy. Thank you for all you do.

Thank you to my family: To my parents, who supported my dream of becoming a chef since I was sixteen. I know you are looking down with smiles and tears of joy (and hopefully a couple of pickle brine martinis, page 32). To my brother, Marty, who agreed to be a partner in this crazy company and keeps us on a great path. To my daughter, Sophia, and my grandson, Ryland, thank you for putting way too many miles on your car, running errands to get whatever we needed to make the crazy ideas we had work. You are the reasons Sylvia and I get up each day.

Lastly, Sylvia, thank you for being my partner in life. I am forever grateful for your kindness, drive, passion, and strength. We set out to open a restaurant where we wanted to eat, and it turned into so much more. I am grateful to go to work with you every day and night, creating magic in our restaurants. You are my best friend and the love of my life, and the stories in this book are not possible without you. There is no Cured without you.

Paula Forbes

Thank you, Steve, for trusting me with your words and your story. This was one hell of an ambitious project, but dare I say it turned out better than we ever imagined! That sweet spot where Wisconsin and Texas overlap will not be defeated. Thanks to Kelly Snowden and everyone at Ten Speed for believing in us—the number of times I've heard "I cannot believe someone is actually letting you write this book" from colleagues during this process underscored just how lucky we were to end up in your very capable hands. Thanks to Denny Culbert for seeing what we saw in this book and making our dream photography a reality. To my agent, Angela Miller, who has believed in me from the jump and has proved an invaluable resource, I am grateful as ever. Thank you to Sylvia McHugh and everyone on the Cured team: Steve thanked you much more eloquently, but I am so proud to be able to count you among my dear friends. Thanks to my friends in Austin and farther afield for being game recipe testers (and recipe test eaters!). And finally, thank you to my family: Mom, Dad, Madeline, and most of all Raphael, who puts up with me hosting endless dinner parties and washes countless dishes, even when he has to get up at 5:00 a.m. the next day. I couldn't do any of this without you, I love you so.

About the Team

Steve McHugh is a six-time James Beard Foundation Award—nominated chef based in San Antonio. His first restaurant, Cured, opened its doors to guests in December 2013 and since then has been joined by Landrace in San Antonio and Luminaire and Las Bis in Austin. McHugh is known for his work with preservation, and his restaurants turn the best local, seasonal ingredients into house-made pickles, fermented foods, jams, mustards, vinegars, and famously intensive charcuterie. He grew up on a farm in southern Wisconsin and spent the early part of his career in New Orleans, before he and his wife, Sylvia, settled in San Antonio.

Paula Forbes is perhaps best known for her work on Texas food and cooking, but she grew up far from the Lone Star State in Madison, Wisconsin. She is the author of 2018's *The Austin Cookbook* and helped write *The Big Texas Cookbook* by the editors of *Texas Monthly*. Formerly an editor at Eater and Epicurious, and cookbook critic for *Lucky Peach* magazine, Forbes is currently a writer at large for *Texas Monthly* magazine and the editor of *Stained Page News*, a cookbook newsletter. She lives in Austin.

Denny Culbert is a (mostly) food photographer based in Lafayette, Louisiana. He built his career photographing the culinary landscape of South Louisiana over the last ten years. His work appears on the pages of *Bon Appétit*, *Garden & Gun*, *Saveur*, and an ever-growing list of food and cocktail books. He also co-owns Wild Child, a natural wineshop in downtown Lafayette, with his wife, Katie.

Index

Note: Words in *italics* indicate Base Ingredients.
Page numbers in *italics* indicate photos.

Typefaces: Grilli Type's Super, TypeType's Ramillas, Monotype's Touvlo

Library of Congress Cataloging-in-Publication Data
Names: McHugh, Steve, 1975- author. | Forbes, Paula, author. Title: Cured : cooking
with ferments, pickles, preserves, and more / Steve McHugh with Paula Forbes;
photographs by Denny Culbert. Identifiers: LCCN 2023014099 (print) | LCCN
2023014100 (ebook) | ISBN 9781984861467 (hardcover) | ISBN 9781984861474 (ebook)
Subjects: LCSH: Cooking (Fermented foods) | Smoking (Cooking) | Pickled foods. |
Food—Preservation. | LCGFT: Cookbooks. Classification: LCC TX827.5 .M34 2024
(print) | LCC TX827.5 (ebook) | DDC 641.6/1—dc23/eng/20230331
LC record available at https://lccn.loc.gov/2023014099
LC ebook record available at https://lccn.loc.gov/2023014100

Hardcover ISBN: 978-1-9848-6146-7
eBook ISBN: 978-1-9848-6147-7

Printed in China
Editor: Kelly Snowden | Production editor: Serena Wang
Editorial assistant: Gabriela Ureña Matos
Designer: Emma Campion | Production designers: Mari Gill and Faith Hague
Production manager: Dan Myers | Prepress color manager: Jane Chinn
Photography assistant: Joseph Vidrine
Copyeditor: Heather Rodino | Proofreader: Hope Clarke | Indexer: Jay Kreider
Publicist: Kristin Casemore | Marketer: Monica Stanton

10 9 8 7 6 5 4 3 2 1

First Edition